AF560001

THE SHORT STORIES OF SHERWOOD ANDERSON
A THEMATIC STUDY

THE SHORT STORIES OF SHERWOOD ANDERSON

A THEMATIC STUDY

By

Dr. B. Mohan, *Ph.D.*

Associate Professor in English

S.V. College of Engineering & Technology, Chittoor

Andhra Pradesh

(India)

DISCOVERY PUBLISHING HOUSE PVT. LTD.

NEW DELHI-110 002

Published by:
Tilak Wasan

DISCOVERY PUBLISHING HOUSE PVT. LTD.
4383/4B, Ansari Road, Darya Ganj
New Delhi-110 002 (India)
Phone : +91-11-23279245, 43596064-65
Fax : +91-11-23253475
E-mail : discoverypublishinghouse@gmail.com
sales@discoverypublishinggroup.com
parul.wasan@gmail.com
web : www.discoverypublishinggroup.com

***First Edition:* 2014**

ISBN: 978-93-5056-508-7

The Short Stories of Sherwood Anderson
A Thematic Study

Printed at:
Dynamic Printers
Delhi

Preface

The present undertaking, **The Short Stories of Sherwood Anderson – *A Thematic Study*** is a modest attempt to examine the predominant themes in the Short Stories of Sherwood Anderson. To facilitate the study of the stories selected, they are grouped according to their thematic affinity rather than the order in which they were written or published.

The thesis is conveniently divided into Seven Chapters.

Chapter one is introductory, it states the theme of inquiry, its scope and limits.

Second Chapter entitled Lonely grotesques of Winesburg is an exploration into some of Anderson's Short Stories which deal with men and women who feel trapped in their loneliness and isolation and who fail to establish communication with others, whether it is a form of what has been called "Metaphysical Homelessness" caused by some defects in the nature of the characters, is examined.

This Chapter entitled Winesburg, Ohio as bildung-sroman, is devoted exclusively to examining Winesburg, Ohio as a bildungsroman presenting the growth and development towards maturity, of unifying character, George Willard. In view of the distinction of Winesburg, Ohio the special place it occupies in Anderson's canon, special attention has been given to it.

A study of Young Peoples Initiation into adulthood in some post-Winesburg Stories is discussed in the Fourth Chapter.

Fifth Chapter entitled Stories on Man Woman Relationship deals about the perplexities, turmoils and confusions in the relationship between men and women, who are stifled in the claustrophobic atmosphere, is discussed.

Stories about Frustrated Men and Women and Unlived Lives is discussed in the Sixth Chapter. The materialistic and commercial environment in which he had to live and function and which often made him feel alienated is dealt in this chapter.

Seventh Chapter By Way of Summing Up with which the present study concludes, the main line argument presents in the preceding chapters regarding Anderson's exploration of life through different related themes, are summed up.

–Author

Contents

Contents

CHAPTER – 1

Introduction

After all ups and downs of critical favour and disfavor during his own life time and afterwards, Sherwood Anderson (1876-1941) has now come to his own as a creative writer. At the time of his death in 1941 he had been "relegated to a minor position in American Literary history", his "influence" on his contemporaries "discredited", and was regarded as one who had failed to fulfill the promise he had shown in his earlier work, Winesburg, Ohio in particular. In the recent decades, however, there has been a revival of considerable scholarly critical interest in his life and in all that he wrote including his writings as writer of advertising copy for different companies. Anderson studies are continuing at an accelerated pace. He is recognized as one of the really important and significant creative writers of the first few decades of the 20th century. Further, it is acknowledged that he "remained a profound, provocative and perceptive writer to the end, and that he has much to say"[1] to the present time.

Anderson was a prolific writer and the total corpus of his creative work is substantial, although he was on the wrong side of thirty when he turned to creative writing. He wrote novels (seven in all), a few plays (Winesburg and Others), some volumes of autobiographical and confessional narrative and nearly a hundred short stories. He also wrote number of articles for trade journals before he emerged as a writer of fiction. He had already published two novels before he brought out Winesburg, Ohio (1919), the cycle of short stories and sketches, which established his reputation as a writer and marked him out for short fiction. There have been differences of opinion among critics regarding the merit of Anderson's novels and his achievement in the field of long fiction. However there is near unanimity of opinion now regarding his distinction and achievement as a writer of short stories, despite some reservations among a few critics.

"An orphan without a name at the beginning of the nineteenth century"[2], the short story became the most popular of fictional forms at the beginning of the twentieth century, especially in America. Almost every important writer of fiction during the first half of the century-Scott Fitzerald, Ernest Hemingway, William Faulkner and others among them handled this form of short fiction with distinction, exploring and revealing its possibilities to give expression to contemporary life and sensibility. Frank O'Connor, who had an acute sense of national values, was led on to declare way back in 1963 that "Anderson have handled the short story to wonderfully that one can say that it is a national art form".[3] (emphasis added). The contribution of Sherwood Anderson to this phenomenal development was by no means ordinary, although critical opinion, as it could be expected, has not been uniform in regarding the precise nature and extent of his influence on other writers of short stories among his immediate contemporaries and those of the newer generations. To cite just two differing opinions in illustration, Walter Litz who has reservations about Anderson's achievement and influence, writes: "There are some signs of Anderson's influence in the apprentice work of Faulkner and Hemingway, but —(his) impact up on his successors was general rather than specific".[4] on the other hand, Robert Papinchak, in near superlative praise of Anderson, says: "unwilling to accept the direction of the American short story, Anderson developed what we now regard as its modern incarnation by making revolutionary contributions to its form and content. He reshaped the American short story, making it his own, and at the same time prepared the groundwork for the revolutionary writers who would follow them".[5] And Papinchak lists a number of writers of short fiction who owe a debt, direct or indirect to Anderson.

Extreme views apart, what seems certain is that Anderson was a sort of 'trail blazer' who pioneered many changes in the art of the American short story in theme, technique, form and content, and opened up for the writers of short fiction in America, fresh possibilities in subject matter, narrative technique and style for introspective and intuitive exploration of the inner life of men and women of the present day. Malcolm Cowley says of him: "What Anderson did for younger writers was to open vistas by finding new depths of breadths of feeling in everyday American life—. He gave them each a moment of vision, and then the younger writer trudged off toward his separate destiny—".[6] Cowley has also said elsewhere of him that he: "became a writer's writer, the only storyteller of his generation who left his mark on the style and vision of the generation that followed. Hemingway, Faulkner, Wolfe, Steinbeck, Caldwell, Saroyan, Henry Miller—each of these owes an unmistakable debt to Anderson, and their names might stand for a dozen of othrs".[7]

The story of Sherwood Anderson, Head of the Anderson Manufacturing Company in Elyria, abruptly breaking off in the middle of a sentence he was dictating to his secretary and walking out of his office making a dramatic exit, and also walking out of a phase of his life, abandoning once and for all his moderately successful business career for the uncertainties of an artist's life, is now well known. Anderson himself told this story with a touch of drama about it more than once.[8] A decade after it happened, chose to describe it as an act of conscious pre-meditation and deliberate act or rebellion against the compulsion of modern life, and as rejection of materialistic values and the standards of the market place, in favour of a writer's career, its uncertainties of money, of survival, and of inspiration. Now it is known to all that Anderson consciously cultivated a legend about himself and his so-called desertion of his business enterprise. This blend of some fact and much more of fiction, this myth was perpetuated by Anderson and his friends and critics too, for different reasons and with different interpretations.

Actually Anderson's decision to give up the business world was neither sudden nor was it total. It took shape in his mind over some months, as he was increasingly getting dissatisfied with what he was doing, while the urge to be a writer was growing strong in him. Having left his office on the 27th of November 1912, he wandered for a few days, was found and hospitalized for nervous breakdown. After recovery he did return in early 1913 to the business world again, though not in Elyria, but in the metropolis of Chicago to write advertising copies once again for an advertisement office, as he had done some years earlier. He remained in the business world for nearly another decade. Though inaccurate as fact, Anderson's version of his break with that world, has nevertheless an essential truth concerning him and the direction his thinking was taking inwardly about that time. He regarded his action always as having 'a major significance'. It was symbolic of what he was ambitious of, and aspiring to do with himself, his life and art. In the words of Ray Lewis White, Anderson went to Chicago for the third time he had lived there between 1896 and 1898, and again during 1900-1907- "to reshape his existence as a quest for inner happiness through art and beauty instead of quest for the external pleasures that money and its attendant power could provide. At thirty-six, free at last to be poor and creative and content, Sherwood Anderson faced the adventure of the rest of life"[9]. The step he had taken was decisive.

David D. Anderson has put succinctly the entire episode in perspective and pointed out the significance it had for Anderson and his art. He writes:

> *His break with business was certainly not a literal break, although he clearly implied that it was. But to Anderson the physical continuity was meaningless. The reality of the move that which he had tried to make clear in his fiction as well as (the) allegedly factual account, had nothing to do with what he actually did. The real break was spiritual and allegorical; not only did he never give a lasting allegiance to anything except his art and his craft, but at the same time his experience became for him the archetypal experience of the artist, of American, of the human being in the twentieth century, who must consciously reject materialism if he is to survive and pursue his vision of happiness.*[10]

Anderson' abandonment, as Ray Lewis White puts it, "marked the turning point of his life, a turning away from the quest for money and social power and a turning toward the satisfaction of literary creation and social freedom".[11]

When Anderson went to Chicago again in early 1913, he was going there for a much longer stay than before. The change from Elyria to the metropolis "served not only as a change of place more deeply as a change in the texture and direction of (his) whole life".[12] His Chicago experience brought him positive gains both as man and creative writer. He also wrote numerous articles for trade journals like Agriculture Advertising in which he wrote to column called "Rot and Reason". Now during his current stay he continued to write advertising copy for some more years, much of it in the same boosting vein of his former advertising copies. But his heart was no longer in it. He had come to Chicago as a writer of fiction though, that fiction was not yet published. He had begun to regard himself as a creative writer and view his writing as a artistic end in itself rather than as means to communicate to convince or sell goods or ideas. What he needed was proper direction to his efforts. This as well as the sympathy, encouragement and stimulus, he found at Chicago where he was initiated in to the group of young artists who comprised the "Chicago Renaissance".

The Chicago Renaissance was a movement of liberation, which was to have lasting effects on American literature. Anderson became imbued with its aesthetic atmosphere and its spirit of personal and artistic liberation. Among the friends and acquaintances he made, there were people who were unconventional and intellectually provocative and who were free thinkers from who he could learn much. Although he did not go the whole hog with them and accept all that they stood for, he profited from their criticism of his work. In particular, through his association with those of the 57th street artistic colony, he made the discovery "that a writer must find himself, his subject matter, and his own means of expression rather than imitate others".[13] through an intimate knowledge of himself. Before he joined the Chicago group, Anderson as a writer "had been primarily a propagandist focusing on issues rather the people". In his early novels, *Windy Mc Pherson* and *Marching Men*, his protest against materialism and his rejection of it, though instinctive and direct, had been couched in the diction and style of the late 19th century popular literature. He learnt from his association with the Chicago group that he had to move in a different direction. He had begun to search led him "to focus on people, as individual human lives" that made up the generations of America.[14] Another important discovery that Anderson made was that a sense of craft and devotion to it were indispensable for imaginative creation pursued for its own sake. The positive gains he made and the growth he achieved in Chicago both as man and writer became manifest in Winesburg, Ohio, his mature and outstanding work which "marked his emergence as a serious, native mid-western literary artist'.[15]

The mature Anderson, the writer of short fiction, had three concerns most essential for every earnest creative writer: concern for life, for form, and for language the medium of his creative endeavour. In all these concerns he distinguished himself, and left his indelible impress on American short fiction. A heightened sensitiveness to contemporary life in America and openness to the myriad experiences of life became central to all his writings. Kate Swift, a character in *The Teacher*, one of the Winesburg, Ohio stories, tells earnestly George Willard, one of her former pupils who is ambitious of becoming a writer: 'You will have to stop fooling with words. The thing to learn is to know what people are thinking about, not what they say'. This revealing statement could very well be Anderson's own because it actually expresses his own mature approach to writing fiction, and reveals his concern for people as human individuals, It was his conviction that a writer must get closer to the people and experiences that gave him the impetus to write rather than ride on his unbridled imagination. Like Walt Whitman and Mark Twain before him, he found a vast and an essentially worthy source of literary material in the lives of the many obscure little people who generally went unnoticed, uncared for, and were ignored like twisted apples in an orchard. In the ordinary and undistinguished lives of average people in an orchard. In the ordinary and undistinguished lives of average people who were un-pretentious, naïve, grotesque, inhibited, inarticulate, simple, perplexed and confused, and whose experience of life grew with our own, he found universally relevant meaning and significance. It was indeed a challenging task to transform this material into satisfying fictional art.

It was natural if Anderson was critical of the writers of popular fiction of the day who, he believed, merely pandered to the average reader's desire for adventure, romance, and the so-called moral upliftment. It was his contention that these writers either shunned or shied away from areas of everyday experiences, which deserved and demanded to be explored and expressed imaginatively. He was possessed by a hunger to understand and obtain an insight into the meaning of the lives of people around him. Then again, he was not satisfied with the American models of short story writing available to him. There were "the realists" (William Dean Howells, Henry James, Mark Twain) and the naturalists (Hamlin Garland, Stephen Crane, Theodore Dreiser). It was Anderson's view that while the realists "explored" "the source of things", the naturalists "followed" "deterministic treatises".[16] although he did learn much from both, he tried to steer clear of the realists as well as the naturalist, in his own practice. It was his contention that fiction should capture life honestly rather than distort it. While the creative imagination certainly had its part to play and keep fiction distinct from real life, it had to feed and sustain itself upon the actual and the real.

Anderson further believed, as he tells us in his autobiographical work, *A Story Teller's Story,* that "the true history of life is but a history of moments. It is only at rare moments that we live".[17] Consistent with this belief, he held that to articulate this vision, this revealing moment or epiphany, authentically, the writer required an appropriate short story form, which was natural and close to life's experience, psychologically suggestive, and yet distinct from the observed reality. Since such a form was not available to him, he had to seek out a new one for himself. His attempt was to find a form of short fiction. Which was as inclusive and accommodative as possible of themes and experiences hither to un attempted in this form as he found it in America.

Anderson was bitterly critical of the trickery of what he called the "poison plot", the tightly knit plot and structure seen in abundance in popular magazines, which had little or nothing to do with the life that people lived. He distinguished what he called "form" from the popularly established notion of plot. He wrote in *A Story Teller's Story*:

> *There was a notion that ran through all story telling in America, that stories must be built about a plot and that absurd Anglo-Saxon notion that they must point a moral, uplift the people, make better citizens, etc... The magazines are filled with these plot stories— the plot notion did seem to me to poison all story telling. What was wanted— was form not plot, an altogether more elusive and difficult thing to come at.*[18]

For his own stories he devised a seemingly from less form without plot and pattern, as these terms were generally understood. He particularly despised the highly plotted stories of O. Henry. The form he forged for himself was intended to suggest the halts and starts and gropings of life, its dreamlike passiveness as well as its loose flow. In this form, as Rex Burbank points out, "the principle of order or organisation was psychological rather than external and linear".[19]

Anderson's search for a new form entailed a search for a new idiom and narrative style appropriate to his subject matter and his conception of the short story. Probably he first learnt from his garrulous and richly imaginative, though somewhat irresponsible; father Irwin Anderson, the art of narrating stories. Irwin was a gifted raconteur, could spin fantastic yarns and hold his audience spellbound. He was known to entertain people in saloon bars with tales of his adventure, real and imaginary, in the Civil War. He entertained rural folk with romantic tales and parlour skits. Anderson's first impulse was to speak, orally narrate, histories, rather than write them. For his narrative style he drew upon the oral tradition, which influenced his notion of what a story should be, and how it should be told. The purpose of the oral story teller was, as David Anderson explains, to seek and to hold the attention of his listeners while he found his way to the point he was trying to make:

> *This is the tradition of the Middle West of the eighties and nineties, when the countless counterparts of Irwin Anderson were holding forth in harness shops, general stores, and barbershops scattered across the rural countryside. When Anderson turned his writing loose to seek its own style, it turned instinctively to that tradition. Often exasperating in its meandering and hence unsatisfactory to a reader accustomed to crisp directness, it is nevertheless true tradition of native Mid-Western technique that is not studiously correct but spontaneous, unsophisticated and honest. It is a style that would naturally attract a man who was tired of dishonesty, artificiality and trickery in the use of words as well as human affairs.*[20]

Anderson adopted for his stories a style spontaneous, simple, colloquial, un ravished and even flat at times, based on the oral narrative pattern and its unhurried pace, which was capable of conveying, despite its apparent meanderings, feelings and psychological insights, and of seeing beneath the surface of lives. This was in marked contrast to the imitative style and rhetorical flourishes of his first novels. He adopted the native American speech and rhythm as the basis for his style. Thus by the time Anderson turned to writing short fiction and made it his forte, his notion of what it should be in content, form and style had clearly formed in his mind. The lessons he had learnt by assimilating the spirit of the Chicago Renaissance bore fruit. And his "form and style infused new life into the American short story".[21]

That Anderson drew largely upon his own rich and varied experiences in life, in the farming town of Clyde, Elyria, the big turbulent city of Chicago and elsewhere for his raw material in fiction, is now critical commonplace. He was in his late thirties when he embarked on his writing career, and was "admirably equipped in range and variety of experiences to explore the possibilities and limitations of Mid Western American life",[22] during a significant period, which he knew first hand and best. By his own admission in his letters and memoirs, his works were essentially autobiographical. For instance a number of his fellow lodgers in 735, Class Street in Chicago served as models and became prototype for characters in his tales. While making this admission, Anderson also made an important distinction. He pointed out that "his autobiographical writing was not intended to focus on facts but on feelings not on names, dates, and places, but on meanings". As result, Daniel Anderson points out, "his works as a whole comprise a — spiritual autobiography that records and analysis the impression of generic man during the unique period that saw America transformed from an Agricultural to industrial state. This change in the American scene took place during Anderson's own life time and was felt most suddenly and spectacularly in his own Midwest".[23]

It was never a smooth sailing life for Anderson. Apart from his own emotional and financial insecure life at home in his boyhood and early youth, with a romantic, talkative but improvident father, and an affectionate but stoically resigned mother who suffered loneliness and isolation quietly in the small, quiet, tradition-bound town of Clyde, Anderson experienced the ups and downs of life in the huge and tasted in no small measure success, hope, frustration, failure, disappointment, perplexity and confusion. He witnessed the rapid changes taking place in the American society of his times, particularly the dissolution of small town life and transformation of his country form a quiet place of farms and country houses with man close to nature, into a big urban, industrialized and commercial society with materialistic and commercial values taking precedence over the time-honoured human and spiritual values. For a time he too shared the agony and aspiration of young people caught by the mad craze for progress and success, and their anxious striving to adopt themselves to a fast moving industrial life. He experienced the adverse effects of industrialization and urbanization; the restless drift towards confusion, frustration, estrangement, loneliness and dehumanization. He witnessed the rapid and extraordinary shift in the American ethos and the sudden displacement in sensibility it created. He became incisively aware of the human consequences of the changes and developments taking place in American society as they affected in particular the ordinary and average, the culturally underprivileged, the "grotesque" as he chose to call them with real affectionate concern for them rather than derision.

If Anderson was averse to the machine, which had displaced the human hand (which, as many of his stories show, for him was a most expressive means of communication) and the industrial civilization of his times, he also discovered, as he grew mature, that beneath the meaninglessness and ugliness of the industrial and commercial surface of America, "there was still a slid core that was worthwhile".[24] it is true that he was nostalgic about small town life and wished for a return to a state of human society, pre industrial and uncomplicated. But he also realized that such a return was not possible. Moreover, it also dawned on him that even that society was not perfect and that human isolation and loneliness was as much a pervasive problem there as it was elsewhere. People there, then as well as now, died alone, many of their lives unfulfilled and frustrated. In the words or Burgees Meridith, Anderson was never fooled about our small town life, and its ugliness and pettiness and limitations, but he was never fooled about its good side either. He saw its beauty too, its courage and its never ending struggle for a free life–".[25]

All these left their deep impress on Anderson's mind and art, and provided the impulse for his creative activity. Majority of those people in his fictional world, men and women, young and old, whether they belong to the little world of his imaginary small town of Winesburg or Chicago or any other town (for most of whom there were counterparts among those known to Anderson) are of the ordinary and average. There are among them a few, or course, who profess to have intellectual brilliance that is focused on. All of them without exception are subject to the pressures exerted by their consequences. Apparently these men and women are nothing special, but each is a distinct individual and deserves attention and concern. To enter deep into their common everyday lives, understand their yearnings, beliefs, hopes and deprivations, unfulfilled aspirations and frustrations, their keen sense of living in a claustrophobic and tense atmosphere, their experience of incurable loneliness and isolation, and of failure of communication, and their anxious but vain attempts to free themselves from them all, and portray them all authentically in his fiction was Anderson's life-long creative endeavour. He sought and found in their lives the themes for his fiction, the short stories in particular. He made the short story an artistic medium for serious, moral and psychological exploration rather a mere instrument for superficial, light and escapist entertainment. In this effort he was certainly breaking new ground.

Certain themes recur all through Anderson's works, as it happens in the works of most writers. They are all closely connected, mutually dependent and therefore affect each other. Therefore one theme leads on to one or more of the other themes. Often they overlap and form a complex and have to be separated only for purposes of analysis. Some of the more pronounced themes of Anderson's are human loneliness and isolation, failure of communication, thwarted potential, frustrated, defeated, unfulfilled and unlived lives, longing for and loss of love, sex and repression because of taboos, outmoded conventions and false notions, breakdown of human relationships, the dichotomy between appearance and reality, confusion of value, search for enduring values in a materialistic world, goal and purpose of life, adolescents growth towards maturity, artist's sense of alienation in a commercial setup etc. these related themes are part of contemporary experiences and are of universal interest. Other writers too are concerned with these themes. But there is something distinctive in Anderson's handling of them. In exploring them he is rarely concerned with theories and ideas in the abstract. His focus is on people, ordinary men and women mainly, in ordinary and everyday situations in the concrete. They are his milieu. He tries to look beneath the surface of their apparently humdrum lives with compassion and concern to reveal the hidden depths of their lives.

The present undertaking is a modest thematic study of Anderson's short stories. The attempt is made to examine how he explores some of the recurrent themes mentioned above in them in terms of the art of short fiction. Anderson wrote very nearly a hundred short stories including those published posthumously. However, to keep the present study within manageable limits, only a selection of the more important ones are studied, which are found in the story cycle Winesburg, Ohio (1919) which is Anderson's first major and lasting achievement, and in such collections of his short stories as The Triumph of the Egg (1921), Horses and Men (1923), Death in the Woods (1933) and Certain Things Last (selection of Anderson's short stories made by Charles E. Modin, 1992). Of Anderson's themes mentioned earlier the most recurrent and most impressive, and found virtually in all of his woks, is human loneliness and isolation. It is a very complex issue as it is at once the cause as well as consequences of the several human problems his characters encounter. Therefore it forms the ground bass of his entire work, early as well as late. He provides several specific and subtle instances of loneliness and isolation to suggest how complex and pervasive men and women into "grotesques", impoverishing and breaking their lives. He also probes implicitly the psychological, sociological, historical and cultural factors responsible for this phenomenon, in the American society of his times in particular.

The approach of the present thematic study is literally critical rather than sociological. The aim has been to examine how Anderson examines and recreates in concrete terms of fiction the different themes he handles in his short stories. Themes in a work of fiction cannot be meaningfully studied without reference to the narrative strategy the author employs in it. It is the narrative strategy devised and the point of view from which the story is told that is, who tells whom when and why, whether it is first person protagonist narrative or third person omniscient authorial narrative, how reliable is the narrator etc., that transforms the theme or themes chosen into art. Anderson's devotion to his fictional craft was total. Ray Lewis White has aptly described it thus; "—the road to artistry for (Anderson) had been too difficult and too meaningful for him ever to become trivial or cheap or worthless in his writing; of all American writers, no one cared more about craft and faithfulness to that craft than did Anderson".[26] The locales used, and the images, symbols and other devises employed, suggest cumulatively the intended meaning. In the present study of Anderson's themes, an attempt is made to pay due attention to these factors in the short stories while analyzing them thematically. Further, as Anderson explores his themes in terms of characters-men and women, young and old- and their situations, attention has to be focused on them in nay analysis of different characters become necessary in the present study too bring out the sharpness of Anderson's perception and the depth of his understanding.

To facilitate the study of the selected stories off Anderson, they are grouped according to their thematic affinities rather than the order in which they were written or published. It is clearly recognized that each story combines several motifs in varying degrees rather than develop or focus on a single theme exclusively. Therefore here the stories are grouped tentatively according to what seem to be their dominant themes. It goes without saying that it is always possible to group them legitimately in other and different ways for study, even from a thematic point of view. And the chapter division of the present study is based on the thematic groups adopted here, and the stories chosen in each group for analysis are mentioned in the brief accounts of the chapters, given a little later in the present chapter.

It is necessary to point out that there is a recurrent theme of importance, dear and significant to Anderson, which is not taken up for examination in the present study. As noted already, Anderson, as a conscientious writer to whom writing was a vocation in the sense of the most meaningful activity of his life, was particularly concerned with the problems, difficulties and dilemmas faced by a creative writer in an unhelpful environment, In particular he was exercised about the extreme difficulty of articulating authentically what one wanted to say and communicating it to others without distortion in a materialistic and commercial environment in which the writer had to live and function. He often felt alienated. It is natural and appropriate that this experience of the creative writer anxious to preserve his artistic integrity, should form the theme of some of Anderson's stories such as *The Book of the Grotesque, Milk Bottles, Certain Things Last*, and *The Red Dog*. This significant theme and theses stories which embody it have not been considered din the present study, the only justification for it being that they may make it even more unmanageable than it already is. However they are mentioned here to indicate that the presence of this theme as well as its importance to Anderson is recognized.

There is yet another aspect of Anderson's short stories which has to be considered as a preliminary to any study of his work, it concerns his attitude to people in general, and the many characters, both men and women, he has created to people his fictional world, for his imaginative exploration of human problems, both psychological and moral. Anderson prefers to portray mainly fragmented persons or individuals who struggle hard, though with little success, which is spiritually undernourished. They are defeated people whose lives are dislocated and whose emotional hunger is ungratified. They are lonely and isolated, and their condition is more pathetic than tragic. Some of them are pathetic and comic at the same time. As human beings they are good, and even lovable. Many of them are very sensitive. But they are treated with indifference, and are neglected and uncared for. Thereby they are prevented from reaching their full potential as human beings, and effectively cut off from their fellows. Such people are not unique to any particular place. They may be found anywhere, in a big city, or small town or village, they deserve to be understood with compassion, empathy and intuition.

Anderson calls such people "grotesque", charging this familiar word with an altogether new, special and profound meaning. In common parlance "grotesque" means 'strange in a way that is unpleasant or offensive', 'extremely ugly in a strange way, often causing fear or laughter' [Oxford Advanced Learners Dictionary of Current English (200)]. But for Anderson the word not only does not at all connote disgust or revulsion in reference to human beings but suggests its very opposite. It is also very clear that this word is of particular importance to him. The grotesques of his conception are to be found in plenty among his characters, noteworthy in Winesburg, Ohio. In *Paper Pills,* the second story in that volume, he likens such people to 'gnarled' or twisted apples in an orchard, which are deliberately rejected and left behind despite their being delicious, all their sweetness gathered in a little round place at the side of the apple, "only the few know the sweetness of the twisted apples". This seemingly common place but most expressive analogy suggests the lot of the grotesques in society. It also indicates Anderson's approach to people in his stories. For him "the sources or natures or their deformities are unimportant compared to their intrinsic worth as human beings needing deserving of understanding". Further, one dare not reject them "because of mere appearance, either physical or spiritual", since "appearance may mask a significant experience made more intense and more worthwhile by the deformity itself".[27]

In *The Book of the Grotesque,* the first sketch of fantasy in Winesburg, Ohio which s intended to be a sort of general prologue to the stories that follow, and also serve as "a statement of purpose", Anderson "points out his approach (to people) in symbolic terms".[28] the narrator in it says:

> *It was the truths that make the people grotesque, the moment one of the people took one of the truths to himself, called it his truth, and tried to live his life by it, he became a grotesque, and the truth she embraced, a false hood.*[29]

This theoretical statement is not of much help because it does not clarity sufficiently the stories in which the conception of the grotesque is recreated and developed in concrete terms. As Irving Howe points out "the conception of the grotesque, as actually developed in the stories, is not merely that it is an unwilled affliction but also that it is a mark of a once sentient striving— the grotesques are those who have sought 'the truths' that disfigure them", and "whose humanity has been outraged".[30] Furthermore their distortion results not only from the narrowing of their vision but also that of others. But what is of importance is that the grotesques should be approached as people, as human beings, worth knowing and understanding rather than as curious specimens or psychological or spiritual deformity. In Anderson's handling of the themes and characters (including the grotesques), there is considerable variety and no monotony, as the analysis that would follow in the present study would show. Be it loneliness and isolation, frustration and disappointment, failure in relationships or in communication, each character of Anderson experiences it in his or her own distinct way, and there is no repetition. This is no mean achievement for anyone.

There are seven chapters in all in the present exercise, including the present one which is introductory and forms Chapter One, in which the theme of enquiry, its scope and limits have been stated, and the theoretical framework adopted for analysis explained. It also explains the rationale of the grouping of the short stories of Anderson's selected for analysis, adopted here. Briefly it also considers the relevance and usefulness of Anderson's concept of the "grotesque" for an understanding of his fiction.

In view of the distinction of Winesburg, Ohio and the special place it occupies in Anderson's canon, particular attention is given to it in two chapters. Chapter Two is concerned with some of the stories in this volume which deal with the "Grotesques" among men and women who feel trapped in their loneliness and isolation, and who fail to establish communication with others for reasons psychological and circumstantial. The nature of their sense of loneliness, whether it is a form of what has been sometime called 'metaphysical homelessness', or caused by some shortcomings in their own nature and forces of circumstances, is examined. The following stories are considered with reference to this theme: *Hands, Paper Pills, The Philosopher, Loneliness,* and *The Untold Lie,* all of which have men of their protagonists, and *Mother, Adventure, The Teacher, An Awakening* and *Death* which have women protagonists.

Chapter Three is devoted exclusively to examining Winesburg, Ohio as a *bildungsroman,* presenting the growth and development formulate adolescence towards maturity, of George Willard, the unifying character of different narratives in the volume, who shares with others at the suburban place of Winesburg several crippling traits, which he however manages to outgrow. How George's psychic and moral consciousness emerges and grows as he encounters and engages himself with different people in that small place, is highlighted.

Chapters Four, Five and six are mostly concerned with Anderson's post- Winesburg, Ohio stories. Chapter Four continues an examination of the theme of growing up as fond in the following stories which forms more or less homogeneous group: *I Want to Know Why, I am a Fool, The Man Who Became a Woman, An Ohio Pagan* and *The Sad Horn Blower*. All these stories are concerned with the growth of adolescents towards maturity and adult realization. The awakening of sex impulses figures in some of them. Some are retrospective narratives and draw attention to Anderson's narrative strategy. All these stories are episodic and therefore hint at development rather than elaborate on it as in Winesburg, Ohio.

Anderson was particularly concerned deeply about the perplexities, turmoil's and confusions in the relationships between men and women, and more often than not about failure of understanding between the married. Rarely does one find among Anderson's many stories one which presents a happy, harmonious and successful marital relationship. An almost impenetrable wall seems to separate men and women, and makes communication and understanding between them almost impossible. Mrs. Wife seems to be the solitary exception in this regard among the short stories, as it presents a middle aged couple who do achieve loving understanding between them. Chapter Four is concerned with this theme of man-woman relationship, and the following stories are considered with reference to it: *The Other Woman, The Door of the Trap, There She is She is taking her Bath, The Man's Story,* and *Mrs. Wife.* In fact failure of understanding and communication between men and women also figures in many of the other stories of Anderson's as the themes generally overlap.

Anderson has many stories, early and late alike, in which he dwells on men and women whose lives are filled with frustrations and disappointments, who live in loneliness and isolation stifled by the claustrophobic atmosphere of the places they live in, and who feel that their potentialities are all wasted and therefore have not lived their lives at all. Some of the Winesburg, Ohio stories which deal with this aspect of human experience are examined in an earlier chapter. Among such post Winesburg, Ohio stories *The Egg* is the most famous. But there are others which are equally moving and even appear tragic. Among them the following stories which explore this universal experience are focused on in Chapter Six: *Seeds, Unlighted Lamps, Out of Nowhere into Nothing, The New Englander,* and *The Egg*. These stories have different locales, and their protagonists belong to different age groups.

In Chapter Seven with which the present study draws to a close, the main line or argument presented in the previous chapters regarding Anderson's fictional recreation of the different related themes, is summed up. The study has no claims to have any original insights into Anderson's works. Nor does it claim to have made any new discoveries. Drawing liberally on the published scholarly critical commentary on Anderson's works, a selection of his short stories have been studied from a thematic point of view, for a better appreciation of the issues involved. This modest study hopes to have reaffirmed the continuing human relevance of Anderson's stories, his insights into the "grotesques", even at this date. In this context it is extremely apposite to cite David D. Anderson's summing up in the following words about the significance of Anderson's work:

> *The spirit of Anderson's work is the spirit of life—. The wonder of human life, a compassionate regard for it, and a compelling sense of discovering significance in the commonplace permeate his works, giving rise to a lyric beauty even in despair. Love, Compassion, Sympathy and understanding are the human virtues that*

raise man above his animal origins and prevent him from being a machine—Life is not only the great adventure for Anderson; in the final analysis it is the universal value-(As) a man who approached life with reverence, who spoke of it with love and who provided some of the most eloquent expressions both in his time, his place is secure.[31]

NOTES AND REFERENCES

1. David D. Anderson, "Introduction", *Critical Essays on Sherwood Anderson.*, ed. D.A. Anderson [Boston: G.K. Hall and Co., 1981], pp.1 and 9. Hereafter referred to as *Critical Essays.*
2. Walter Litz, ed, *Major American Short Stories* [New Delhi: Allied Publishers, 1975]. p. 443.
3. Frank O'Connor, *The Lonely Voice: a Study of The Short Story* [Cleveland: world, 1963], p. 41.
4. Walter Litz, p. 445.
5. Robert Allen Papinchak, *Sherwood Anderson: A Study of the Short Fiction* [New York: Twayne, 1993], p. ix.
6. Malcolm Cowley. *Anderson's Last Days of Innocence, the Achievement of Sherwood Anderson,* ed. Ray Lewis White [Chapel Hill: The University of North Carolina Press, 1016], p. 225. Hereafter Referred to as *The Achievement.*
7. Malcolm Cowley, "Introduction", *Winesburg, Ohio,* ed. Malcolm [New York: Viking Press,1960], p. 1.
8. See Anderson's *A Story Tellers Story,* and "Why I left Business for Literature", Century, August, 1924.
9. Ray Lewis White. *Sherwood Anderson: Early Writings* [Kent, Ohio: Kent State University Press, 1989], p. 115, Hereafter Referred to as *Early Writings.*
10. "Anderson and Myth", *Critical Essays,* p. 274.
11. Early Writings, p. 114.
12. Bernard Duffy, "The Renaissance in American Letters", *The Achievement.* p. 56.
13. David D. Anderson, *Sherwood Anderson: An Introduction and Interpretation* [New York: Holt Rinehart and Winston, 1967], p. 27. Hereafter Referred to as *Introduction and Interpretation.*
14. David D. Anderson, "Sherwood Anderson After 20 years", *The Achievement,* pp. 252-53.

15. David D. Anderson, "Sherwood Anderson's Moments of Insight", *Critical Essays*, p. 155.
16. Papinchak, p. 3.
17. Sherwood Anderson, *A Story Tellers Story* [New York: Garden City Publishers, 1924], p. 309.
18. Ibid., p. 352.
19. Rex Burbank, *Sherwood Anderson* [New York: Twayne, 1964], p. 63.
20. Introduction and Interpretation, p. 31.
21. Papinchak, p. 7.
22. Rex Burbank, p. 7.
23. *Introduction and Interpretation*, p. 2.
24. Ibid., p. 36.
25. Quoted by D.D Anderson, *Critical Essays*, p. 282.
26. Early Writings, p. 171.
27. David D. Anderson, "The Grotesque and George Willard", *Winesburg, Ohio: Text and Criticism*, ed. John H. Ferres [Middle Sex, England: Penguin Books, 1977], p. 423.
28. *Ibid.*, p. 421.
29. *Ibid.*, pp. 25-26.
30. Irwing Howe, "The Book of the Grotesque", *Winesburg, Ohio: Text and Criticism*, pp. 412-413.
31. *Introduction and Interpretation*, pp. 172-73.

CHAPTER – 2

Lonely Grotesques of Winesburg

It was pointed out in the previous chapter that the most recurrent and most impressive theme of Anderson which appears virtually in all his works and forms their ground bass is human loneliness and isolation and all the feelings that accompany it. Anderson explores this theme with particular reference to the American society of his times. However, experience of loneliness is as old as man and known to mankind form times immemorial. But at no time in human history it was as widespread and pervasive as it is in modern times. It may even be said that it has not only become the badge of contemporary life all over the world but is being experienced by a number of men and women with a keenness of edge and intensity as never before. Today throughout the world we are familiar with lonely crowds, loneliness in crowds, anonymous and lonely existence in crowded towns and cities. One is reminded of the 'crowd', which flowed over London Bridge, and 'each man' with his 'fixed' 'before his feet' in T.S. Eliot's The Waste Land. Philosophers, men of religion and social scientists have been deeply concerned with this phenomenon and are trying to trace its root cause and discover, if possible remedies for it in the modern world. In the world of letters, here is hardly a writer worth the name in the west or East, who is not anguished over it. It has become one of the central concerns of modern literature as of life.

For all its universal presence each society, country, and each individual experiences loneliness in a distinct way. They are all lonely but lonely in different ways. Sherwood Anderson, like other important writers of his generation, on either side of the Atlantic- James Joyce, T.S. Eliot, Katherine Mansfield, Ernest Hemingway, William Faulkner and others-contends with the problem of human loneliness and tries to come to grips with it.

Loneliness is the most striking symptom of the malaise afflicting man in the contemporary world. It is a sickness, which is mental and spiritual rather than physical. Gregarious as man is by instinct, he feels deeply the need to be related to the outside world, his family, his community or society and the world at large. He feels mentally and emotionally secure when he feels this relatedness others, however small the group comprising others be. This relationship need not always mean physical contact with one another. When this relationship snaps, one feels not only utterly lonely but also alienated. In Coleridge's Rime of the Ancient Mariner we have the most impressive example of such a spiritual condition. The Mariner's experience is exceptional in that he feels most acutely that he is estranged from man, all creation and God and cursed to live in the claustrophobic prison house of his own sterile guilty self. Only when he is able to pray, his anguish is transformed into joy and he is restored to human community. His suffering loneliness and alienation as well as his restoration takes place within a moral and supernatural order.

All loneliness need not necessarily be a symptom of sickness, spiritual or otherwise. For, one may choose deliberately to be alone and withdraw from society and all social contact with others, to an isolated and lonely place to live a life of a meditation and contemplation. Monks who retire to their remote monasteries and *sanyasis* who make their way to distant places in the Himalayas in India to live the life of recluses are of this kind. If they are not in touch with the outside society or world, they are in contact with or strive to be in contact with a higher power. Therefore they are never alone. It is possible that a political prisoner, condemned for life to live in a solitary cell, may not feel lonely, however oppressive and narrow the goal, because he feels a sense of solidarity with his fellow fighters who share with him his faith in an ideal, a new political order. In a significant sense he is in spiritual contact with others who are like minded. His shared faith sustains him. He experiences his loneliness and estrangements, which actually forced on him, chiefly at the physical level. In fiction there is the famous example of Robinson Crusoe, created by Daniel Defoe, who is forced to lie alone on a desolate island for an unbelievably long period of twenty-eight years before he is able to return home and to civilization. Though frightened out of his wits at the prospect of utter loneliness in a lonely island, Crusoe soon recovers, reconstructs there a miniature version of the ordered Protestant society he knew, devises his own calendar to guide his everyday life and lives according to it. His faith in God and his countrymen remains unshaken all through the years of his lonely existence and struggle to survive. What he experiences in essence is physical estrangement and not loneliness. Recent American history itself provides the example of Henry David Thoreau who deliberately chose to live all by himself in a hut which he himself built for a couple of years (1845-47) by the side of Walden pond to live as a recluse according to the values of the society he had come away from. Thoreau was in complete harmony with himself, and in constant contact in spirit with those of his kind, past and present. He neither felt lonely nor estranged. The distinguished thinker Enrich Fromn observes: 'Religion and nationalism as well as any custom and any belief however absurd and degrading if it only connects the individual with others, are refuges from what man most dreads: isolation'.[1] one could be living amidst people and yet experience overpoweringly utter isolation and loneliness when there are no related values, symbols and patterns of living shared among them. This spiritual isolation and loneliness is the most agonizing. Several branches of modern thought such as sociology, psychology and others have shown conclusively that modern man has lost his moorings in nature, in religion and simple human relationships which sustained him in former ages through thick and thin, and that these changes have affected him so profoundly that he feels lonely, insignificant and lost. Erich Fromn raises the question, which suggests its own answer, "whether there is not something fundamentally wrong with our own way of life and with the aim toward which we are striving".[2] most thinkers would endorse his view.

The experience of loneliness and isolation has remained a constantly recurrent theme in the American literary tradition, but the nature of this experience and how it is experienced, and its motivating factors have changed from generation to generation. The factors responsible for this recurrent phenomenon are bound up with American history, and its first manifestation dates back to the time when the first pilgrims from England landed in the New World and were challenged by an overwhelming sense of isolation, separated as they were form the old world by a vast ocean, and faced by a hostile environment. These first settlers were sustained by their faith in God, and they viewed their estrangement and loneliness as a test of their faith and potentialities, as the entries in the personal journal of William Bradford reveal.[3] Tracing historically in any detail the changing phases of this experience of isolation and loneliness and its significance as it finds expression in American literature is outside the scope of the present study. For its purposes it is enough to take note of the recurrent phenomenon and its presence in writers like Sherwood Anderson and others of his generation, so that it may serve as a scaffolding to approach Anderson's exploration and expression of it in his short stories.

If a broad generalization could be made at the risk of over-simplification, in the American literature of the 19th century- the period proceeding Anderson's-the hero sought loneliness as it were as a necessary precondition for self fulfillment, and for establishing his distinction and identity. To his counterpart in the 20th century, loneliness is his badge of defeat, an impenetrable barrier to self-fulfilment. He appears often as a pathetic figure, deprived of faith in himself, in his self-confidence and his identity. In contrast, *Huckleberry Finn* of the 19th century walks out of a particular society-though not form the human community that wants to 'civilize' him. By deliberately isolating himself from it he is able to articulate his dissent and define his own moral position. He has a viable goal to pursue, although it is precarious under the circumstances, since the indications are that he has almost reached the end of his tether. Nevertheless , he lights out for the "territory ahead of the rest'.[4] in Nathaniel Hawthorne's Hester Prynne (*The Scarlet Letter*) we have a character who is despised and ostracized by her decadent puritanical society, and thus forced to experience isolation as well as loneliness. But she remains imperturbable and defiant, for deep down within herself she knows and feels convinced that she is innocent, pure and inviolable. The price she has to pay for choosing her loneliness is the pain of isolation for no fault of hrs. it is a mark of her moral courage and inner strength that she does not feel defeated. Her loneliness enables her to preserve her integrity and individuality heroically.

Loneliness as it has been noted by many an Anderson critic is the keynote of his first major work Winesburg, Ohio. This work consists of twenty-one tales. The tables, as Rex Burbank points out, are "self-contained and complete in themselves and may be read individually with enjoyment". However "they gain an added and important dimension when read consecutively as episodes in a single narrative".[5] They are thematically related sketches about individuals whose lives are in some way connected. Thus the stories together present, as one of the first viewers of Winesburg, Ohio noted, "a continued picture of life in a small inland town".[6] Winesburg is a wholly imaginary Midwestern small country town of Anderson's creation (somewhat similar to Malgudi created by R.K. Narayan, one of the leading Indian novelists in

English, but very different in content and spirit form it). Its known layout and clearly defined topography offers a tremendous advantage to the creative imagination of one like Anderson who is deeply concerned with human beings. Within the small town's manageable limits, attention can be focused on individual men and women, their experiences and the problems vexing them-loneliness in the present instance-and probed into with imaginative sympathy. Anderson's own aim is to commiserate and understand through compassion and a loving concern for them, rather than judge or revile or satirize them.

The men and women who live in Winesburg are ordinary, average and unspectacular people, inconsequential and obscure. It could even be said that it is a small town of solitary persons. There is nothing special about them to attract attention except perhaps some harmless oddities and eccentricities. They are 'grotesques' in the sense Anderson uses the term charging it with a new meaning. There are men and women, young and old alike, among them. For one reason or another, either willfully or because of certain circumstances which they are unable to control, they have become isolate form others and lonely. As a result they are "closed off form the full range of human experience".[7] There is not normal sociability between men and women. People move about in Winesburg, come across their acquaintances or strangers, sometimes collide with one another, but rarely establish any meaningful communication and understanding with each other. "There is indeed more muttering than talk".[8] As observed by Waldo Frank. Not only does the word 'lonely' occur again and again in the course of the several narratives, but one of the stories is even given the title *Loneliness*. Almost everyone, regardless of age, experiences in one way or another, and in different degrees, an acute sense of isolation and loneliness, with little or no opportunities for building up enduring and fruitful human and personal relationships. They hardly participate in each other's lives, and those who try seem to fail invariably.

Surrender, one of the parts of the larger tale *Godliness* in Winesburg, Ohio, illustrates the points made. It is a story of misunderstanding and loneliness. Lousie Bently, a young country girl, the daughter of ' a delicate and overworked mother and an impulsive, hard and imaginative father', is sent to live with the Hardy's in Winesburg, where she attends school. As a child she is 'silent', 'moody', 'over sensitive' and 'neurotic' and not happy because her father looks upon her with disfavor. She wants, therefore, 'love more than anything else in the world', but does not get it. At the Hardy's place too she is not happy, as her dreams of freedom do not come true:

> *For years she had dreamed of the time when she could go forth into the world, and she looked upon the move into the Hardy household as a great step in the direction of freedom—. It had seemed to her that in town all must be gaiety and life, that men and women must live happily and freely giving and taking friendship and affection—. After the silence and cheerfulness of life in the Bently house she dreamed of stepping forth into an atmosphere that was warm and pulsating with life and reality.*[9]

But in the Hardy household she feels lonely and is treated with coldness and disfavor by the Hardy girls. The sharp pain of her childhood loneliness continues there too. "It seemed to her that between herself and all the people in the world, a wall had been built up".[10] Possessed by a vague and intangible hunger roused in her by her loneliness, and in her desperate need for love which was denied to her all these years, she risks writing to John Hardy, the son "I want some to love me and I want to love someone".[11] The next step is to take him for a lover, but her hunger for love remains ungratified. Marriage with him does not make matters any the better, because John neither understands, nor does he make an attempt to understand her unfulfilled longing. She becomes so much frustrated that "she did not know what she wanted".[12] she refuses to give their son David any of her love. Her sharp rejoinder to her reproaching husband is. "It is a man child and will get what it wants anyway. Had it been a woman child there is nothing in the world I would not have done for it".[13] Several other women in Winesburg go through similar experiences and echo Louse Bently's troubled feelings. Men and women alike share her agonized feeling that each individual is walled in and has to live in loneliness without communication or understanding.

The sense of loneliness is so subjective an experience that it seems easier to sense than define it. It is a state of mind and touches upon a variety of feelings It is experienced as separation, misunderstanding, failure, feelings of unworthiness, vague hunger, impotence, lostness and lack of communication etc., the grotesques of Winesburg, both men and women belonging to different interests as such, but is their ordinary humanity rather than at their intellectual brilliance that is stressed by the author. These denizens of Winesburg have their innate weaknesses and limitations, human as they are. However all are subject to the pressure exerted on them by their circumstances of which some of them are victims. They all seek love, fulfillment, and communion in a world where they feel alienated. There is hardly anything heroic about them, despite some of them like Dr. Reefy of *Paper Pills* exhibiting a quiet courage. All are seemingly minor characters, naïve, simple, pathetic, sometimes shrinking into themselves, caught as they are in struggle, conflicts and thwarted desires. Most of them grope for joy and happiness in life, which elude them. They are either inarticulate or half-articulate, but feel the urgent need to make human contact and break away the loneliness and isolation of their broken lives. This is the best seen in almost everyone of them eagerly seeking the sympathetic company of the young reporter George Willard, who seems to be the only person in Winesburg who has not yet become a grotesque. The irony of their lives is that they live in a small country town where everyone is likely to be known to everyone else, and therefore where there should be a sense of community, and yet feel lonely, and isolated because there is nothing in their society to connect them with each other.

Contrasting with these sensitive back street grotesques whose humanity has been outraged, are those conventional and banal people who dominate the official life of Winesburg, and exert an intangible but decisive and unhealthy influence over the less fortunate. These clods "present a background of moral decay, calculation, and artifice, of a rampant egoistic individualism".[14] For Tom Willard, young George's father, husband of Elizabeth Willard, and proprietor of the 'New Willard House" (*Mother*), and John Hardy the insensitive husband of Lousie Bently and banker (*Surrender*), the new American ideal of success is their religion. Will Henderson, editor of The Eagle and his saloon keeper friend Tom Willey, both are banal creatures and gossip-mongers. The middle aged Henderson (*The Philosopher*) is a "sensualist" and enjoys talking of women. Henry Carpenter, father of Belle Carpenter and Book Keeper in a local bank (*An Awakening*), is such a petty minded bully that he makes life almost unbearable for his daughter. The two persistent suitors of the rich "tall dark girl", who later marries Dr. Reefy (*Paper Pills*) profess love for her but actually lust for her body. Three are in Winesburg women like Wash William's mother-in-law (*Respectability*) and Helen White's mother (*Sophistication*) who "exploit sex with varying degrees of crudity and subtlety to draw young men to their daughters".[15] the Hardy sisters (*Surrender*) crush the sensitive country girl Lousie Bently by their hypocrisy and crafty use of sex.

Portrayal of such people as these reveals a society which is culturally moribund and socially degenerating. It appears as a society "that has no cultural framework form which to draw common experience no code of manners by which to initiate, guide and sustain meaningful relationships among individuals, no art to provide a communion of shared feeling and thought, and no established traditions by which to direct and balance their lives. They live in the midst of cultural failure".[16] what a decaying and degenerating place Winesburg has become may be gathered from the stories themselves, apart from the occasional but clear hints given in the narrative and dialogue. It has a dreary face, and is streets and alleys are cluttered with rubbish and broken glass. The housed and public buildings present a bleak and depressing spectacle. The New Willard House, never a flourishing hotel. Now looks a mere ghost of what a hotel should be, it is a disorderly old hotel, its wall paper faded, its carpets ragged, and the beds soiled (*Mother*) Bill Carter's lunch room, housed in a small frame building where Dr. Parcival dines is dirty and filled with flies, and Bill's 'white' apron is dirties than the floor (*The Philosopher*). Biddlebaum lives in a small frame house with a "half decayed veranda" (*Hands*). More examples can be cited to show how gloomy and barren of joy Winesburg is especially for the neglected and uncared for, but the instances given should suffice.

Anderson's endeavour in Winesburg, Ohio is to enter into the apparently uninteresting, defeated and frustrated lives of his characters with imaginative sympathy and empathy to understand and portray authentically their earnings, hopes, deprivations, frustrations and their sense of being alone in a stifling atmosphere. He does not develop their characters fully. Instead he focuses on the crucial and revealing moments their lives. But they are all distinct individuals without exception deserving sympathetic attention and understanding. Anderson is aware of the social and historical factors, which contributed greatly to the plight of these individuals. He senses that a repressive Puritanism without its relation God and the concomitant materialism are the chief social forces lurking behind the prevailing lifeless individualism and gross materialism. However, David D. Anderson presents in the right perspective Sherwood Anderson's approach to the grotesques and their problems in Winesburg, Ohio. He remarks: "In the short stories of Winesburg, Ohio Anderson is determined to treat isolation as a phenomenon of the individual rather than as a manifestation of social evil. As such, he approached the problem in its simplest level, seeking understanding through intuitive perception. This was to be accomplished not through analysis, but through empathy, his purpose being not to diagnose and to cure, but simply to understand and to love—".[17]

Against the background presented in the preceding paragraphs the stories selected from Winesburg, Ohio, may be briefly examined with particular reference to loneliness and isolation. Anderson's preoccupation with this theme , as is obvious, is not the result of any philosophical or literary influence. It springs directly form his own observation and experience of life as it was lived during his times. The stories of Winesburg, Ohio form one unit, and are knit together however seemingly loosely. The idea of the first tale, *The Book of the Grotesque* sets the tone for the subsequent narratives. The imaginative figures, apart from their shared suffering of loneliness, isolation and frustration are related in their environment. Though search story focuses on one individual man or woman and reflects and presents some emotional reality, the tales are thematically related and interconnected because of some common characters. George Willard the young reporter of the Eagle, for instance, appears in a majority of the stories. He is sought after by others in Winesburg to communicate with or confide in. Helen white, the attractive rich banker's daughter, is a presence of varying importance in more than one story. she is seen in *The Thinker, Drink, Sophistication* and *Departure,* Kate Swift, the teacher is a crucial presence in *The Strength of God,* and is the chief character in *The Teacher, Mother* and *Death* tell the sad and painful story of Elizabeth Willard, mother of George, and Dr. Reefy of *Paper Pills* also figures in one of her stories. Thus the common characters, common environment and psychic atmosphere, and shared experiences with the stories of Winesburg, Ohio into a whole. Of them only ten are chosen in the resent study for analysis, only as a measure of convenience. Six of them are concerned with men and five others with women. This division also is a measure of 'convenience'. All the protagonists are, as noted already, lonely, isolated, alienated, defeated and frustrated persons, their lives distorted, fragmented and broken, their emotional hunger, longing for love, communion, and fulfillment ungratified. They feel estranged from the basic sources of emotional sustenance, living as they do in a claustrophobic atmosphere. However, as human beings they are indeed like the twisted and gnarled apples rejected, but whose delicious sweetness is gathered at the side.

Now a close look at the stories of Winesburg, Ohio chosen for study may be taken. To begin with the stories of men, the following, as noted earlier, have been selected: *Hands, Paper Pills, The Philosopher, Loneliness, The Thinker*, and *Responsibility*. Among the chief characters of those stories there are old and young alike. There is considerable variety among them and their incisive experience of loneliness. To begin with *Hands,* it is as Rex Burbank has justly remarked, "one of the best tales around epiphanies can be seen in the portrayal of/wing Biddlebaum:.[18] it is about an unfortunate school teacher who comes to live as a recluse in Winesburg from a town in Pennsylvania literally hounded out of it in disgrace because of a complete misunderstanding of his nature and misinterpretation of his gestures. The story is presented as a third person omniscient authorial narrative and told form the point of view of Biddlebaum, who is the first in the series of lonely, isolated and alienated grotesques in Winesburg, Ohio who have suffered psychic damage and whose potential is thwarted. His actual name was Adolph Myres, which he changed into Wing Biddlebaum in Winesburg to suit his desire for anonymity. This timid and forever frightened man, "beset by a ghostly band of doubts", feels so lonely and alienated that he does "not think of himself as in any way part of the life of the town", where he has lived alone for "twenty years". His presence in Winesburg remains a "mystery".[19] So complete is his withdrawal from the people and society there. No one seems to be particularly interested in him, except as an occasional but of laughter. He was driven into this condition of helplessness and loneliness by an insensitive, unimaginative, unthinking and narrow-minded community of a town in Pennsylvania where he worked for some time, years ago as a school teacher. The harassment he was subjected to did him permanent psychic damage.

All of Biddlebaum's troubles began with his hands. It is "a story of hands".[20] says the narrator in a brief pregnant statement. Before telling the reader how it all happened, the narrator gives a brief description of the silent Biddlebaum's walking restlessly up and down in the dilapidated veranda of his lonely ramshackle house near the edge of a ravine in front of which is a long field with only a dense crop of weeds. The boisterous and laughing berry pickers, youths and maidens, returning from the fields, make fun of him. One of them from a distance commands this awkward bald man who had grown prematurely old, to "comb" his hair. He is so unnerved by it that his "nervous little hands (fiddle) about the bare white forehead as though arranging a mass of tangled locks".[21] this description suggests not only Biddlemaum's alienation from the town but a possible connection between his twitching and nervous hands and his loneliness. The dense crop of weeds grown in ht long field in front of his house also hints at his thwarted potential for creativity.

As the narrative makes its progress, more and more attention is focuses on Biddlebaum's hands, so that they acquire cumulative meaning and symbolic significance to justify the statement that this is "a story of hands", and hence the title given to this story. the lonely and alienated Biddlebaum hs one and only acquaintance in Winesburg in the young reporter George Willard with whom he has a sort of friendship. He looks forward to the youngster's visit to him and even ventures to walk with him in Main Street now and then breaking the shell of isolation. In his youthful company he becomes articulate his imagination is enlivened, and he talks excitedly about his dreams, his hands in their excited activity keeping pace with his talk:

The voice that had been low and trembling became shrill and loud. The bent figure straightened—Biddlebaum the silent began to talk, striving to put into words the ideas that had been in his mind during long years of silence. (He) talked much with his hands. His slender expressive fingers, forever active, forever striving to conceal themselves in his pockets or behind his back, came forth and became the piston rods of his machinery of expression.[22]

Talking to George makes Biddlebaum feel at ease and comfortable. He becomes wholly inspired. In his eagerness to advise him he forgets his hands, which steal forth, rest upon the young man's shoulders, and rise further to caress him. But suddenly as if he is thunder-struck, horror sweeps over Biddlebaum's face, and he thrusts his hands into his trousers pockets. Unable to talk any more, he abruptly leaves his company. George who is both perplexed and frightened, senses that there is "something wrong" and that "his hands have something to do with his fear of me and of everyone".[23]

It is this point of the narrative, the hidden story of Biddlebaum's hands and the secret of his loneliness and isolation are reveled. In his youth he was a school teacher in a town in Pennsylvania. By nature he was meant to be a teacher, and was much loved by the boys under his care. Of his exceptionally gentle nature the narrator says: "He was one of, those rare, little-understood men who rule by a power so gentle that it passes as a lovable weakness. In their "feeling for the boys under their charge such men are not unlike the finer sort of women in their love for men".[24] Biddlebaum walked with the students or sat with them upon the schoolhouse steps in the evening and "lost in a kind of dream". He talked to them in a voice "soft and musical", while his hands went "caressing the shoulders of the boys, playing about the tousled heads". The voice, the hands, the stroking of the shoulders and the touching of the hair were "part of the school master's effort to carry a dream into the young minds". By the caress in his fingers he expressed himself.[25] Unfortunately his loving touch upon his pupils was misinterpreted by a half-wit boy who had become enamored of the teacher, and the crude, obscene men of the town. He was beaten black and blue and driven out of the town in the dark and raining night, by indignant men, one of whom would have loved to hang the schoolmaster. Poor Biddlebaum did not understand what had happened but felt that his hands were to blame since every one of the furious attackers had warned him to keep his hands to himself. Since then he strove hard to conceal his hands, which had become a source of shame to him.

Having sought refuge in Winesburg, Biddlebaum had turned a day labourer, a berry picker, for his survival. His hands, however, could not escape attention, and even became famous despite his frantic effort to hide them, because he could with amazing speed pick "as high as a hundred and forty quarters of strawberries in a day".[26] In Winesburg his hands become his distinguishing feature and the source of his fame. The irony is that this country town is proud of his hands in the same spirit in which it is proud of the race winning bay stallion Tony Tip. The narrator comments appropriately that the hands "made more grotesque an already grotesque and elusive individuality".[27] In Winesburg, Biddlebaum lives a buried life, lonely and isolated, and afraid of being victimized. He also, it must be recognized, is a victim of his own timidity and naivete. A part of his isolation stems from his human shortcomings. All the same, this battered man rouses our sympathy. Forced to withdraw himself the lives of others, his psyche bruised by insensitive people, he is unable to find as outlet for his creative and imaginative life. Disillusioned and defeated he becomes a human fragment, all because of his hands, which were actually his means of expressing love. The nature of his love was creative and as long as he was a teacher it found an outlet in communication to his pupils though his gentle caresses, and in his own tendency to dream. But these gestures were misinterpreted.

As the narrative progresses the hands "change from image to symbol and the themes of alienation, fear, love and shame become in turn associated with them. And at the end of the narrative Biddlebaum appears as "a kind of defeated strangely perverted priest of love".[28]

Dr. Reefy of *Paper Pills* is the second grotesque to appear in the gallery of grotesque presented in Winesburg, Ohio. It is in telling his story of isolation and loneliness that Anderson used the very expressive analogy of twisted apples, which are discarded by fruit pickers, to render in terms of a concrete image, the grotesques of his conception. If Wing Biddlebaum presents one kind of psychic unfulfilment or limitation and thwarted potentiality, Dr. Reefy offers another. *Paper Pills* is an unemphatic story and told after effortlessly in a brief compass of five pages. Te basic problem in this story too is loneliness and isolation of human beings resulting in an inability to communicate. Anderson's approach to his characters is amply suggested by the image of twisted apples. It is his conviction that "the sources or natures of their deformities are unimportant compared to their intrinsic worth as human beings needing and deserving of understanding". He also believes "that one dare not reject because of mere appearance, either physical or spiritual; that appearance may mask significant experience made more intense and more worthwhile by the deformity itself".[29]

There is a contrast between Dr. Reefy's outward appearance and his inward nature. He is a tall old man with a white beard and huge nose and hands. The knuckles on his hands are "extraordinary large", and when the hands are closed they look like "clusters of unpainted wooden balls as large as walnuts fastened together by steel rods".[30] as if to match his awkward outward appearance, he is indifferently dressed. For ten years he has "worn one suit of clothes", "frayed at the sleeves" and with "little holes" "at the knees and elbows".[31] What is more, this country doctor who drives a buggy drawn by a faded horse, has chosen to live alone in his musty office in the Heffner Block above the Paris Dry

Goods Company's store. Nevertheless inwardly Dr. Reefy is a different man, sensitive,, understanding, insightful and thoughtful. There are in him "the seeds of something fine",[32] which however have not been allowed to sprout and grow to their full potential. The beauty of his inner life is revealed when he marries quietly and thus helps the tall dark girl who comes to confide in him and seeks his help in a desperate situation. Dr. Reefy understands what has happened to here and therefore does not ask her any questions. He merely takes her out for a ride in the countryside in his buggy. We hear nothing of their talk together. She discovers in him "the sweetness of twisted apples". When she dies and leaves all her wealth to him he is least affected by it. What difference her death after an all too brief married life makes for him and the stunning effect it has had on him is revealed in the following passage:

> *He smoked a cob pipe and after his wife's death sat all day in his empty office close by a window that was covered with cobwebs. He never opened the window. Once on a hot day in August he tried but found it stuck fast and after that he forgot all about it.*[33]

Dr. Reefy problem is the extreme difficulty of communication with others. Long before he married the young lady he had formed the habit of jotting down on scraps of paper in an epigrammatic form "thoughts, end of thoughts, beginning of thoughts".[34] During winter he read out to his wife all of the odds and ends of thoughts he had scribbled on bits of paper. He had formed the habit of thrusting these bits into the large pockets of his linen duster, which in course of time became hard pellets and balls. After his wife's death, Dr. Reefy has none to whom he can communicate his thoughts except John Spaniard, an old man and his only friend and his only human contact for ten years. But instead of reading the thoughts to him, he throws the paper pills on him. Dr. Reefy hears that others, unthinking and insensitive as they are, may not understand his thoughts properly and even misinterpret them. it is also possible that he himself feels the inadequacy of his thoughts in the face of the complexity of life. Either way, he has to prefer lonely silence to communication and allow his potentialities thwarted.

Characteristically Winesburg forgets this old man and ignores him because he has no use for it. The *Paper Pills*, which Dr. Reefy prefers to vain attempts at communication, "represents the barriers of isolation that surround human minds". He voluntarily isolates himself rather than try to over some those barriers and he "lets himself to become a grotesque because he is unable to find a satisfactory means of communication".[35] In a later story, Death, in which Dr. Reefy once again appears, he is shown not only as an understanding and compassionate man but as one who achieves real communication with another kindred soul in a moment of insight, although it does not last long, as death snatches away both of them.

In *The philosopher* Anderson presents another but a slightly different person whose outward appearance is a sharp contrast to his inward nature. Dr. Parcival, who is ironically called Philospher though he can hardly think coherently, is yet another specific instance of a grotesque character who, like Wing Biddlebaum and Dr. Reefy, acquiesces in his loneliness, living as the others do, in a shabby corner of life. he is said to be a doctor by profession, but by his own confession to George, he has "might few patients" and he does not want patients either, although he claims to know as much medicine as anyone in Winesburg.[36] Outwardly Dr. Parcival's appearance is literally ugly. He is "a large man with a dropping mouth covered by a fellow mustache". He always wears "a dirty white waistcoat", its pockets filled with "black cigars". His teeth are "black and irregular", and the lid of his left eye constantly twitches, falling down snapping up.[37] his office is 'unspeakably dirty'. The place where he dines, Bift Carter's lunchroom, is worse, it is "filled with flies", it is implied, is stale and uneatable. But Dr. Parcival is indifferent to all of them, and with a show of bravado tries to make a joke of it; "It makes no difference to me. I am a man of distinction, you see Why should I concern myself with what I eat".[38] All these factors would make Dr. Parcival appear if not revolting, if more about him, especially the turmoil and confusion in his mind and his lack of confidence, in himself are not known. The first hint that inwardly he may be a different person who deserves sympathetic understanding is indicated in his liking for the boy George Willard, his seeking on his own his acquaintance and trying to communicate with him. Interestingly, to Dr. Parcival and others like him in Winesburg, George "represents— the opportunity to restore communication with the world form which they all feel "excluded". They see in him "the key that will release them from their personal prisons and enable them to resume normal human forms—through understanding, acceptance, denied to them. therefore they feel confident and Love" which have been in George's presence.[39] If the lonely and frightened Biddlebaum feels sure of himself and walks freely with him through the town, Dr. Parcival feels confident to reveal the secrets of his life to him, hidden behind the mask of indifference and even hatred he puts on. he opens up and talks to him freely and uninhibitedly; "Why I want to talk to you of the matter", that is his not wanting patients although he knows as much medicine as any other in Winesburg 'I don't know. I might keep still and get more credit in your eyes. I have a desire to make you admire me, that's a fact. I don't know why. That's why I talk'.[40]

Sometimes this fat unclean-looking doctor tells George at great length tales about himself. But for all the urge he has for communicating with someone who would listen to him and despite his previous experience as a 'reporter' he is poor at it. The tales he tells George "began nowhere and ended nowhere" and sometimes they seem to contain "the very essence of truth".[41] He begins to tell about himself but soon digresses to speak about his drunkard brother of uncontrollable temper who never said a kind word either to him or to their mother and who roared and threatened them, though once in a while bought presents to them. in his own incoherent way the doctor reveals his past: how he grew under very insecure circumstances with an insane father kept in an asylum and a poor mother who scrubbed people's dirty clothes to make ends meet, and who loved her threatening and intemperate older son more than her younger son. He also tells him of his studying to be a minister though he did not become one, his stealing a dollar or two from the money left by his brother on the table and his experience as a reporter. Like some of the other grotesques of Winesburg, Dr. Parcival also wants to warn George against making a fool of himself as a reporter. It seems to the young man that the doctor has one object in view", to make everyone seem despicable".[42] The doctor's company is so engaging to George that for a month he goes to him every morning to spend an hour when the doctor reads to him from the pages of his book in progress. Significantly there is no mention of the doctor completing the writing of it.

An accident and the unexpected response of the doctor to it jerks the mask that he has been wearing and reveals him to be, for all his affected indifference and bravado, an utterly frightened man, carrying the burden of a guilt, and afraid of being victimized and persecuted. The incident mentioned above is reported at the close of the narrative. The little daughter of a farmer is thrown from a buggy and killed on Main Street. When someone runs to Dr. Parcival for help, he bluntly refusal passes unnoticed. It is also an indication of Winesburg's indifferences to him. But he feels so guilty that he is filled with terror. He tells George: "Word of my refusal will be whispered about. Presently men—will come here. We will quarrel and there will be a talk of hanging". And he feels convinced that he "will be hanged to a lamppost on Main Street", sooner or late[43] from the tenor of his incoherent narration of his past, it would seem that his present fear of being made a victim is a hangover of a past experiences when he was unjustly victimized. To cover up his haunting fear he appears to have put on the mask of indifference, and live as a recluse and an outcast in Winesburg. His failing to complete the book he began writing hints at his frustrated potential. The beauty of his nature hidden hitherto is momentarily glimpsed when e tells George that the theme of his incomplete book is "that everyone in the world in Christ and they are all crucified".[44] Obviously this generalization is in part a projection of his own experience of being unjustly victimized as Christ was: It also reveals his compassion, sympathy for several other lonely victims like him, who deserve sympathy and understanding. His nature has been distorted by his loneliness and isolation and the neglect and indifference he has experienced in Winesburg and elsewhere. Yet there remains in him, as Rex Burbank points out, "a weird, perverted beauty understanding of the human situation in his consciousness of profound that emotions laceration is a condition of life".[45]

Wash William of *Respectability*, which is serially the ninth story in Winesburg, Ohio, is outwardly perhaps the ugliest of the ignored and neglected men of the place who have become revoltingly ugly to look at by a traumatic experience, which has completely distorted his amiable and loving inward nature and his view of life making it macabre. In this story Anderson presents a straightforward authorial narrative with few digressions. Before telling the reader what particular experience damaged Wash William's inward nature, its goodness and beauty, and twisted it out of shape almost beyond recognition, the narrator dwells on his hideous physical appearance, his immense girth, thin neck, and feeble legs, and the dirt all around him. As in the case of Dr. Reefy of *Paper Pills*, the description of his physical appearance is intended to anticipate his inner beauty. He is likened to a caged monkey seen in city parks, " a huge, grotesque kind of — creature with ugly sagging, hairless skin below his eyes and a bright purple body". Children are fascinated by this creature".[46] It is the citizens of Winesburg who see the similarity between the beast in his cage and Wash Williams, the telegraph operator as he sits in the station yard after his office hours. This comparison between him and a caged monkey clearly suggests how much isolated: lonely and claustrophobic he must have felt in Winesburg, were no one pays any attention to him. He does not associate himself with anyone either. After drowning himself in been he staggers off to his bed in his room in the new Willard house of George's father.

There cannot be a more disquieting picture of a person than the above. The only relieving feature in the ugly, dirty and unclean person of Wash is the carve he takes of his hands. His fingers though "fat" are "sensitive and shapely".[47] This reference to Wash William's hands is very significant. Walter B. Rideout has pointed out that Anderson repeats certain elements throughout to give sufficient unity to Winesburg, Ohio while maintaining the 'looseness' of life as he sensed it, and also to give meaning and significance to the several stories individually and collectively. One such element or device is his frequent use of 'handi' in the singular or plural. "Very often— it suggests, even symbolizes, the potential or actual communication of one personality with another. The hands of Wing Biddlebaum and Dr. Reefy come immediately to mind",[48] but there are several instances also and Wash Williams is one among them. but sometimes the hand, may in fact express aggression rather than communication as in the case of Elmer Cowley in the story *Queer*. And as in *Hands*, it may also indicate murderous instincts: one of the men who attack poor Biddlebaum has a rope in his hands, for reasons obvious. Ironically "hands" also suggest personal isolation and loneliness. How his sensitive hands drive Biddlebaum into them, since few understand peoperly the significance of their activity, has already been seen. In the case of Wash Williams his sensitive hands, which have made him the best telegraphic operator, underline his loneliness and failure of communication. Partly because of his own withdrawal from social contact and largely because of the indifference and neglect of the residents of Winesburg, he has hardly anyone to communicate with, except perhaps the lifeless telegraphic instrument on which fingers play to send messages to others.

Only one or two people seem to care for Wash Williams and he interested in him. One of them is the Superintendent of telegraph operations of the railroad who appreciates his skill and efficiency as an operator and ignores the snobbish banker's wife's complaint against him and allows him to stay in Winesburg. The other is the young reporter George Willard who becomes curious about this man with a 'leering" and "hideous" face, wash too is drawn to George. Otherwise this man who had chosen to be lonely and isolated would not have gone out with him as other lonely and neglected people of Winesburg have desired. But he shrinks back though both are at the point of talking a "dozen times". George, sensitive and eager to understand others, senses that lurking in the blank staring eyes of others": he "had nevertheless something to say to him".[49] Therefore he ventures to draw the older man into a conversation and make him tell about his married life, which actually turns out to be a bitter and painful story. Wash Williams wouldn't have opened his mouth had he not suspected to his chagrin a romantic attachment developing between George and Belle Carpenter who worked in a milliner's shop. In an outburst of rage he tells George his own story to warn him against entertaining "foolish notions" about women. It is a story of unabashed infidelity and cuckoldry.

Years ago Walsh had married a beautiful girl and lived with her in Columbia, Ohio. He loved her madly and doted on her with an unfailing and blind devotion. He admits to George that he is fool enough to love her still, in spite of the raw deal he has received at her hands. The shock of her betrayal was made intense by the fact that he had remained "virginal" until he was married. When he learnt about her infidelity, he merely sent her to her mother and gave her all the money he had including what he got by selling their house. He was so naïve that he continued to love her even after he sent her away. He was "sick of living alone and wanted her back". He "ached to forgive and forgot".[50] So when his mother-in-law sent for him, he went to Dayton eagerly to make it up continuing to believe that his wife was innocent but wronged by her lovers. Having made him wait for hours, his wife was pushed into his presence naked by his mother-in-law. Walsh had the rudest jolt of his life. His sensibilities were so rudely shocked by the crudity and the obscenity of this move that he was revolted by what he saw rather than he impressed favourably by it. His mother-in-law was treating him outrageously as though he were a seducer.

This traumatic experience of personal disappointment and betrayal colours his vision of life and of all men and women. It is this, which makes a grotesque of him, a misogynist and hater of all life. he hates them all with an abandon. All women, past and present, are "rotten" for him and "dead". He spits forth a succession of vile oaths against them. They are a trick played by nature on men to "prevent men making the world worthwhile". Men are mere helpless victims of women. The extent of his bitter hatred of women is revealed in the following words: "They are creeping, crawling, squirming things, with their soft hands and their blue eyes. The sight of women sickens me. Whey I don't kill every woman I see I don't know".[51] in the white heat of his age and indignation, Wash Williams not only breaks his silence to communicate but also even become eloquent. Obviously George's sympathetic attention helps him in this process.

It is significant that Wash Williams narrates his pitiable story, which is a sort of confessional narrative, in the darkness of the evening. Biddlebaum and Dr. Parcival reveal themselves in their essential nature in semi-darkness. The interior of Dr. Reefy's office is always without any light. In the other stories of Winesburg, Ohio too, darkness or semidarkness or absence of light prevails especially when the moments revealing the character's inward nature are presented. On this aspect of the stories Irving Home makes the following helpful observation:

> *Winesburg is a book largely set in twilight and darkness, its background heavily shades with gloomy blacks and marshy grays as is proper for a world of withered men who, shattered by night, reach out for the sentient life they dimly recall the racial inheritance that has been squandered away.*[52]

It has to be added that after George listens to Wash William's story, he becomes aware of the inward beauty of Wash, which has been almost entirely damaged. As he listens to the older man, the young reporter finds himself imaging that he is sitting "besides a lonely young man with black hair and shining eyes". He also finds "something beautiful in the voice of Wash Williams", though he tells a "hideous" story [53]

Wash's deepest need is love and understanding. Not only are they denied him, but his love is treated with callous disregard and indifference. His misogamy, which is an aspect of his psychic deformity, is the consequence of this crucial failure in his life. he seeks love but finds it perverted into sex. Socially too he is defeated by the insensitivity and unresponsiveness of the Winesburg community. It seems inevitable that he seeks his isolation and loneliness. It is quite possible that his hatred of life in general and his misogamy are an unconscious self-protecting mask he wears for his survival. His concern for George Willard suggests that notwithstanding his bitter experience, there are remnants of his essential humanity still in him.

Winesbur, Ohio is full of insights into the buried life, into the thoughts of the repressed, the inarticulate, and the misunderstood. Most frequently frustrated is the desire to establish some degree of intimacy with another person". Writes Charles Child Walcutt.[54] Seth Richmond of *The Thinker* provides one more instance of such a buried life in the small country town of Winesburg. Elmer Cowly of *Queer* is yet another of this kind. He is literally inarticulate with frustration. He feels isolated, and thinks that he is condemned to go through life without friends. He is so self-conscious that he feels that no one says anything to him, although everyone stands around and laughs and talks with others. "I feel so queer that I can't talk either. I go away. I don't say anything I can't".[55] Ironically the only person he can talk to freely and with great freedom is a half-witted old man who held long conversations with farm animals.

Meek and reticent Seth Richmond the only child of his parents and brought up by his widowed and overworked mother Virginia Richmond with a singular protectiveness, feels lonely and isolated. He belongs to Winesburg since the time of his birth. The location of their housed in a little valley far out at the end of Main Street hints at the loneliness as well as isolation experienced by the young man who watches only form a distance the wagon loads of berry pickers, boys, girls and women, going to fields in the morning and returning in the evening. Their chatter and rude jokes irritate him and at the same time he regrets that he cannot laugh boisterously like them and "make himself a figure in the endless stream of moving, giggling activity".[56] In her attempt to protect her son whom she loves and prevent him from listening to gossip about his dead father, unwillingly his mother contributes to his isolation and loneliness. Therefore Seth lives aloof from everyday activities and cannot share in the lives of others or the life of the community.

Seth is a sensitive spirit and self-conscious youth, and has a tendency to nurture grievances against others of his age for isolating him. Actually he is isolated partly by his own timidity and awkwardness, which render him unable to break out of his isolation. His inability to communicate worsens it. His mother, despite her unlimited love and affection for him, remains "for the most part silent in his presence" because of an "almost unnatural respect for the youth".[57] When she does not react in the expected conventional way when she reprimands him causing uneasy doubts in her mind. Seth's adolescent escapade of running away from home along with a couple of boys and his return at the end of the week, once again illustrates the failure of communication between the mother and son. During his absence she is beside herself with suspense and anxiety. She even contemplates giving stinging reproofs to him. But when he actually returns and tells her frankly what he did and why he returned home, she "half resentfully" tells him that she is glad for what he did, and pretends to busy her with some work. She does not say anything more. In her inability to communicate and articulate, she seems a match to her son.

In Winesburg, Seth is of course greeted by men and boys with respect, but he is called the deep one like his father in the sense that he is not only a silent man but one who hides his real feelings and opinions. Actually Seth is no deeper than others of his age. His silence, which marks him out from others, is mistaken for some deep emotion and ideas. In actual fact, "no great underlying purpose" or "no definite plan for his life", lie back of his "habitual silence".[58] He is not particularly interested in what goes on and he himself wonders whether he would ever be particularly interested in anything. He sometimes wishes that he might be thoroughly stirred by fits of anger or excited by politics. It may do some good to him who is lonely, isolated and inarticulate. As he walks along to meet his friend George, he begins to think that loneliness is "a part of his character, something that would always stay with him".[59] In George's presence too he talks very little and all the talk is done by his effusive friend. He is unbearably irritated by George's condescending suggestion to him that he should tell Helen White the banker's daughter that chosen to fall in love with her and report back to him how she takes it. He has sets for whom silence has become habit, resents George and the men of the town who are "perpetually talking of nothing, and most of all against his own habit of silence".[60] He feels desperate. He is hurt by George's taking him for granted by asking him to be his messenger to Helen, without ever considering that he (Seth) too may have his own feelings about her. But the pity is that he cannot articulate them. All that he does, as he abruptly goes away from the place, is to mutter to himself that George is a "profound fool" and wishes that he could tell him so.

Actually Helen White has often been the subject of Seth's thoughts. He feels that she is "something private and personal to himself".[61] They have known each other since their school days and there has been " a half-expressed intimacy between them". though outwardly Seth makes his acquaintance with her to be "casual". As he walks away from George, his self-analysing habit, which can be paralyzing makes him think of his own inadequacies and depresses him. It is borne in on him that while George takes keen and enthusiastic interest in little everyday occurrences, he cannot. He is 'an outcast', not "a part of the life in his own town". Therefore he resolves on the spur of the moment that he will get out of the town without making any fuss. But he also smiles at "the absurdity of his thoughts".[62]

Seth goes to Helen White's house and knocks on the door feeling awkward and foolish. Helen who comes out 'blushing with pleasure' happy to see him. He feels so awkward and unsure of himself in her presence that instead of telling what he feels about her, he blurts out his plans to get away from the place, not knowing precisely what he really wants to do and where he wants to go. One also gets the doubt whether Seth really cares for his so called plans. In the process the tender romance of the occasion is destroyed. As they walk along, the half-embarrassed youth and maiden, the makes bold to put her hand into his, which gives him a strange and giddy feeling. In his confusion, instead of speaking about himself, he blurts out to her George's silly message to her. Her silence is her response to it. Daring thoughts come to his mind and he regrets his decision to get out of town: "It would be something new and altogether delightful to remain and walk often through the streets with Helen White".[63] He even imagines his lying on a summer evening under a tree with Helen by his side, her hand lying in his. Even in this imagined situation a "particular reluctance" keeps him from kissing her. Now sitting with her on a bench in the garden, he uneasily released her hand and thrusts his hands into his trousers pockets.

By this gesture Seth misses once for all the best opportunity to communicate his feelings to her. The potential for silent communication has hand has, goes waste. When he opens his mouth it is only to impress upon her the importance of his resolution 'to strike out' and 'get to work' in some other place. The narrator says that Helen too is duly impressed and sees in him not a boy but a strong purposeful man. The romance of the moment fizzles out for her too. The garden "with Seth beside her might have become the background for strange and wonderful adventures", but now t seems "no more than an ordinary Winesburg backyard".[64] Except repeating once again his impatience with the town where everyone merely talks, and his wish to go away from it, Seth has nothing more to say to her. Helen wants Seth to leave her alone to herself, and go to his mother to tell her about his plans.

Seth Puzzled and perplexed by her action stands there staring. As he walks slowly back home the feeling of loneliness possesses him once again. He tends to find fault with Helen for his disappointment: "That's how things will turn out. She will be like the rest— when it comes to loving someone, it won't never be me. It'll be someone—who talks a lot, someone like that George Willard.[65] Inarticulateness is certainly Seth's problem. But he is much too preoccupied with himself and his loneliness that he hardly makes an attempt to understand what goes on in Helen's mind. In complete disregard of her feelings he goes on to tell her of his future plans. And therefore perhaps she wants to be left alone. Rex Burbank makes the perceptive observation about Elmer Cowley (Queer) and Seth Richmond that "Neither has enough real insight or imagination to guess that others might be as lonely as they and their resentment about real insight or imagination to guess that others might be as lonely as they and their resentment about their isolation intensifies their dilemma".[66] for Seth Richmond's turning a lonely grotesque, his own innate limitations and his upbringing are partly responsible. He cannot articulate his loneliness and therefore is hopelessly defeated. Had the people of Winesburg taken some interest in him instead of commenting on his silence, he might have tried to break the shell of his inability as well as reluctance to communicate. Charles Child Walcutt has a plausible explanation for the confusion and constricted emotions of Seth and Helen at a critical moment. He attributes it to the absence in a small town like Winesburg of "a tradition of manners" which would have provided "a medium through which acquaintance could ripen into intimacy".[67] therefore sensitive spirits like Seth draw into themselves.

The last of the stories concerning men's loneliness to be considered is *Loneliness* which tells the story of Enoch Robinson, a real grotesque, both physically and mentally. An accident had made him lame. His own diffidence, his inability to understand others and to make others understand him, his desires and aspirations, his deep and instinctive need for love thwarted either because of misunderstanding or indifference or by a repressive conventionalism, make him inwardly too grotesque. His too is a buried life and his is a more agonizing and intenser experience of loneliness than Seth Richmond's. a boy form the farm near Winesburg, Enoch never grows up and remains a sort of child-man even into his old age. He is a self isolated personality. But his isolation began even in his childhood. This is suggested by the fact that his farmhouse in Winesburg was located two miles beyond the house limits, and that "the blinds to all of the windows facing the road were kept closed". It would seem that he grew up in a claustrophobic environment form the start. At school he was known to be a "quiet smiling youth inclined to silence".[68] more or less alone.

Enoch is an artist, a painter or sorts. As young man he "could draw well enough and had many delicate thoughts hidden away in his brain that might have expressed themselves through the brush of a painter".[69] But nothing came of it. Inspite of his long stay in New York and his going to an art school there, he failed to make the grade. He always remained a child, happy in the world of his fantasy, and never grew up. Money, sex opinions did not matter to him. In New York he had a number of friends among young artists, men and women, who came to his room. While they all talked of art passionately and feverishly Enoch sat in a corner silently and said nothing. He wanted to talk too but he did not know how". When ever he tied his sputtered and stammered. "He knew what he wanted to say, but he knew also that he could never by any possibility say it".[70] When a picture of his is admired by his artist friends, he was so much irritated that he wanted to tell them that their understanding and interpretation of it both were wrong. But he just could not say it. Self conscious as he was began "to doubt his own mind. He was afraid the things he felt were not getting expressed in the pictures he painted".[71] it must have been a harrowing agony to him to be not only incapable of expressing himself in both speech and painting but also bed aware of that fact.

Enoch's solution to his predicament was to shut himself in his long narrow room, which looked more like a hallway than a room, and shun all company. The narrator of the story makes the significant remark. "The story of Enoch is in fact the story of a room almost more than it is the story of a man".[72] Enoch's room is this story becomes a most expressive symbol of his claustrophobic loneliness and isolation , his inability to communicate and understand as well as make others understand him. Alone in his room, Enoch filled it with the people of his fancy and invention, an odd lit comprising two dozen, and freely and eloquently talked to those shadow people, 'happy as a child is happy'. With an absurd air of importance he talked to them aloud, giving instructions, and making comments upon life. but even then his sense of loneliness did not leave him. To get over it he married and marriage did not help him. Living with his wife and two children in an apartment made him feel choked as he had felt when his artist friends visited him. He had to invent excuses to be alone. He rented once again the same narrow room, locked himself in and felt happy in the company of the figures of his fantasy, talking to them to his hearts content. Then

Enoch freed himself to his wife and children. His wife was happy t go away although she cried and made a fuss about it, because she had begun to doubt his sanity.

To send Enoch back to the small town of Winesburg something else happened. Another woman entered his life. She sat with him looking at him and said nothing. After sometime she too got on his nerves. She, he thought, was an encroachment on his privacy and individuality. But his attitude to her was ambiguous. He wanted her to understand him and at the same time he could not let her understand him.[73] As if he cherished his loneliness and isolation, in mad fury and frenzy he drove her out. But it had a totally unexpected result. All creatures of his invention also vanished along with her, never to return, leaving Enoch to taste his bitter loneliness. He bemoans to George, whom he has cultivated and finds in him a sympathetic listener who would understand him, " I am alone, all alone here. It was warm and friendly in my room but now I'm all alone".[74] Enoch Robinson's is a peculiar and most pathetic case isolation and loneliness have damaged him and brought him to the very edge of mental derangement, "his loneliness is such a powerful force in his life", observes Rex Burbank aptly, "that it becomes a kind of demon and crushes his effort to overcome it".[75] Apart from Enoch's own inherent limitations which are partly responsible for his becoming a grotesque, there are to her external factors contributing to it. He hungered for love and understanding and both were denied. His artistic potentiality and sensibility were thwarted. With particular reference to this aspect of his character David Anderson makes the following pertinent observation with which the present analysis of Enoch Robin's story may close:

> *Loneliness describes a twofold manifestation of human isolation so severe that it drives Enoch Robinson into the supposed security of a single room and then denied him even that security. An artist who had returned to Winesburg after an unsuccessful marriage Robinson tells George the peculiar isolation of the artist in a society*

that makes special demands on him while it denied understanding until finally he flees, driven from his work and losing the only means whereby he can reveal his dream. Robinson's isolation is not only that of other men, it is also the peculiar isolation that only the unfulfilled artist can know.[76]

Next the stories concerning women and their incisive experience of loneliness and isolation, which make them also grotesques, may be taken up for brief analysis.

In Winesburg, Ohio there are only a handful of stories with women as their protagonists and the foci of attention, the stories concerning men out numbering them. But they are very moving deeply touched by the pathetic and the tragic. Women of these stories experience unbearable loneliness, isolation, thwarted potential, frustration, misunderstanding, failure of communication, inarticulateness etc., and live buried lives, and become grotesques for much the same reasons as men of the place do. All of them face the same predicament. But they are far more constricted than their men counterparts. They have few opportunities to free themselves from the constraints largely imposed on them by their social environment, conventions and traditions, which condition their lives. They wish for elbow room for themselves if not absolute freedom. They seem to have little or no scope in Winesburg to develop their individualities or potentialities. Above all they all long for love, and want to be loved much more than have a mere lover. In their minds they make a clear distinction between being really loved for their own sake a having a lover who merely gratifies a psychological need. This hunger for love remains unfulfilled though they go through travails and some of them even take risks. Disappointment and frustration remains by and large their lot. There is yet another factor, somewhat strange, common to all the women. Unlike, at least some of the young men of Winesburg like George Willard, Elmer Cowley and Seth Richmond, few women think of leaving the country town to seek a new life elsewhere. Kate Swift the teacher, for example, who has travelled in Europe and lived in New York City for two years, returns to Winesburg to settle there. Elizabeth Willard's ardent with to travel in the wide world remains only a frustrated dream. Alice Hyndman for a time thinks of going to the city to search for her lover Ned Curie, but she gives up the scheme.

The first focus chiefly on the mother-son relationship and her ambition for her son, which go contrary to her husband's in addition to drawing attention to the other handicaps of life that Elizabeth Willard has to live with. *Death* covers her early life, her youthful romantic dreams, her disillusioned married life, the lucid interval of her friendship with Reefy and her death for which she longs. Unlike the woman in *Paper Pills,* she hungers to express herself and articulate all that she feels and thinks, but she is no less silent and no freer, having been defeated in life and turned into a grotesque very early in life. When she is introduced in *Mother* again she is forty-five years old, tall and gaunt with smallpox scars on her face, suffering from some obscure wasting disease, which has taken away all the vitality form her life, She is listless and goes about their old disorderly hotel looking at the faded wall paper and ragged carpet, which serve as a faithful image of her own life. To her husband Tom Willard, who is "a slender, graceful man with square shoulders, a quick military step, and a black mustache", she is no more than 'a tall ghostly figure' and a 'reproach' to his life. He puts her out of his mind as far as possible, for him both the old house and the woman are things defeated and done for".[79] Their marriage is a thorough failure, an utterly disillusioning experience, especially for her. There is neither love nor respect for each other. There are few instances of tolerably happy married life in Winesburg. Whether it is Elizabeth Willard or Lousie Bently or Ray Pearson's wife (*The Untold Lie*), not one of them has the semblance of a happy married life though for different reasons. There is, it is implied, something in the environment which makes a happy marriage and harmonious relation between husband and wife extremely difficult.

Elizabeth Willard hates her husband for more than one reason. Her hatred is so intense that even murderous thoughts pass through her mind once.[80] There is no indication in either story that her husband has ever felt any concern for her. There is hardly any communication or even perfunctory conversation between them. He has always been insensitive to her feelings and longings. He has a passion for village politics and entertains ambitions of a political career too. But what is most hurting to Elizabeth is his dramatizing himself as a "successful man" despite their hotel never doing well, and wanting their son George to "succeed", which means going to the city to 'make money', become a business man perhaps, and "be brisk and smart".[81] This is precisely what Elizabeth detests. She too has ambition for her son in whom she is completely involved. She does not want him to catch the itch of "success". She hopes to see her youthful dreams fulfilled in her son in whom she senses "a secret something that is striving to grow".[82] Her prayer to God, challenging in its tone and fervor, is that her son should not become a meaningless and drab figure", a defeated person like herself: "I will take any blow that may befall if but this my boy be allowed to express something for us both—And do not let him become smart and successful either".[83] She anxiously watches her son's activities and movements.

Strangely, notwithstanding the "deep unexpressed bond of sympathy" between the mother and son based on a girlhood dream that had long go died", there is hardly any communication between them. In his presence she is "timid and reserved", and "communion" between them again is "outwardly a formal thing without meaning".[84] Inarticulateness is an agonizing problem for her and it is not restricted to her insensitive and understanding husband but extends to her son too. Again it seems odd that the son George visits his sick mother only occasionally though they live under the same roof. When they actually meet there is more of silence than any exchange of words.

Left alone and isolated, both mentally and physically, Elizabeth has to spend days of dullness on end, and brood over her lot. In the contest between the bearded baker Abner Groft and the clever eluding gray cat in the Alleyway and the prolonged and ineffectual outburst of the baker against the cat which safely hides itself behind a barrel, she sees "a rehearsal for her own life, terrible with and become eloquently articulate is Dr. Reefy. The two grotesques discover in each other kindred spirits who can understand perfectly and sympathetically their dreams, hopes, defeats and frustrations. It is to him that Elizabeth opens up her past frankly and uninhibitedly. The first and last time in her life she tastes what true love is as both as he and Dr. Reefy fall in love with each other. The doctor is the only man she really loves, and all the other men in her youth she came into contact with including tom whom she later married, did not even touch the fringe of true love.

Dr. Reefy knows how to listen and encourage others to express themselves freely in his presence. When Elizabeth talks to him she comes to life, and feels revived and strengthened against the drabness of her life. the gaunt, sickly and tired woman of forty-one seems to become young in spirits, when she walks while talking to him, there is a "swing, a rhythm: to her whole body.[86] it is to him that she tells the story of her life from her childhood, childhood onwards reconstructing in words some of the crucial moments of her life in the past. It is then Dr. Reefy discovers how sweet, and dear is her nature. He cannot but declare, "You dear! You lovely dear!".[87] which she cherishes till the end of her life, though she does not meet him again alive. Left motherless when she was just five years old, and living with a father who was sickly and wished to be left alone, Elizabeth's girlhood was "lived in the most haphazard manner imaginable".[88] It was a sad, insecure and inarticulate childhood and girlhood. A great restlessness and confusion possessed her, which expressed itself in "an uneasy desire for change, for some big movement in her life". she tried to be "a real adventurer in life".[89] That was the time when she was 'stage struck' and dreamt of joining a theatrical company and "wandering over the world seeing always new faces and giving something out of herself to all people".[90] Naturally she was disappointed as few of the theatrical people encouraged her though they sympathized with her romantic dream. Then came her relations with young men, including Tom Willard whom she later married. She had half a dozen lovers, but none understand and gratified her longing for a "real lover". "Always there was something she sought blindly, passionately, some hidden wonder in life— In all the babble of words that fell from the lips of the men with whom she adventured she was trying to find what would be for her the true world".[91]

Her unconventional ways had brought Elizabeth "a somewhat shaky reputation in Winesburg".[92] Like most girls she thought marriage would change the face of life. she married Tom Willard because "he was at hand" and her rather was ill and near death at that time. She herself was perplexed by the meaningless outcome of an affair she had been involved. Inspite of her father's warnings against her marrying Tom and against the "muddle" of marriage itself she married him. As she confessed to Dr. Reefy, the marriage "did not turn out", "It wasn't Tom I wanted, it was marriage.[93] With in months after marriage, which was a failure almost from the start, her restless and her irrepressible longing for something she could not define possessed her again. How desperately she sought release and freedom are revealed in her description of her buggy ride to Dr. Reefy: "I wanted to get out of town, out of my clothes, put of my marriage, out of my body, out everything—I wanted to run away from everything, but I wanted to run towards something too".[94]

Elizabeth Willard does not go to meet Dr. Reefy again, probably because that rare moment of understanding they both had reached may not be renewed again. She longs of death with the eagerness of a lover, which comes t her a few months afterwards. Death brings her the much needed release, but her wish to tell her son before she dies about the hidden money remains unfulfilled as death overtake inspite of her pleas to this lover. It may be assumed that she has at the time of her death the consolation that her son will not be like his father. His words to her during one of their rate meetings were, "Don't know what I shall do. I just want to go away and look at people and think— something that father said makes it sure that I shall have to go away", [95] is some hope of her dreams being fulfilled in her son. All the same, hers is a lonely life of unrelieved tensions, thwarted hopes and aspirations. The stifling and narrowly conventional Winesburg community could not show an opening, an outlet for her potentialities to manifest themselves creatively and fruitfully.

Mother and *Death* present most impressively the terrible poignancy of loneliness and isolation of a mother who is denied live, understanding, companionship, and whose potential for a normal life of joy and happiness has been stunted who is left with a vague ungratified hunger and frustration, and in whose life nothing happens inspite of anticipation. In recreating Elizabeth Willard's life, Anderson demonstrates what it would be like if one is denied love and experiences the death of love. Instead of real love for which she hungers, she is forced to listen to the babble of words from them any lovers she has known. It is her plight that she cannot even communicate her love for her son George, but express to him only vaguely her anxious concern for his future. When mother and son meet, either there is a tense silence between them despite spent up feelings or there are, when they attempt to speak, only a few inconsequential words. The mother tells the son, "I think you had better be out among the boys. You are too much indoors". In reply he says, "I thought I would take a little walk".[96] She is the worst hit by the stifling atmosphere of Winesburg which successfully neutralizes all her longings for a life of adventure. Elizabeth Willard is alienated from everything that gives meaning, purpose and joy to life, and she is conscious of it. Waldo Frank remarks: "The form of the mother, frustrate, lonely, at last desperate, pervades the variations that make the rest of the book".[97]

The story of Elizabeth Willard who yearned all her life true love and a real lover and was left defeated, leads to the story of Alice Hindman (*Adventure*) who too experiences a like hunger with equal intensity, gets disappointed because her lover deserts her, suffers psychic damage and grows old and queer even by the time she is twenty seven. She is one of the loneliest in Winesburg, and experiences all the consequences of loneliness that other grotesques like her in the country town experience. Alice Hindman's story is given an expressively ironical title *Adventure*. In her life nothing really happens, and nothing can happen. The one and only "adventure" she risks in her otherwise passive life of "waiting" for a lover who has cheated her, is rushing out naked on a rainy night in the despair of her loneliness "to find some other lonely human and embrace him". Ironically it ends in an utter fiasco. This is worse than nothing happening. This "adventure"[98] drives home to her the defeat and futility of her life.

Alice Hindman is outwardly quiet and placid, but she experiences a continual ferment inwardly. Ned Currie, with whom she fell in love when she was sixteen, and who promised before going away to Cleaveland to get a place in a newspaper that he would return to Winesburg to take her with him and marry, never returns having forgotten her altogether. Alice never reconciles herself to this fact ad keeps on waiting for him. She even starts saving money so that she can go to the city to find him and claim his love. For a long time she regards herself as Ned's wife whether he comes back or not. Therefore she refuses to have anything to do with other young men. Tearfully she whispers to herself: "Oh Ned, I am waiting" though the creeping fear in her grows stronger that he would never come back.[99] She cannot understand "the growing modern idea of a woman's owning herself and giving and taking for hr won ends in life".[100]

With the passage of time, Alice realized that her freshness and youth are fading away. Fear of age and ineffectuality possess her, and she becomes more and more lonely. He mother's second marriage emphasizes her isolation even at home. Prayer at home is of little help. Attending Sunday prayer meeting and the meetings of the Epworth League to get acquainted with people hardly helps her. To overcome her increasing loneliness she adopts eccentric ways. She becomes attached to the furniture in her room and cannot bear to have anyone touch it because it is her own.[101] She continues to save money though she gave up the scheme of going to the city to find Ned. As in the case of George Eliot's Silar Marner, saving money becomes a habit. For her emotional gratification she clings on t inanimate objects as substitutes to the lover she has lost. In her desperation to get a new hold on life she even walks with the middle-aged clerk Will Hurley. Even this does not work. His company becomes tedious and she sends him away. Her fear is that he may not understand her real need: "It is not him that I want. I want to avoid being much alone".[102]

Alice remembers Ned now and then but she does not depend on him any longer, nor does she want any other man: "She wanted to be loved, to have something answer the call that was growing louder and louder within her". She mutters to herself again and gain: "Why does not something happen? Why am I left here alone?".[103] this refrain voices the agony of all lonely people in Wiinesburg as well as elsewhere. One rainy night, distraught by her loneliness, a wild and desperate mood taking possession of hr, she tries something adventurous, she rushes out of the house naked and stands in the cold rain. She thinks that "the rain would have some creative and wonderful effect on her body". She feels "so full of youth and courage" that she wants "to leap and run, to cry out", and above all "to find some other lonely human and embrace him".[104] The bitter irony of her one and only adventure is that the lonely man she finds and embraces is an old man somewhat deaf who cannot hear what she says or understand her desperate longing and hunger. Frightened she drops to the ground unable to understand the meaning of her own act. She dare not get her feet, but crawls on all flours to her room. Broken hearted she weeps. She reflects on her hysterical conduct and realizes that there is no way out of her loneliness. In a moment of resignation she comes to the conclusion "that many people must live and die alone even in Winesburg".[105] Life appears as blind alley of loneliness from which there seems to be no escape. She derives some consolation in that thought.

Commenting on Alice's approach to her life and loneliness Marilyn Atlas remarks: "She at no time considers finding a healthy outlet for her needs, but rather she demands that instinct be controlled, she doesn't consider being larger and learning to own the various parts of her nature, but rather demands that she be smaller and survive that smallness".[106] This critic also complains that Anderson "is not allowing women many options".[107] It is true that Alice does not look for options, but the blame for it does not lie with Anderson. It is plain form Alice's story that apart from the limitations of Alice's own nature, her understanding and intelligence being average, then narrowly conventional environment, with suggestions of a puritanical bias, into which she is born and in which she grows up. Allows her a few options to look for. By nature she is not rebellious and the one act of revolt she tires on the rainy night demonstrates the futility of her effort. Moreover Alice is so lonely and isolated, so much withdrawn into her own self, that she has none even to communicate with. Let alone seek advice from. She has not even George Willard to listen to her tale. At home her mother is preoccupied with her own life and has little thought for the daughter. Her stepfather is indifference. And the one-man she loved, trusted and hoped fervently to marry, lets her down badly. In view of these facts could she have been other than a grotesque? Anderson seems to imply all these in narrating her story. It is easy to dub Alice a sexually frustrated spinster to explain her eccentric behaviour. Even so sensitive a critic of Anderson as Rex Burbank says that her "years of loneliness and sexual frustration displays itself as she rushed naked out into the rain at night".[108] There is no need to labour the presence of sex and its disappointments in her life. but that alone cannot account for her queer 'adventure': "—the impulse that drives her to this antic behaviour is not as has been suggested sexual frustration. Her desire for communication transcends the sexual—In her extremely Alice wanted to find and embrace some other lonely human".[109]

The Teacher is a most delicately and suggestively told story in Winesburg, Ohio. It is a story of subdued pathos. Kate Swift the school teacher is regarded by some as one of the most lovable of women created by Sherwood Anderson. Without a doubt she is one of the most sensitive and articulate of the grotesques in Winesburg whose desires and aspirations are thwarted and who have few opportunities for fruitful human relationships and therefore become outcasts or recluses. Kate Swift is very much of a recluse. She is first introduced to the reader indirectly through *The Strength of God* which precedes *The Teacher,* and tells the story of the devour Presbyterian minister Curtis Hartman, who ironically becomes a peeping tom and spies on her in her bedroom form the bell tower of the church. It is through his eyes that Kate is presented. She is a school teacher, she is thirty years old and has " a neat trim looking figure". She has few friends and she bears "the reputation of having a sharp tongue".[110] She had been to Europe and had lived in New York city for two years before she came to settle in Winesburg. She also smokes. Some of these facts indicate that Kate Swift is somewhat unconventional in the conventional Winesburg society. They also suggest that she is much unlike the other women of Winesburg analysed so far.

In *The Thinker* Kate Swift is first seen through the eyes of George Willard, the young reporter, who was once her pupil, in whom she has taken great interest. She "had talked to him" on four or five occasions "with great earnestness and he could not make out what she meant by her talk". He begins to believe that this former teacher of his "might be in love with him".[111] For him it is a pleasing as well as an annoying thought. At the same time there is here an indication that Kate has difficulties of communication despite her being articulate, and that George, and perhaps others too, cannot understand her meaning. Difficulties of communication and misunderstanding are the problems that most men and women grotesques experience.

In the eyes of Winesburg, Kate Swift is an old maid, conventional, and unattractive with something biting and forbidding in her character. She is usually cold, stern, and withdrawn in the class room. But when she tells stories t her students she becomes animated and spellbinds them. Both the teacher and her pupils share the happiness of the occasion. In telling stories she can be very inventive and imaginative. Once she talked to her students about Charles Lamb making up strange, intimate little stories about that lovable writer, as if she knew all the secrets of his private life. She also talked to them about the old artist Benvenuto Cellini presenting him as "a bragging, blustering, brave, lovable fellow, inventing humorous anecdotes about him. The students and the teacher laughed heartily. But suddenly she stiffened up, became cold and stern again,[112] withdrawing herself into her shell.

Behind her cold exterior and appearance of lacking in human feeling, Kate Swift has actually a nature eagerly passionate and insensitive "yearning for companionship and significant achievement".[113] She aches for a full life and gropes towards it. Feeling lonely and isolated, she is almost always restless, a storm raging inwardly. She goes out long walks even on stormy nights so that she may contain her inward agitation. As she walks along "grief, hope and desire" fight within her.[114] Whatever adventure there was in her life seems to be a thing of a past. Going for long walks even on cold nights against the doctor's warning to hr is the only adventure seen in her present life. Why did Kate Swift, who was well educated, had travelled to Europe, and lived for two years in New York, choose to settle an enigma. Perhaps some crucial failure and defeat in her life has been responsible for it. There is no indication that she has any intention of leaving this small suffocating town. Like Dr, Reefy in his dusty office, Enoch Robinson in his fantasy-crowded room, and Elizabeth Willard in her sick room, she too is alone in her bedroom. Her isolation of herself in her room, which is as barren of joy as the town itself, appears to be largely voluntary. The room is used by Anderson as a symbol for the stifling loneliness and isolation of these people.[115]

Kate Swift's hunger like that of Wing Biddlebaum and unlike that of Alice Hindman is not vague. It is for meaningful communication. But "there is no man of her sensibility in Winesburg". She also knows like Dr.Reefy that "the only way to abate loneliness is through absorption in others".[116] Having recognized "a spark of genius" Like Elizabeth Willard's schoolboy essays, she wants "to blow on the spark".[117] Like Elizabeth Willard she too wants to be a serious writer and express something for the people of the town. Judging by her lively imagination and gift for narration especially in talking to her pupils about Lamb and Cellini, it is quite possible that she had ambitions of becoming a writer herself, which for some reason or other was not fulfilled. And therefore, like George's mother, she too is trying to nourish his talent hoping unconsciously to see her own dreams fulfilled through him. She speaks to him in great earnestness more than once to bring home to him the difficulties he would have to face as a writer. She urges him to equip himself for the task. She warns him against his egocentric fascination with words, and wants him t immerse himself in life, and look into the minds and hearts of people before writing about them.[118]

On that particular cold and rainy night when Kate Swift caught in an inner storm takes a long and unpremeditated walk, her mind is ablaze with thoughts of George. She seeks him in his office and talks to him about his responsibilities as a writer in such passionate earnestness that it becomes "something physical".[119] She had noticed earlier that he was rapidly becoming a man combining the winsomeness of the boy and something of a man's appeal. Now as she looks at him "the passionate desire to be loved by a man that had a thousand times before swept like a storm over her body", takes possession of her. George appears to be " a man ready to play the part". She allows him to take her into his arms. But both become confused, and she breaks away from him hitting him in her fear and frustration, and runs away.[120] Could it be that in that moment of confusion her sexual urges were suddenly released and immediately frozen by embarrassment? Or was she, like Biddlebaum, trying to communicate her experience of life through caress but could not express herself adequately? Reflecting on that experience George, due to the growth of intuitive wisdom realizes that it is not sex that she was seeking and that perhaps he has "missed something Kate Swift was trying to say",[121] what was actually on her mind and what was she trying to tell him, remain uncertain. There is, to be sure, an element of sex in Kate Swift's concern for George, but much stronger is the anguish to help him to become a responsible writer. Her loneliness that is partly self imposed, and inability to articulate fully and properly make her pathetic.

Winesburg, Ohio as whole conveys the feeling of loneliness, isolation and defeat through twenty and odd specific instances of people, both,, men and women of Winesburg, who have been transformed into grotesques. Anderson understands them through intuitive understanding and empathy, and presents their tales through the omniscient authorial point of view. In the foregoing pages of this chapter eleven of the lonely people Biddlebaum onwards, have been analyzed. For one reason or to her lonely men and women have become, either witfully or because of circumstantial pressures, isolated and closed off from the full range of life's experiences, and they live narrow, lonely, lives. Denial of love or the death of it is a common experience for most of them. And their yearning for love is frustrated. Women are the worst affected in this respect. Elizabeth Willard, Alice

Hindman, Kate Swift, and Louise Bently are all poignant instances of it. Of course men too have their share of it. The lives of Biddlebaum, Dr.Reefy, Wash William and Seth Richardson are empty because of it.

Further, few of them have any friends. None has nay active relationship with the society in which they live, and they have no sense of community, which for them is sterile, insensitive and in capable of any understanding. Probably because of his freshness and as yet uncorrupted youth and sensitiveness many of them seek George Willard to confide in. they live lonely buried lives, because of their thwarted potentialities and the absence of an out let and an opening for their energies. Inarticulateness is a curse they all labour under. Their defeated inner lives are full of agitation and turbulence. Loneliness drives some of them to the edge of despair. Religion in their society is reduced to sterile and empty conventional moralism. Few pray because prayer seems ineffectual. As a result they do not have the consolation of philosophy or the comfort of faith. Nothing happens in their lives, as there is little scope for anything to happen. They know inarticulateness and silence rather than meaningful communication. Culturally Winesburg presents a decayed and deteriorating society. The social and historical factors, which have helped to shape the grotesques, are implied in the narrative. But Anderson focuses on the limitations of human nature, ignorance and cruelty as seen in individuals and the community, largely responsible for the psychological damage done to people, and for their sense of isolation and loneliness. Therefore theirs is not metaphysical homelessness. However the twilight and darkening world of Winesburg, is not entirely without hope. That there is still the possibility of love, affection and human understanding, though they are often disfigured and dislocated, is indicated by the growing and maturing young lovers, George Willard and Helen White. The next chapter takes up for consideration George's growth from adolescence towards maturity.

NOTES AND REFERENCES

1. Erich Fromn, *Escape from Freedom* (New York: Aaron Books, 1967), pp. 34-35.
2. Erich Fromn, *The Sane Society* [London: Routledge and Kegan Paul, 1956], p. 10.
3. *American Literature Survey*, Vol. I eds. Milton R. Stern and Seymour L. Gross; Indian rpt. [New Delhi: Light and Life Publications, 1975], pp. 11-33.
4. Mark Twain, *The Adventures of Huckleberry Finn* [Middle Sex: Penguin, 1968], p. 369.
5. Rex Burbank, *Shewood Anderson* [New York: Twayne, 1964], p. 66.
6. H.L. Meneken, Review, Smart Set, August 1919, Reprinted in *Winesburg, Ohio: Text and Criticism*, ed. John H. Jeferres [New York, Penguin Books, 1966], p. 257. Hereafter Referred to as *Winesburg, Ohio: Text and Criticism.*
7. Rex Burbank, p. 67.
8. Waldo Frank, *Winesburg, Ohio After Twenty Years*, and *Winesburg, Ohio* Text and Criticism, p. 372.
9. *Winesburg, Ohio: Text and Criticism*, p. 88.
10. *Ibid.*, p. 91.
11. *Ibid.*, p. 94.
12. Ibid., p. 96.
13. *Ibid.*
14. Rex Burbank, p. 74.
15. *Ibid.*
16. *Ibid.*, p. 73.
17. David D. Anderson, Sherwood Anderson: An Introduction and Interpretation (New York: Holt Rine Hart and Winston, 1967), p. 40.
18. Rex Burbank, p. 64.
19. Winesburg, Ohio: Text and Criticism, pp. 27-28.
20. *Ibid.*, p. 28.
21. *Ibid.*, p. 27.
22. *Ibid.*, p. 28.
23. *Ibid.*, p. 31.
24. *Ibid.*

25. *Ibid.*, pp. 31-32.
26. *Ibid.*, p. 29.
27. *Ibid.*
28. Rex Burbank, p. 65.
29. Some of Biddebaum's Gestures may Suggest a Homosexual Strain in him. But the Real Point of the Story is not in it, but Elsewhere, to Overstress his Strain in Biddlebaum's Character would Lead to a Through Misunderstanding of his Pathetic Story of Loneliness, Isolation, Thwarted Potential and Mute and Unjustified Suffering.
30. David D. Anderson, Sherwood Anderson's Moments of Insight", Critical Essays on Sherwood Anderson, ed. David D. Anderson (Boston: G.K. Hall and Company, 1981), p. 160. Hereafter Referred to as Critical Essays.
31. *Ibid.*, pp. 35-36.
32. *Ibid.*, p. 35.
33. *Ibid.*, p. 37.
34. *Ibid.*, p. 37.
35. David d. Anderson, Critical Essays, p. 102.
36. *Winesburg, Ohio: Text and Criticism*, p. 5.
37. *Ibid.*, p. 49.
38. *Ibid.*, p. 51.
39. David D. Anderson, Critical Essays, p. 103.
40. *Winesburg, Ohio: Text and Criticism*, p. 50.
41. *Ibid.*, p. 51.
42. *Ibid.*, p. 55.
43. *Ibid.*, p. 56.
44. *Ibid.*, p. 57.
45. Rex Burbank, p. 75.
46. *Winesburg, Ohio: Text and Criticism*, p. 121.
47. *Ibid.*, p. 122.
48. Walter B. Rideout, *The Simplicity of Winesburg, Ohio*, Critical Essays, pp. 149-150.
49. *Winesburg, Ohio: Text and Criticism*, pp. 123-24.
50. *Ibid.*, p. 127.
51. *Ibid.*, p. 124.
52. Irving Howe, *The Book of the Grotesque*, Critical Essays, pp. 94-95.

53. Charles Child Walcutt, "Sherwood Anderson: Impressions and the Buried Life", *The Achievement of Sherwood Anderson: Essays and Criticism*, Ed. Ray Lewis White [Chapel Hill: University of North Carolina Press, 1966], p. 164.
54. *Winesburg, Ohio:* Text and Criticism, p. 125.
55. *Winesburg, Ohio: Text and Criticism*, p. 197.
56. *Ibid.*, p. 125.
57. *Ibid.*, p. 120.
58. *Ibid.*, p. 130.
59. *Ibid.*
60. *Ibid.*, p. 135.
61. *Ibid.*, p. 136.
62. *Ibid.*, p. 137.
63. *Ibid.*, p. 140.
64. *Ibid.*, p. 141.
65. *Ibid.*, p. 142.
66. Rex Burbank, p. 73.
67. Charles Child Walcutt, *The Achievement of Sherwood Anderson*, p. 161.
68. *Winesburg, Ohio: Text and Criticism*, p. 167.
69. *Ibid.*
70. *Ibid.*, p. 167.
71. *Ibid.*, p. 170.
72. *Ibid.*, p. 168.
73. *Ibid.*, p. 177.
74. *Ibid.*, p. 178.
75. Rex Burbank, p. 75.
76. David D. Anderson, *Sherwood Anderson: An Introduction and Interpretation*, p. 47.
77. Winesburg, Ohio: Text and Criticism, p. 39.
78. Marilyn Judith Atlas, *Sherwood Anderson and Women of Winesburg*, Critical Essays, p. 256.
79. *Winesburg, Ohio: Text and Criticism*, p. 39.
80. *Ibid.*, p. 45.
81. *Ibid.*, p. 45.

82. *Ibid.*, pp. 47-48.
83. *Ibid.*, pp. 40-41.
84. *Ibid.*
85. *Ibid.*, p. 41.
86. *Ibid.*, p. 227.
87. *Ibid.*, p. 223.
88. *Ibid.*, p. 46.
89. *Ibid.*, p. 224.
90. *Ibid.*, p. 46.
91. *Ibid.*, p. 224.
92. *Ibid.*, p. 46.
93. *Ibid.*, p. 226.
94. *Ibid.*, p. 227.
95. *Ibid.*, p. 48.
96. *Ibid.*, p. 42.
97. Waldo Frank, *Winesburg, Ohio: After Twenty Years,* Winesburg, Ohio: Text and Criticism, pp. 372.
98. *Winesburg, Ohio: Text and Criticism,* p. 119.
99. *Ibid.*, p. 116.
100. *Ibid.*, p. 115.
101. *Ibid.*
102. *Ibid.*, p. 118.
103. *Ibid.*, p. 119.
104. *Ibid.*
105. *Ibid.*, p. 120.
106. Marylin Judith Atlas, *Sherwood Anderson and Women of Winesburg* Critical Essays, p. 260.
107. Ibid., p. 259.
108. Rex Burbank, p. 75.
109. George D. Murphy, "The Theme of Sublimation in Anderson's *Winesburg, Ohio Modern Fiction Studies,* XIII, 2, 1967, p. 119.
110. *Winesburg, Ohio: Text and Criticism,* p. 149.
111. *Ibid.*, p. 158.
112. *Ibid.*, pp.161-162.

113. David Stock, "Winesburg Ohio, As a Dance of Death", Critical essays, p. 188.
114. David Stock, *Winesburg, Ohio, As a Dance of Death*, Critical Essays, p. 188.
115. Winesburg, Ohio: Text and Criticism, p. 162.
116. Irving Howe, *The Book of the Grotesque, The Achievement of Sherwood Anderson*, p. 101.
117. Rex Burbank, p. 73.
118. Winesburg, Ohio: Text and Criticism, p. 164.
119. *Ibid.*
120. *Ibid.*, p. 164.
121. *Ibid.*, p. 165.
122. Ibid., p. 166.

CHAPTER – 3

Apprenticeship to Live
Winesburg, Ohio as a Bildungsroman

In a letter of his t Waldo Frank dated November 14, 1916, Sherwood Anderson made what seems to be his earliest comment about Winesburg, Ohio: "It is my own idea that when these studies are published in a book form, they will suggest the real environment out of which present day American youth is coming".[1] Much later in his Memoirs (1942) he wrote: "I felt that, taken together, they (i.e. short stories) made something like a novel, a complete story (which have)—the feeling of the life of a boy growing into young manhood in a town".[2] These statements and a reading of the work indicate that the "boy" Anderson refers to is obviously George Willard. But Winesburg, Ohio is not entirely about him, though he has certainly an important function to perform in the work, which, as Malcolm Cowley put it, "lies midway between the novel proper and the mere collection of stories".[3] George Willard is a central figure and performs a unifying function in it as he appears and reappears in more than half of Winesburg, Ohio either as a leading character or as an audience or as a casual observer, and thus shares importance in the narration with other characters. In developing the theme of loneliness, isolation and defeat, which is the burden of the work, George Willard's role is indeed important, as he serves since "a symbolic counterpart to the grotesques of

Winesburg".[4] As David Anderson put it" in the last analysis it (i.e Winesburg, Ohio) is about people and George Willard is secondary in importance to the individual on whom each story centers".[5]

However, if Winesburg, Ohio is approached from the direction not of the subjects of the tales but form that of George Willard, a boy growing to manhood and becoming involved in the perplexing world of adults, developing from an aimlessly curious boyhood to an intensely conscious adulthood, the work composes as a *buldungsroman*, the 'novel of formation' or 'novel of education' which portrays the development of the protagonist's mind and character as he passes from childhood through varied experiences into maturity and the recognition of his identity and role in the world. This approach to Winesburg, Ohio is complementary to approaching it as a collection of tales of so many grotesques-tales of sadness, unfulfillment, thwarted desires, loneliness, absence of communication and communion. George Willard's growth form adolescence to adulthood is made possible by his living amidst those grotesques of the small town, closely observing and getting t know them and listening to their confessions and enjoying their confidence. His growth and development, "as definite as it is unobtrusive" "supplies a pattern for Winesburg, Ohio".[7] As a *bildungsroman*, Winesburg, Ohio presents two mutually related and inseparable aspects of facets of George Willard's growth and development: his growth form adolescence to adulthood and his growth towards becoming an artist or creative writer. Both strands of growth are simultaneous and interdependent.

Among the more famous novels of formation are Charles Dickens, David Copperfield and Great Expectations, George Meridith's The Egoist and James Joyce's Portrait of the Artist as a Young Man. There is a difference between these and Winesburg, Ohio. In all the others the focus is invariably on the growing protagonist, and his growth is traced or is traceable from stage to stage. But Anderson's work is a collection of tales about a number of people and also the story of a growing young man, George Willard, George appears in sixteen of the stories in different capacities. There is no mention of him at all in *Paper Pills* and all the four parts of *Godliness*- In three of the tales- *Adventure, Tandy* and *The Untold Lie*- there is only a passing mention of his name or reference to him. In only four of the tales –*Nobody Knows, An Awakening, Sophistication* and *Departure*- he may be said to be the protagonist. And in the remaining stories he is a secondary character of varying importance. However all those he comes into contact with impinge on his consciousness, particularly the grotesques, and make his growth possible, from adolescence to manhood and form a superficial observer of trivialities and peddler of words towards becoming a responsible writer, covering "the period preceding his final discovery of métier".[8] Before George can hope to become a writer worth the name, he must serve his apprenticeship to life itself. Anderson's method of portraying a character in Winesburg, Ohio may be remarked here. As David Anderson points out:

> *Although Anderson's people are highly individualized in their microcosmic setting, characterization is not fully developed. Instead, each person is defined by controlling characterstic and the nature of his grotesqueness—characterization in these stories are achieved through depth rather than breadth: each is a narrow area deeply explored.*[9]

George, who appears frequently sometimes listening to another's experience and sometimes involved in an experience, seems to be the only character who is in a way developed. But even he is not portrayed linearly form scene to scene, episode t episode. His character emerges from glimpse and flashes provided in the varied situations in which he appears.

George, son of Tom Willard and Elizabeth of the New Willard House, grows up in the small country-town of Winesburg, which is full of solitary persons who have become grotesques. They are, as seen already, a sensitive, lonely, isolated, inarticulate and misunderstood lot who are unable to communicate and experience a sense of communion. They feel a pressing need to make human contact to free themselves of their sense of loneliness and isolation. Though young George lives amidst them, he has not as yet caught the contagion from them. This is rather surprising since even a home, as he himself is aware, the relations between his father and mother are bitter and irreparably strained though there is no open clash or confrontation. He begins as a newspaper reporter for the Winesburg, Eagle, even as an adolescent, curious and enthusiastic about his profession and remains so until he leaves the town to meet the adventure of life in the wider world. Most people are drawn to him because of his moral freshness, his Adamic innocence, capacity for feeling, his responsiveness and openness to experience, his generally friendly nature. From the grotesque point of view, he is bumptious now and then though in a harmless way. They seek him eagerly, surprisingly become articulate in his presence to explain them selves and confide in him. Some of them feel such concern for him that they even advice him and warn him against corrupting forces. For, as he has the gift for language and expression and wants to become a writer, he represents for them" the line of communication and gives them opportunity to restore communication with the world form which each feels excluded".[10] Further it is their hope that he will someday "speak what is in their hearts and then reestablish their connection with mankind".[11] actually George is much too young at that time to understand them, some of whom are much older than him, and their problems and anxieties. In fact understanding of their lives comes to him only gradually when he is shocked and startled into a mood of insight, during his contact with different people. When the book ends with his departure from Winesburg, there seems to be the promise that he will become one day the spokesman of inarticulate men and women like them wherever they may be found.

George Willard appears in the very first story, *Hands* which tells the pathetic story of Wing Biddlebaum. He is introduced as the young reporter of the local newspaper the Winesburg Eagle. Biddlebaum, the nervous alienated recluse who was once a teacher but persecuted and driven out from his place owing to a gross misunderstanding of his nature and gestures, has had to seek asylum in Winesburg. He who has grown old before his time and prefers his anonymity, however chooses to make friends with young George. George who is friendly by nature seeks him as much as he does him. In his presence Biddlebaum loses some of his timidity and occasionally walks with him along Main Street, and eagerly looks forward to spending an evening with him. This young man symbolizes for him innocent love that has been denied to him, and in his presence he feels quite at ease and comfortable. He talks excitedly in a shrill and loud voice striving to put into words the ideas accumulated in his mind during the long years of enforced silence. Observant George is naturally curious about Biddlebaum's eccentricities and his hands. Sensitive as he is, he guesses that there must be a strong reason for the strange restless activity of the other's hands and his anxiety to keep them hidden. But despite his overwhelming curiosity, he wisely refrains from asking his old friend about them because he is touched by the horror sweeping over Biddlebaum's face and the terror in his eyes when he suddenly becomes aware of the activity of his hands. George sympathises with him and does not try to probe into his background. This reveals his capacity for intuitive understanding. What is noteworthy is that old Biddlebaum feels a strong concern for this impressionable young man, who has the gift of imagination and the capacity for intuitive understanding. What is noteworthy is that the elderly man feels a strong concern for this impressionable young man, who has the gift of imagination and the capacity to "dream", but who may ruin himself by imitating others, instead of being himself. Biddlebaum even take the liberty of admonishing him and urges him not to conform to the spurious values of his society: "You are destroying yourself, you have the inclination to be alone and to dream and you are afraid of dreams. You want to be like others in town here. You must try to forget all you have learned. You must begin to dream—"[12]. Biddlebaum hungers for the presence of the boy whom he regards "as the medium through which he (expresses) his love of man".[13] He hopes that George would serve the purpose provided he resists the corrupting influence of the people around him.

George Willard grows both as man and writer-to be over some years. He "grows form passive observer of life t active participant, from aimlessly curious boy to intensely conscious adult".[14] However his growth cannot be traced and graduated from story to story. As Edwin Fussel puts it, "throughout Winesburg runs the slow and often hidden current of George Willard's growth towards maturity, often the stream is subterranean and we are surprised to see where it comes out; sometimes it appears to lose itself in backwaters of irrelevance and naivete. But all the time the book's current is steadily towards the ultimate 'departure' of George".[15]

For the sake of convenience, approximately three stages of development in George may be discerned. The first stage is covered by the early chapters from *Hands* to *Nobody Knows* and *Responsibility*, in which he appears "as the object of actions initiated by other people or as the recipient of their advice". This is a stage of 'passiveness and limited understanding of others'.[16] In the next stage, covered by stories from *The Thinker* to *The Teacher*, George takes on a more aggressive role in the incidents in which he becomes involved". He is still an adolescent, though he enjoys a place of distinction since it is generally accepted that he is to become a writer someday. He begins to understand something of the complexity of human motives and behaviour. Stories from *Loneliness* to *Departure* cover the final stage of his growth. These stories show his sensibility coming to "full maturity as he develops an awareness of the complicated motives and contradictory instinctive demands in life and comes to fed compassion for its victims".[17]

As newspaper reporter, George is readily put in touch with a large number of people in the town, and it gratified his idle curiosity. He is also enabled to receive the confidences of many whom he meets.. He runs here and there as the narrator of the story *Thinker* tells, "as an excited dog" all day noting on his pad of paper little facts of no significance to be published in the newspaper, striving to mention as many of the inhabitants of the country town as possible: "A.P. Wringler had received a shipment of straw hats. Ed Byerbaum and Tom Marshall were in Cleveland on Friday Uncle Tom Sinnings is building a new barn on his place on the valley road".[18] Such jottings as these clearly show that "he is committed to the surface of life, not to its depths", as reporter he is "concerned with externals, with appearances, with the presumably sold, simple, everyday surface of life".[19] But his growth towards adulthood and maturity depends upon his leaning to see beneath the surface of lives and try to understand them, and his outgrowing his earlier immature ideas about his vocation as a writer.

In most of the stories of Winesburg, Ohio in which George Willard has a role to play, he is seen either in the office of the *Eagle* or in the company of his friends or walking outdoors alone or with someone else. Only two stories, *Mother* and *Death* show him in relation to his family and within the four walls of his house for a short while. Significantly, the former story is placed almost at the beginning of the work and the latter almost at its close, spanning considerable length of time. The distance George traverses emotionally and intellectually between these two points, indicate his growth towards attaining maturity. In both stories, which are primarily concerned with his mother Elizabeth Willard, he is a secondary but important character. In either story the mother-son relationship is an important strand of the narrative, and sheds light on the growth and development of young George. The tragedy of Elizabeth Willard's life her loneliness, isolation and estrangement, her futile groping for happiness and fulfillment, frustration and defeat, and her intense but inarticulate bond with her son, and her strained relation with her husband have already been discussed in the previous chapter in a different context. But some repetition of those facts is unavoidable here.

Among the several factors responsible for the discord between Elizabeth and her husband tom Willard, George is one in the sense that they have sharply conflicting expectations about their son. Each wants that George should shape himself after him or her. Tom Willard wants him to succeed in life rather than be a mere reporter or writer. His contempt for either profession is betrayed by his voice when admonishingly and flatteringly he tries to persuade George to aim at success: "I guess You'll get over it—You're not a fool and you're not a woman. You're Tom Willard's son and you will wake up—".[20] Elizabeth wants to protect her son form his father's influence. She too is ambitious for him. She does not want him to be under any circumstances "a meaningless drab figure"[21] like herself or become "a dull clod, all words and smartness",[22] like his father. Unlike the overbearing Tom Willard who has little thought of his son's nature, aptitude and aspirations, and who threaten to destroy his potential for a rich imaginative life, she has "a more intimate and more comprehensive understanding of his needs".[23] Unable to love or respect her husband, she directs all hr interest and love on her son in whom "she sees the potential for the individual fulfillment that her role as woman and as head of the household had denied her".[24] She knows that her son has the gifts to be a writer and wants him to be a serious writer. And hence the appropriateness of her prayer to God that he should keep her son from cheap smartness and success seeking, the twin vices of Winesburg typified by Tom Willard so that he is free "to express something for (them) both".[25] The prayer she articulates is representative of the prayers of all the grotesques who come into contact with George. It echoes the feeling of Biddlebaum, Dr. Reefy, Dr. Parcival and Kate Swift, who have great expectations of him. What these and other characters who cannot communicate "want of George Willard is to have their stories told (they are quite literally characters in search of an author)".[26]

Elizabeth is continually afraid for her son whose future is at stake because of her husband. It is her fervent hope that George somehow understands, and fulfils the long-forgotten dreams of her girlhood. But for all her intense involvement in her youthful self, there is hardly any communication and communion between them. As David Anderson puts it, "The relationship between the two is completely inarticulate".[27] He is as much tongue-tied in her presence as she is in his. In awkward and long silence they spend the evening whenever he visits her in her side room. In a sense, George has every reason to feel, lonely and isolated because of the disharmony between his father and mother, and the silence, which virtually reigns at home. But his sociable nature and the exuberance of his youth save him from such a feeling at this stage of his life. Generally the conversation between them is formal. Sitting beside his mother, George begins to talk. He tells her: "I am going t get out of here. I don't know where I shall go or what I shall d but I am going away". Trembling at this unexpected revelation for which she has been waiting for long and yet unable to believe it she asks him: "You think that? You will go to the city and make money, eh? It will be better for you, you think, to be a business man, to be brisk and smart and alive?". Dispelling her fears he tells her earnestly.

> *I suppose I can't make you understand, but oh, I wish I could. I can't even talk to father about it. I don't try. There is not any use. I don't know what I shall do. I just won't to go away and look at people and think—I suppose it won't be for a year or two but I've been thinking about it. Something father said makes it sure that I shall have to go away.*[28] *(emphasis added).*

It is quite clear that his mother's inarticulate phrases and stunted declarations have made an impact on his impressionable and growing sensibility. This wish of his is realized only after his mother's death months later, when he is no longer an adolescent. But even at this stage of his adolescence he is sensitive enough to understand something of his mother's anguish about his growth and development and the choices he has to make in life. as yet he has no ideas or plans for his future. But it seems clear that he has begun to think on the right lines and that his mother's hopes, expectations and values are his. It is also clear that his growth is still in nascent condition.

The sensitiveness and understanding that George reveals in *Mother* is missing in the immediately following stories. *The Philosopher, Respectability* and *Nobody Knows.* In the first two he is a secondary character very much the audience, listening to the confessions and confidences of their protagonists. In *Nobody Knows* he is the chief character. In this phase, as noted already, he is still adolescent, immature and his understanding of others and of himself is limited. His relations with Dr.Parcival (*The Philosopher*) and Wash Williams (*Respectability*) have already been considered in the previous chapter. Therefore the analysis here is limited to considering how far they aid the formation of George. To both of them George serves the function of an ear into which they pour their fears, hopes and dreams. Moreover they seek him out with a purpose to listen to their confessions and confidences. Apart from finding in him a line of communication with the outside world from which they feel estranged, they feel a genuine concern for this young man and do not him to commit the mistakes they have made in their lives. They present to him their own lives as examples to warn him against the pitfalls he is liable to.

Dr. Parcival is a recluse tortured by guilt. On his own he seeks George and makes his acquaintance. He senses that George has in him the waking of a good writer. He does not want him to waste his gifts as a mere reporter. So he warns him: "You are a reporter just as I was once and you have attracted my attention. You may end by becoming just such another fool. I want to warn you and keep on warning you. That's why I seek you out".[29] Dr. parcival has yet another objective, apart from advising George on "the advisability of adopting a line of conduct that he himself (is) unable to define".[30] And that is like, George's mother, he too hopes that the young man will fulfill a dream of his. Behind the mask of indifference and hatred of men, there lurks in Dr. Parcival a highly troubled soul sympathizing with all those who are made victims undeservedly. And he wants George to write a book, that he himself may never write, on the theme that "everyone in the world is a Christ and they are all crucified". Dr. Parcival makes this not just a request but a command to George: "That's what I want to say. Don't you forget that whatever happens, don't you date yet yourself forget".[31] It is doubtful whether George at this stage understands at all the meaning and implication of Dr. Parcival command. But what must have been clear to him is that this grotesque of a doctor wants George t enlarge his sympathises and deepen has understanding of people, especially those who are victimized and made to suffer if he really wishes to be a responsible writer. Later his teacher Kate Swift too advises him on similar lines.

In cultivating Wash Williams, George shows his desire to understand others, particularly those who are solitary, lonely and who avoid or shy away from company. But he is not entirely free form idle curiosity. Wash too has been eager to communicate with this young reporter for more than one reason. Like Dr. Parcival, he too wants to caution George against a foolish romantic entanglement he is likely to be caught in. his own bitter experience of love and disillusionment in married life and the consequent hatred of all women urge him to warn him not to have any foolish notions about women. Wash has seen George moving with Belle Carpenter, a trimmer of hats in a millinery shop, and he suspects that they are in love. It is his confirmed belief that all love affairs end as disastrously as his own. Therefore he tells him his story, though he had not divulged it to anyone in Winesburg, making it an illustrative example only to save George from disaster: "It is because I saw you kissing the lips of that Belle Carpenter that I tell you my story. What happened to me may next happen to you. I want to put you on your guard. Already you may be having dreams in your head. I want to destroy them".[32]

Nobody Knows concerns George more immediately than the other stories preceding and some following it. It tells the story of his 'adventure' with Lousie Trunnion, whose letter he mistakes for an invitation to a mere sex adventure. He is still so adolescent and immature that it never occurs to him that the brief letter to him may have a different implication and that possibly it is Lousie's ineffective and unsuccessful attempt at communicating with someone outside her narrow orbit. He never considers even once that her needs may be something other than mere sexual gratification. As David Anderson remarks, this episode "demonstrates that George at this stage, like the society of which he is a part, does not understand the grotesque attempt at communication".[33] George does not at all try to understand what Louise really hungers for or what she is seeking in her lonely and restricted life. What makes her pathetic is that she herself does not know what she wants or how to get at it. In response to her letter George goes to meet her secretly, walking stealthily along the dark lanes avoiding people like a nervous thief. When they are by themselves he initially lacks self-asssurance and bursts forth with a flood of words. Then he behaves towards her like a bold aggressive male. But in her heart he has "no sympathy for her".[34] He is "coldly insensitive" and after the encounter "he is simply impressed that his pleasure is free", as Marylyn Judith Atlas notes".[35] Once it is over, he dismisses the girl and exults over his first sexual conquest. This experience perhaps gives him some physical satisfaction but nothing more. After he sends her away he begins to get nervous and worry about his reputation and what would people think of him. But he feels relieved and sighs a cowardly sigh of relief as he remembers: "She hasn't got anything on me. Nobody Knows".[36] As Rex Burbank remarks, George's "nervous effort to assure himself—indicates that his adolescent responsiveness to public opinion—rather than a mature understanding still dictates his moral consciousness".[37] If his encounter with Louise Trunnion gives him a feeling of entirely self centered masculine pride, it also leaves him with a sense of guilt for having violated the overt moral code of the community.[38] George who adulates himself and power now learns little from this experience. But, as it will be seen in some of the later stories, he has to encounter in his career towards maturity some more women of different dispositions who make an impact on him and from whom he derives some healthy capacities.

There are two closely related and mutually informing aspects to George Willard's growth and development towards maturity: his efforts to understand with sympathy other people and their essential but buried lives, and his desire to become a creative writer and his growing awareness of the meaning of this vocation. *The Thinker* is mainly the story of Seth Richmond in which George figures as an important secondary character. It also directs attention to George's growing interest in creative writing not mentioned till then. His mother and Dr. Parcival know that he has a gift for writing, which he has to develop, so that he can become a competent writer and be their spokesman. But George himself does not refer to it until this story, though writing appears to have been an interest he has had for some time. He talks about it continually to Seth Richmond. With this story George emerges as a respected person in Winesburg where he is given "a place of distinction" because it is established that he "would someday become a writer".[39] Two facts concerning George are revealed in this story: his conception of writing and his attitude to his profession as writer; secondly his interest in Helen White, the Banker's daughter. In general he appears to be so much absorbed in himself that he does not seem to take any interest in Seth Richmond and his vexing problems although he has been courting this younger man. In Winesburg it is the grotesque that generally seeks George, but in the case of Seth it is the other way about Seth deserves, sympathetic attention and listening. George seems to prattle in his presence endlessly about himself rather than make an attempt to encourage him to talk understand him.

George appears to be conscious of the attention shown to him in the town as a promising writer, and is both vain and complacent about it. He is supremely satisfied with himself and rather supercilious towards others. "At this point his conception of writing", as Walter Rideout points out, 'centers in externals, in the opportunities the writer's life offers for personal freedom and for public acclaim".[40] Writing is a matter of fun and fame, and as writer he is his own master wherever he may be. He tells Seth boastingly: "It is the easiest of all lives to live. Here and there you go and there is no one to boss you. Though you are in India or in South seas in a boat, you have but to write and there you are. Wait till I get my name up and then see what fun I shall have".[41] That this view of himself and writing, is naïve and myopic if not silly, hardly needs to be pointed out. It is quite characteristic of his immature youth to think of writing a love story to start with. But his plan to fall in love first and then write the story and the cocksureness with which he speaks of it to Seth is utterly ridiculous: "I know what I'm going to do. I'm going to fall in love. I have been sitting here and thinking it over and I am going to do it". Going a step further with supreme complacency he says that he has chosen Helen White to fall in love with, for "she is the only girl in town with any get up to her",[42] as if he is doing her a favour by doing her a favour by doing so. Though no overt comment is made b the narrator on George's plan to fall in love first and then write a story about it, is implied that it is not how one writes a story and that it is a naïve and superficial view of both love and creative writing. It is time that one ought to write from experience in the naïve manner of George. This story reveals his immaturity, inexperience, vanity and complacency. He is yet to learn the fundamentals of creative writing, notwithstanding the distinction he enjoys in the town as a writer of promise. As an individual he is a complete contrast to Seth Richmond who is introspective, thoughtful, analytical and unpretentious, whatever be his other limitations.

The next two stories, *The Strength of God* and *The Teacher*, shed light in the growing George, and show that his "adolescent attitude toward love and literature changes to puzzled wonderment".[43] In *The Strength of God* there is only a fleeting glimpse of the change gradually and unobtrusively coming over him. First he is seen one night in the office of the Eagle "tramping up and down in the office undergoing a struggle of his own",[45] when Rev Curtis bursts into his room to tell him about the revelation he has been granted by God. His struggle could be about how to write the story he has in mind as well as the confusion in his mind about his view of his teacher Kate Swift, as the next story shows. In any case he is not any longer the merely self-satisfied adolescent of the story *The Thinker*, and does seem to have made some advance.

The Teacher which has been examined from the point of view of Kate Swift in the previous chapter, also tells us much about George Willard who seems as much preoccupied with thoughts about his former teacher as she is about him, her former pupil. *The Teacher* begins with him as if it is his story that it tells. But halfway through Kate Swift is brought in and thereafter it becomes her story, her impassioned advice to George and his eventual confusion. The young reporter is pleased with his own charms. Having listened to Kate Swift talking to him four or five times with great earnestness although he cannot make out her meaning, he begins "to believe that she must be in love with him", registering a typical adolescent response. The thought both pleases and annoys him. When he is alone he boldly declares to him self: "Oh, You're just letting on, you know you are. I am going to find out about you. You wait and see".[46] Obviously he is still cocksure of himself and his ability to understood what goes on in others minds. Wrapped up in thoughts of love of Kate Swift and Helen White, he sits in his office pretending to be at work but in reality indulging in romantic thoughts about them.

As for Kate Swift, she had recognized the spark of genius in one of George's schoolboy exercises and wanted to blow on the spark and nurture his talent. She knows about his ambition to be a writer and become famous. On an occasion she takes him out to the Fair Ground and tries to bring home to him "some conception of the difficulties he would have to face as a writer".[47] She endeavours to impress upon him that the writer's is not "the easiest of all the lives to live", as he supposed once and told Seth Richmond so, but rather one of the most difficult and responsible. He has to immerse himself in life before he can try to write about it. In a trembling voice with earnestness she declares to him:

> *You will have to know life. If you are to become a writer you I have t stop fooling with words. It would be better to give up the notion of writing until you are better prepared. Now it's time to be living—I would like to make you understand the import of what you think of attempting. You must not become a mere peddler of words. The thing to learn is to know what people are thinking about, not what they say.*[48]

Kate Swift is anxious to warn George against "his egocentric fascination with words and to urge him to immerse himself in life before writing of it".[49]

On this particular stormy night Kate Swift once again possessed by a passionate desire "to have George understand the import of life to learn to interpret it truly and honestly". She thinks that the boy may "possess a talent for the understanding of life". "A great eagerness to open the door of life" to him seizes her. Her interest in his talents is perfectly genuine and unselfish. Impulsively she walks into his office and speaks to him persuasively about the thoughts preoccupying her concerning him. In the embarrassment of the moment when George appears to her not a boy but a man ready to play the part of an adult lover. She lets him take her into his arms. But recovering almost immediately from her confusion, she gives him two sharp blows on his face and runs away from the place.[50] George too is confused and furious at the unexpected behaviour of his former teacher. As noted in the previous chapter while analyzing Kate Swift's peculiar sense of loneliness and isolation, there is an element of sex-just an element and nothing more than that in her conduct in the situation. The turmoil in her bosom results from a mixture of interest, desire, enthusiasm and love. Possibly she is half in love with her former pupil, as David Stouck suggests. But it is equally likely that she cannot express herself adequately[51], imperfect articulation if not total inarticulateness being as much her problem as that of the other grotesques of Winesburg. Her physical touch, as Walter Rideout remarks, "symbolizes an attempt to create the moment of awareness in George regarding the demanding principles by which earnest writer must live".[52] she is as much earnest as his mother was that he should become an earnest and responsible writer and speak for the like of her in the world.

As George broods over the experience in the darkness of the night, his resentment and bafflement gradually leave him. Initially he interpreted her fervent appeal to him as a tribute to his personal charms. But on reflection, though he is not yet mature as a person and writer, he begins to realize intuitively that it is not sex that his former teacher is seeking but something else. He tries to understand. Earlier in the ease of Lousie Trunnion (*Nobody Knows*) he had completely misinterpreted her lonely plea as an invitation to an "adventure". But after this encounter with Kate Swift, he sets aside his self-congratulations, and he begins to realize how complex human motives and behaviour can be. And before dropping off into sleep he mutters to himself: "I have missed something. I have missed something Kate Swift was trying to tell me".[53] as David Anderson remarks, George begins "to realize that there is a truth about human life that he is missing. For (him) it is the beginning of wisdom".[54] the maturity he needs comes to him lonely at the end of Winesburg, Ohio for which he has to wait for some more time and go through some more experience.

In *The Strength of God* George appears only at the end of the narrative. When he is pacing up and down in his office going through a struggle of her own because he is confused and bewildered by Kate swift's unexpected violence against him when he thought that she was perhaps in love with him, ironically Curtis Hartman the clergyman bursts upon him to declare with fervor, "God has appeared to me in the person of Kate Swift— Allthough she may not be aware of it, she is an instrument of God, bearing the message of truth".[55] George is confounded and naturally thinks that the minister must have gone insane. No less puzzling is Kate Swift's own behaviour towards him. Receptive though he wishes to be, he cannot understand the miracle that Curtis has seen, or the message Kate swift has tries to impress on him. He is set thinking in a manner none of his previous encounters with people had. He has to ask himself how much does he really know about others and himself, as his muttering to himself at the end of *The Teacher* indicate clearly.

The remaining stories of Winesburg, Ohio, in which George appears as a character of secondary and primary importance, show him growing visibly towards maturity outgrowing his adolescence. All those whom he has met so far and whose confidence and confessions he has listened to, have impinged on his consciousness. But it is in the last phase that the impact they had others make on his sensibility sharpening it becomes visible in his responses to them and in his understanding of their conflicting behaviour and motives and his sympathy and compassion for them. More importantly, this development is seen in his attempt to know himself, because of his realization how little he knows about himself and how much more he has to know about himself and life. to trace this phase of his development it is convenient to take for consideration first *Loneliness, Queer* and *Drink* together in which his role is secondary, and then take up *An Awakening, Death, Sophistication* and *Departure,* in three of which he is the protagonist.

George has his first real encounter with a lonely man in Enoch Robinson of *Loneliness* though he has met other lonely creatures. Enoch is an elderly, frustrated artist, oppressively lonely and isolated, who feels that he is condemned to be lonely forever. His is a buried life and hungers for love and understanding. He is diffident about his ability to make others understand him as well as his own ability to understand others. Enoch is a very complex instance of a grotesque, who is twisted out of shape psychologically and otherwise. Despite his inability to communicate properly he has an urge to talk to someone and tell him his unfortunate story. he chooses George who seems to be "in a mood to understand" and who may be a sympathetic and understanding listener of his story and also understand it. Enoch finds enough encouragement in George for his confessional narrative. The authorial narrator explains this peculiar situation thus: "Youthful sadness, young man's sadness, the sadness of a growing boy in a village at the year's end, opened the lips of the old man. The sadness in the heart of George Willard was without meaning, but it appealed to Enoch Robinson".[56] George himself does not know the precise cause for his sadness, though part of it is certainly due to his mother's illness, who has not been well for a month. But the real cause for his sadness, according to the narrator, is George's thinking about himself. Probably he has begun to be aware of the nature of his activities, the uncertainty about their meaning and purpose, and of the goals of his life. It would appear that he has become introspective. When Enoch asks him to go with him, he becomes curious to know more about him because generally the old man is believed to be a little of his head. But George's is not idle curiosity as it was in the case of Wash Williams.

As for old Enoch, he knows that it is not easy for anyone to understand his complex story, but it is his hope that young George can understand if he tries, while none in Winesburg has ever tried to understand him. He tells George: "You'll understand if you try hard enough. I have looked at you when you went past me in the street and I think you can understand. It is not hard. All you have to do is to believe what I say, just listen and believe, that's all there is to it".[57] George listens with attention to Enoch Robinson's narration of the story of his life of loneliness, misunderstanding and defeat. He is filled with sadness. He feels such deep sympathy for the old man, as he had not experienced before for anyone. He moves over to sit with him on the cot and puts his arms about him. He insists on listening to the entire story to its helpless and hopeless end. George has not listened to anyone, neither to Biddlebaum nor Dr.Parcival not Wash Williams with such absorption and imaginative sympathy.

Virtually all the grotesques of Winesburg that George has come into contact with to find in him a friendly person who, they think, can understand them with sympathy and "ease their passage into the intimacies of human life"[58] from which they have been obstructed so far. Only Elmer Cowley of *Queer* resents him and even gives him a jolt by hitting him hard on his face and chest. Ironically George has this humiliating and bewildering experience when he s eager to understand Elmer with sympathy. Elmer Cowley, son of Ebenezer Cowley, a farmer turned merchant, is not actually acquainted with George Willard whom he knows only as the tall boy who runs about town gathering news for the Winesburg, Eagle. Because his father has not been doing too well as merchant, just as he did not do too well as farmer, Elmer has become very sensitive about his father's continuous failure in life. he suspects that George "who passed and repassed Cowley and son's store and who stopped to talk to people in the street must be thinking of him and perhaps laughing at him".[59] He cannot believe that George too must have "his days of unhappiness", "vague hungers and unnamable desires",[60] like everyone else.

Unlike the other grotesques Elmer has no specific deformity. But he is excessively self-conscious and sensitive t what people in the town may be thinking of him and his people. He himself knows that there is something 'queer' about his father and suspects that perhaps he himself is queer though he does not want to be. At the same time he feels strongly aggrieved that "the public opinion of Winesburg (has) condemned the Cowleys to queerness". And he thinks that George, who walks along Main Street "whistling and laughing", "typified the town (and) represented in his person the spirit of the town". The line of thinking leads him to conclude that by assaulting George's person he might be striking "the greater enemy—the judgment of Winesburg".[61] He is also envious of George who can make friends easily and talk to everyone he comes across. He makes himself miserable further by feeling that he is "condemned to go through life without friends",[62] as he has not been able to make friends in the town although he has been there for a year. His queerness becomes a disabling obsession with him.

The people of Winesburg ofcourse are not concerned about the Cowleys and are indifferent to them, as they have been towards all the other grotesques. Like the grotesques Elmer too is inarticulate and connot communicate with anyone, though he strongly wishes it. He desires to talk to George but loses courage in his presence. Instead he goes away from him and wants to move to an old farmhand and a half-wit known to him: "—no one says anything to me. Everyone stands around and laughs and they talk but they say nothing to me—Do you know why I came clear out here afoot? I had to tell someone and you were the only one I could tell—".[63] Had he not been in real interest, his talking to a half-wit would have been absurd. He resents George but yet wants to have satisfactory relations with him and convince him that he is not queer. George is indeed delighted to be asked by Elmer to go out with him because he has "long been wanting to make friends with the young merchant and find out what (is) in his mind".[64] When Elmer however stands face with George he becomes once again speechless and fails to declare his determination not to be queer. In despair he decides that very moment to leave Winesburg to go to Cleveland where he hopes to find his release. In a last effort at communication before leaving, he asks George to meet him at the railway station, "to tell him about things, perhaps challenge him, and challenge all of Winesburg through him".[65] Unfortunately he becomes tongue-tied, once again and in frustration and defiance, he hits George hard who rolls over on the platform bewildered and half-conscious.

This encounter of George's with Elmer Cowley reveals what the other grotesques, who have been confiding in him, have failed to perceive, that George as yet does not really understand them and their perplexities. As all of them see in him an extension of their different selves, they implicitly believe that he cannot fail to understand them. But he is still too young and inexperienced to grasp their problems and their expectations too. However, his contact with them strengthens his capacity for intuitive perception of the nature and worth of the individual by going behind outward appearances. Further their stories teach him compassion and sympathy, which in time will enable him to know and understand others

In *Drink* George appears only for a short while towards its end, and his role is strictly secondary, since it is the story of Tom Foster. The brief contact George has with him reveals that he has stained some maturity and that he is on his way to fall seriously in love with Helen White. Tom, who is a little younger than George, is an interesting character. He is not a grotesque like the others that George comes into contact with. He is innocent and childlike and knows to be happy wherever he is. When he was at Cincinnati before he and his grandmother moved into Winesburg, he "had found out many things, things about ugliness and crime and lust. Indeed, he knew more of these things than anyone else in Winesburg".[66] For he has far more experience of life than many of his age. Yet retains his childlike nature, "The most absurd little things (make) Tom Foster happy". So gentle is his nature "that he could not hate anything". And what he cannot understand he decides to forget,[67] But he has to try to understand, when he falls in love with Helen White, with whom Seth Richmond too had fallen in love. Like a typical adolescent he loves her for her purity and innocence. He knows that it is an impossible dream to fall in love with her. His way of solving the problem is to let himself think of her and concern himself with the manner of his thoughts. He wants to experience everything without hurting others. For this reason George is drawn to him. Like the other grotesques, tom does not seem to seek George for confessions or for confiding, because he does not have any need for it.

On a spring night Tom Foster gets unusually drunk, Helen White naturally figures in his drunken dreams. Finding him wandering in a drunken condition, George takes him into the Eagle print shop. But Tom's drunken talk about Helen White that he was with her during the evening on the seashore disturbs and confuses George, and makes him angry, because a sentiment concerning her lurks in his own heart. When he takes Tom out for a walk and helps him to become sober, Tom explains to him his strange behaviour and talk particularly concerning Helen subsides and feels drawn towards anyone before. With a motherly solicitude he assists him to his feet and walk about.[69] This gesture of his is significant. It displays, as Rex Burbank remarks, "his maturity by being able to discriminate between conflicting attitudes, without rejecting the unpleasant ones".[70]

George Willard has now reached the last phase of his growth and development. That he is close to attaining maturity transcending his adolescence is seen already in *Loneliness, Queer* and *Drink*. His maturity has been coming on for a long time. In the stories an *Awakening, Death* and *Sophistication*, his passage form adolescence to maturity to complete. It is worth noting that in these stories, two of which have him as the protagonist, women characters figure prominently and they impresses and influence George. We have seen already how Kate Swift had already set him thinking about the limitations of his own understanding. Nancy Bunge has made the claim with a touch of exaggeration that "all of George Willard's healthy capacities derive from his contact with—Winesburg women—"[71] In *An Awakening* George is involved with a woman, as he did in the earlier story *Nobody Knows*, But there is a difference. In *Nobody Knows*, feels happy and even proud of his sexual adventure with Louise Trunnion. His only worry then is about what people may think of him in case they come to know about it, He is otherwise totally indifferent to the unfortunate young woman who cannot express herself properly. In *An Awakening* he is confident of himself and of his masculine power. He feels stronger because of what he believes to be the new insights he has obtained into life which he wants to share with Belle Carpenter, his companion. He has no qualms to disturb him in his approach to her. There is, however, an ironical reversal of his expectations, even before he expects her to surrender herself to him. He has to learn the lessons that experience of humiliation, hurt pride, disappointment, disillusionment and the puncturing of his ego, brings. This experience proves salutary for his growth.

Belle Carpenter, daughter of a bank cashier, and employed in a millinery shop, and George are friends. Occasionally they walk together in the evenings. Wash Williams (*Respectability*) the misogynist, suspecting that they were lovers had tried to put George on his guard. But actually she is secretly in love with Handby, a bartender, who is socially her inferior. She walks now and then with George "as a kind of relief to her feelings",[72] and is confident that she can keep the young reporter within his bounds. Ed Handy views George as the only obstacle to his getting Belle. George has grown old enough to talk braggingly about women. One evening in January, he falling into the talking vein, tells his friends expecting from them an admiring attention: "—women should lookout for themselves,—the fellow who (goes) out with a girl (is) not responsible for what (happens)",[73] Such is his masculine confidence and arrogance that he dwells on this theme for full five minutes. Form the friends he walks out into the lovely night. When he is in a lonely place, overflowing with youthful energy, he talks aloud picturing himself as a soldier inspecting with a critical eye a long line of men in uniform, and admonishing them for want of order in them. He is hypnotized by his own words. Then lost in reflection he mutters to himself:

> *There is a law for armies and for men too. The law — covers everything. In every little thing there must be order—I myself in touch with something orderly and big that sings through the night like a star. In my little way I must begin to learn something, to give and swing and work with life with the law.*[74]

This train of thought is indeed an advance on his idle curiosity about trivialities in Winesburg as reporter.

George himself is amazed and delighted to find himself thinking such thoughts as one inspired, though he feels with some modesty that some voice outside himself has been talking to him. It does not occur to him how vague and wooly the thoughts are with his head filled with resounding thoughts, he walks along. He has "the curious feeling of one revisiting a place that had been a part of some former existence".[75] He looks at the people in the alleyway. The men and women and crying children, barking dogs and grunting pigs, all make him feel, "oddly detached and apart from all life".[76] He is so much excited that he is unable to bear the weight of his own thoughts. He feels unutterably big and remade. "The desire to say words (overcomes) him and he (says) words without meaning, rolling them over on his tongue and saying them because they (are) brave words, full of meaning": "Death, nights, the sea, fear, loveliness".[77]

In this state of exalted feeling, which is not far away from his inflated ego, he feels that his sympathies have become so large-hearted that he feels like calling, provided he has the courage, "all of the people in the street" "brother and sisters to him" and shaking hands with them. He wishes to share this so-called insight with someone, preferably a woman. To the question, why a woman and not a man, probably he would have no answer. An admiring young woman would feed his vanity which a man cannot. Therefore he goes seeking the company of Belle Carpenter. He thinks that "she would understand his mood and then he could achieve in her presence a position he had long been wanting to achieve".[78] He is confident that he has become too big to be used by her as she did on former occasions. That is where he goes wrong. Belle actually makes use of him not because she has any love for him but to make Ed Handby "suffer". As George and Belle walk bout under the trees, he is full of big words. In fact Kate Swift had warned him precisely against this egocentric indulgence. With the sense of power that has come to him during the previous hour of reflection and inspiration he talks to Belle boldly, swaggering along and swinging his arms about. As Nancy Burge points out, "George wants someone to be his audience for his new found ability to declaim pompous words".[79] He wants to impress upon her that he is a changed person, no longer the adolescent: "You'll find me different—You've got to take me for a man or let me alone".[80] He has no more understanding of her or of her needs than he had of Louise Trunnion's. He is more interested in himself than anyone else at this moment. Suddenly he decides that Belle Carpenter is about t surrender herself to him. The new force which has manifested itself in him he feels, has been at work upon her too and has led to her conquest. This thought makes him "half drunk with the sense of masculine power".[81] Holding her in his arms who is least interested in what he ways, he whispers large words until the passionate, non-verbalising Ed Handby throws him aside and marches off Belle Carpenter. George is left "angered, humiliated, and disgustedly disillusioned with his moment of mystical insight".[82] This escapade with Ed Handby marks a stage in George's growth and development. A good dose of humiliation and defeat is necessary to cure him of his vanity, conceit and his illusory sense of power over women. Because of his preoccupations with himself, the concept of universal order he formulates and his need for living in accordance with it, appear ridiculous. He is most self-deceived at the moment.

George Willard, however, learns much from his foolish involvement with Belle Carpenter and Ed Handby, and also from his contacts with Elmer Cowley and Tom Fisher, which follow one another. His response to his mother's death described in *Death* is on a different footing altogether. It is much more immediately personal touching the core f his being than any of his previous experiences. Her death precipitates his growth into manhood and qualified him for the "sophistication" he acquires subsequently which leads to his departure from Winesburg as an adult. George appears in the last quarter of *Death*, which is mainly a retrospective account of his mother Elizabeth Willard's past and her relations with Dr. Reefy. She dies in the year George becomes eighteen. When she dies he "has but little sense of the meaning of her death",[83] contact and communication between the mother and son being minimal. His visits to his mother in her sickroom are few and far between. Moreover he spends most of his time outside home gathering news for the Eagle. He lives in his own world of adolescent fancies and curiosities. How much his mother is anguished over his future, he has little knowledge of. During the last six days of her life she is paralysed, unable to move or speak, although she thinks only of her son and his future. Therefore she is not able to tell him about the money she has hidden to give him a start in the city.

George is so much thinking entirely of his own affairs that the notion of his mother's death does not get hold of him at once. He is "annoyed" and "half angry" that she should have died on that day because he cannot go to see Helen White,[84] and has to put it off. He is angry with the turn of events. Thought about his own affairs-his decision to leave Winesburg to go to the city and get a job in a newspaper, and the girl with whom he was to have spent the evening get mixed up with the thoughts of his mother's death.[85] But when he looks at the figure of the dead woman he is filled with shame and guilt. For a while the thought that it is not his mother but someone else that lies in the bed before him grips him. She in death looks "young and graceful" and "unspeakably lovely".[86] This vision overpowers him. He wants to lift the sheet and look at her more closely. His courage fails and grief stricken he goes out of the room. But staring at the door through which he has just come out he mutters aloud, "The dear, the dear, oh the lovely dear", the very words used earlier by Dr. Reefy as if so suggest that in the genuine grief that over powers him he too understands like the Doctor what a loving and lovely person his mother must have been. As Nancy Bunge remarks, "The realization that he loved someone who is now dead makes him feel authentic sadness".[87] This impulse that urges him to verbalise his, love comes from outside himself. Geroge's mother's death finally pushed him out of selfish isolation. He begins to realize the significance of her half-uttered expressions to him, her contempt for conventional and mere material success, and her fascination with dreams.

With his mother's death George's education in Winesburg is almost complete. The means of his release are provided by her death, which breaks the ties, which have bound him to the small town. *Sophistication,* the next story of George's formation, :provided the final lesson that leads to George into complete manhood".[88] The full impact of his mother's death, which draws together all the lessons he has learnt unconsciously and half consciously to form a whole, becomes visible now. He is older and wiser now. Emotionally he is mature now. It is possible to read and enjoy independently a good many of the episodic tales in Winesburg, Ohio, stories such as *Hands, the Strength of God, Tandy, The Untold Lie,* for instance. But *Sophistication,* which is exquisitely told, gains in depth of meaning remarkably only when read in relation to and against the background of all the preceding stories in which George Willard appears and in which his gradual growth and formation towards emotional and mental maturity are subterraneous presented. This tale in which George's maturity is fully realized, is most appropriately titled. Anderson uses the word 'sophistication' only in a favourable sense to imply awareness, understanding of one's own self and other people, refinement of feelings and emotions. George Willard on whom attention is chiefly directed acquires all these largely because of the people (the grotesques) he has come into contact with and the experiences he has gone through. The story, which marks the culmination of George Willard Helen White affair, also dwells on the sophistication of growth and development that Helen White also achieves. The relation between these two people touched upon in earlier stories now surfaces as a mature relationship and is given full treatment. However the chief focus is on George, who gets ready "departure" from the small country town into the wide world, form ignorance t understanding, from apparent reality of the face of things to true reality behind or below".[89]

Sophistication is the third of the stories in which George deals with a woman, the other two being *Nobody Knows* and *An Awakening*. Of these Nobody Knows is the simplest, and occurs appropriately early in Winesburg, Ohio. In the story, which briefly recounts George's first experience of sexual conquest, he begins with a lack of self-assurance and ends with a feeling of self-satisfaction and masculine power. He bursts forth into a flood of words, which only betray his want of understanding, inexperience, and absence of concern and sympathy for Lousie Trunnion, the inarticulate girl involved with him. An Awakening records an experience, which happens much later when George is about to cross the threshold of adolescence into manhood. He believes that he has resounding thoughts about life and human existence, and can contemplate men and women with detachment. He wants to share this insight with belle Carpenter. Actually he wants someone who can listen to him as he vexes eloquent on vague things. He has little sympathy or concern for her. He wants to impress Belle that he is now a man, not an adolescent any longer. While talking to her he loses himself in words. He remains vain, self-centered and over-confident. His relations with Belle carpenter becomes complicated further because of the involvement of Ed Handby, who is "laconic, direct and highly physical",[90] and shows George his place, and leaves him hurt, humbled and defeated. *An Awakening* records the story of George's defeat. In *Sophistication* too George has to deal with a woman, Helen White. His relation with him is complicated, as in *An Awakening*, by the presence of another man: it is a college instructor "who is valuable, pompous and has pretentious to be an intellectual. But Helen White is not like Belle carpenter, and knows her own mind. *Sophistication* "records in all ways a triumph".[91] George's meeting with her in this story is brief, but within the short duration he realizes "that sex and love are not synonymous but that they are often confused". This realization makes it possible for him to achieve eventually understanding. In the process he also learns "something of the nature of the human heart, both of others and of his own" and "to open his heart and t listen with it rather than with the ears".[92]

The events of *Sophistication* take place some months after the death of Elizabeth Willard. It is late fall and the time of Winesburg country fair, and Winesburg is full of crowds. His mother's death has sharpened George's sensibilities. The narrative is presented from his point of view chiefly and that of Helen White. He has become thoughtful, introspective and self analytical. Though he does not want to think, new thoughts keep on coming into his head. He is 'fast growing into manhood" and feels grown up. He has already made up his mind to go away to some city. His "new sense of maturity" sets him apart from others. Significantly he wants "someone to understand the feeling that (has) taken possession of him after his mother's death".[93] Obviously that –"someone" he has in mind is Helen White for whom be anxiously waits in that evening, for the first time in his life he "takes the backward view of life", and he also thinks of the future and of what he would be. "Perhaps that is the moment", says the narrator, "when he (i.e. every boy) crosses the line into manhood".[94] Ambitions and regrets awake within him. All the cocksureness of his adolescence has vanished. As he waits "the voices outside of himself whisper a message concerning the limitations of his life". The future becomes uncertain. To his imagination it appears as though countless men have come out of nothing into the world and have disappeared into With a little gasp he sees himself as merely a leaf blown by the wind" who "must live and die in uncertaintly".[95] His mother's death has probably awakened him to both the brevity and loneliness of human existence. Already he hears the call of death. He longs for coming close to another person preferably a woman because "he believes that a woman will be gentle—will understand".[96]

Like the grotesque, now George too needs understanding, and he seeks it in Helen White who has been occupying his mind for sometime. This growing youth has been conscious of this girl growing into womanhood as he has been growing into manhood. When he was eighteen he had taken a walk with her along a country road on an evening. He remembers it now because on that occasion he had yielded to an impulse t boast, "to appear and significant in her eyes". "He had tried to make her think of him as a man when he knew nothing of manhood". Now he wants to meet her, not to use her for any selfish purpose such as writing a love story. (*The Thinker*) but to seek understanding, and "to be with her and try to make her feel the change he believed had taken place in her nature".[97] This train of thought in George shows that he has become modest, humble, free form vanity, conceit, and selfish pride, all seen when he took a walk along with belle carpenter.

As for Helen White, she too has reached a period of change, of transformation into womanhood paralleling George's into manhood. Now what he feels, she also in her young woman's way feels. No longer a firl, she hungers "to reach into the grace and beauty of womanhood".[98] She has come home now from Cleaveland where she is attending college, to spend a day at the county fair. One of her instructors has come along with her on her mother's invitation. At the Fair Helen is glad to be seen in the company of this well dressed person whose presence would make an impression. But it is a credit to her sensitive nature that she gets tired of the company of this young man with a pedantic turn of mind, and his inane talk. She becomes "restless' and wants to drive him away from her presence, if she can. The young pedant has his own designs. He muses: "A scholar needs money. I would marry a woman with money".[99]

Helen remembers George even as her dissatisfaction with the instructor rises. In fact interest in the young reporter has been growing silently in her. She wishes to walk with him again as she did in summer. She too wants him "to feel and be conscious of the change in her nature" since she went to the city. George, who also recalls that particular summer evening, feels "ashamed of the figure he had made of himself" in her presence by his boastful talk. He also realizes that he has been talking a little too much.[100] The medley of sounds created by the crowds gets on his nerves. He feels utterly lonely and dejected". Wandering restlessly for a while he makes up his mind to go to Helen White's house, "and goes running towards her house". Exactly at that time Helen, obliged to sit in the company of her instructor and her mother, feels "restless and distraught". His snobbery, and "pompous and heavy" voice put her out and she abruptly leaves the company and goes eagerly into a little street. It seems to her "that the world is full of meaningless people saying words".[101] In nervous excitement she cries out for George who just at that moment reaches the same place. This is their last meeting in the story. Hand in hand they walk away towards the Fair Ground on the hill. Few words are spoken. The narrator makes the significant observation: "now that he had found her, George wondered what he had better do and say".[102] The feeling of loneliness and isolation, very different from that which the grotesque experience, which he had felt in the crowded streets of the town, paradoxically seems broken and intensified by Helen's presence. What he feels is "reflected in her" too.[103]

Having overflowed with life during the day the Fair Ground, with all life going away from it, hs become terrifying silent since it is night. George's reflective rendency becomes intensified. Where there was hectic activity there s only utter silence. It seems to suggest to him "the meaninglessness of life". but at the same instant he feels that "if the people of the town are his people, one loves life so intensely that tears come into his eyes".[104] With Helen White sitting by his side, he feels "very keenly his own insignificance in the schemes of xistence". Whatever irritation he had felt about people earlier disappears now. He feels renewed and refreshed by Helen's presence. He thinks of "people in the town whee e had always lived with something lke reverence". He feels a like "reverence for Helen" for; "He wanted to love and to be loved by her, but he did not want at the moment to be confused by her womanhood".[105] Clasping each other's hand Helen and George sit rapt and wordless, each revering the other. In the mind of each is the same thought: "I have come to this lonely place and here is this other".[106] This moment during which they reach "a complete understanding" marks the "climax" of the story of the growth and development of both George and Helen. Charles Child Walcott aptly remarks on this situation: "It is most significant that this experience is almost entirely wordless. The shared feeling, indeed, id of seeking and wondering".[107] Just to overcome the embarrassment of the moment, they laugh and pull at each other like children and return home together in dignified silence. The narrator concludes the story thus: "For some reason they could not have explained they both got form their silent evening together the thing needed. Man or boy, woman or girl, they had for a moment taken hold of the thing that makes the mature life of men and women in the modern world possible".[108]

Now that George Willard has learnt all that he can in Winesburg, it is time for his departure from the place. Before he leaves for the railway station to catch the train that would take him to the city, he goes round the town silently touching all the spots he loved there since his boyhood. When he sits in the train, which is to take him out of his town "to meet the adventure of life", appropriately he does "not think of anything very big or dramatic". The "serious larger aspects of his life", such as his mother's death or "the uncertainty of his future life in the city" do not come into his mind.[109] He thinks of little things and of obscure people like Tom Smollet wheeling boards noisily through the main street, Butch Wheeler the lamp-lighter of the town and an unknown quiet a tall woman, beautifully gowned at his father's place. Of course he also remembers Helen White "standing by a window in the Winesburg post office and putting a stamp on an envelop".[110] He is so carried away by his growing passion for dreams that he does not notice Helen running along Main Street hoping to have a parting word with him. The story Departure concludes with the narrator's observation that when George aroused himself from reverie "the town of Winesburg had disappeared and his life there had become but a background on which to paint the dreams of his manhood".[111]

Viewed as a whole George Willard who helps the grotesques of the town to make some sense of themselves by listening to their confidences and advice, receives much more from them than he can ever give them. it is they who unconsciously help him to enlarge his sympathies, become empathetic, and thus make keen his powers of understanding and receptiveness to all human feelings. He also must have realized that they were imposing on him a burden of responsibility for which he is not equal, by expecting him to speak for them. But he begins to learn before he leaves Winesburg the lesson that Kate Swift, his one-time teacher, wanted him to learn-not to be a mere peddler or words, but learn to understand people before he can think of writing about them. By the time the work is brought to a close with departure, which serves as an epilogue to it, George Willard, the man and the potential responsible writer, has grown and developed. The work ends on a note of promise. It is apposite to cite here Malcolm Cowley's observation:

> *All the grotesques hope that George Willard will someday speak what is in their hearts and thus reestablish their*

connection with mankind George is too young to understand them at the time, but the book ends with what seems to be the promise that, after leaving Winesburg, he will become the voice of inarticulate men and women in all the forgotten towns.[112]

NOTES AND REFERENCES

1. Quoted by Jarris A. Thurston, *Technique in Winesburg, Ohio, Winesburg, Ohio: Text and Criticism*, ed. John F. Ferres [Hammondsworth: Penguin Books, 1996], p. 339.
2. Cited by William Phillips How Sherwood Anderson Wrote *Winesburg, Ohio*. p. 286.
3. Malcolm Cowley, *Introduction to Winesburg, Ohio* to his Edition of the Work Reproduced in *Winesburg, Ohio: Text and Criticism*, p. 366.
4. Rex Burbank, Sherwood Anderson [New York: Twayne, 1964], p. 66.
5. David D. Anderson, *Sherwood Anderson and Introduction and Interpretation* [New York: Holt, Rinehalt and Winston, 1967], p. 50.
6. Edwin Fussel, *Winesburg, Ohio: Art and Isolation*, Winesburg, Ohio: Text and Criticism, p. 387.
7. Walter B. Rideout *The Simplicity of Winesburg, Ohio*, p. 294.
8. Edwin Fussel, Winesburg, Ohio: Text and Criticism, p. 294.
9. David D. Anderson *Sherwood Anderson: Introduction and Interpretation*, pp. 50-51.
10. *Ibid.*, p. 45.
11. Malcolm Cowley. Winesburg, Ohio: Text and Criticism. p. 30.
12. Hands, *Winesburg, Ohio: Text and Criticism*, p. 389.
13. *Ibid.*, p. 70.
14. Rex Burbank, p. 69.
15. Edwin Fussel, Winesburg, Ohio: Text and Criticism, p. 389.
16. Rex Burbank, pp. 69-70.
17. *Ibid.*, p. 70.
18. *The Thinker*, Winesburg, Ohio: Text and Criticism, p. 134.
19. Waltere Rideout, The Simplicity of Winesburg, Ohio, p. 290.
20. *Mother*, Winesburg, Ohio: Text and Criticism, p. 44.
21. *Ibid.*, p. 41.

22. *Ibid.*, p. 43.
23. Edwin Fussel, Winesburg, Ohio: Text and Criticism, p. 388.
24. David D Anderson, *Sherwood Anderson's Moments of Insight, Critical Essays on Sherwood Anderson*, ed. David D. Anderson [Boston: G.K Hall and Company, 1981], p. 162.
25. *Mother*, Winesburg, Ohio: Text and Criticism, p. 40.
26. Edwin Fussel, Winesburg, Ohio: Text and Criticism, p. 388.
27. David d. Anderson, *Critical Essays on Sherwood Anderson*, p. 162.
28. *Mother*, Winesburg, Ohio: Text and Criticism, pp. 47-48.
29. The Philosopher. *Ibid.*, pp. 54-55.
30. *Ibid.*, p. 50.
31. *Ibid.*, p. 57.
32. Respectability, *Ibid.*, p. 125.
33. David D. Anderson, *Sherwood Anderson; An Introduction and Interpretation*, p. 45.
34. Nobody Knows, Winesburg, Ohio: Text and Criticism, p. 134.
35. Marilyn Judith Atlas, *Sherwood Anderson and Women in Winesburg, Critical Essays on Sherwood Anderson.* p. 258.
36. *Nobody Knows*, Winesburg, Ohio: Text and Criticism, p. 134.
37. Rex Burbank, p. 70.
38. Walter B. Rideout, *The Simplicity of Winesburg, Ohio, Critical Essays on Sherwood Anderson*, pp. 152-53.
39. The Thinker, Winesburg, Ohio: Text and Criticism, p. 134.
40. Walter B. Rideout, *Critical Essays on Sherwood Anderson*, p. 151.
42. *Ibid.*, p. 135.
43. Rex Burbank: p. 70.
44. *The Strength of God*, Winesburg, Ohio: Text and Criticism, p. 153.
45. *Ibid.*, p. 155.
46. The Teacher, *Ibid.*, p. 158.
47. *Ibid.*, p. 163.
48. *Ibid*.
49. Nancy Bunge, *Women in Sherwood Anderson's Fiction; Critical Essays on Sherwood Anderson*, p. 245.
50. The Teacher, *Ibid.*, pp. 163-65.
51. David Stouk, *Winesburg, Ohio as a Dance of Death, Critical Essays on Sherwood Anderson*, p. 188.

52. Walter B. Rideout, Critical Essays on Sherwood Anderson, p. 151.
53. The Teacher, Winesburg, Ohio: Text and Criticism, p. 166.
54. David D. Anderson, *Sherwood Anderson: An Introduction and Interpretation*, p. 47.
55. *The Strength of God*, Winesburg, Ohio: Text and Criticism, p. 155.
56. *Loneliness*, Ibid., p. 173.
57. *Ibid.*, p. 175.
58. David D. Anderson, The Grotesque and George Willard, Winesburg, Ohio: Text and Criticism, p. 429.
59. *Queer*, Winesburg, Ohio: Text and Criticism, p. 194.
60. *Ibid.*
61. *Ibid.*
62. *Ibid.*, p. 195.
63. *Ibid.*, p. 197.
64. *Ibid.*, p. 198.
65. *Ibid.*, p. 200.
66. Drink, *Ibid.*, p. 215.
67. *Ibid.*, pp. 214-15.
68. *Ibid.*, p. 215.
69. *Ibid.*, p. 218.
70. Rex Burbank, p. 71.
71. Nancy Bunge. *Critical Essays on Sherwood Anderson*, p. 245.
72. *An Awakening*, Winesburg, Ohio: Text and Criticism, p. 180.
73. *Ibid.*, p. 182.
74. *Ibid.*, p. 183.
75. *Ibid.*, p. 184.
76. *Ibid.*, p. 185.
77. *Ibid.*
78. *Ibid.*, pp. 185-86.
79. Nancy Bunge, Critical Essays on Sherwood Anderson, p. 245.
80. *An Awakening,* Winesburg, Ohio: Text and Criticism, p. 153.
81. *Ibid.*
82. Walter B. Rideout, Critical Essays on Sherwood Anderson. p. 153.
83. *Death,* Winesburg, Ohio: Text and Criticism, p. 229.

84. *Ibid.*, p. 229.
85. *Ibid.*, p. 230.
86. *Ibid.*, p. 231.
87. Nancy Bunge, Critical essays on Sherwood Anderson, p. 345.
88. David D Anderson, *Sherwood Anderson: An Introduction and Interpretation*. p. 49.
89. Walter B. Rideout Critical Essays on Sherwood Anderson., p. 152.
90. *Ibid.*
91. *Ibid.*
92. David D. Anderson, *Sherwood Anderson Movements of Insight, Critical Essays on Sherwood Anderson*, p. 165.
93. Sophistication, Winesburg, Ohio: Text and Criticism, p. 234.
94. *Ibid.*
95. *Ibid.*
96. *Ibid.*, p. 235.
97. *Ibid.*
98. *Ibid.*
99. *Ibid.*, p. 236.
100. *Ibid.*
101. *Ibid.*, p. 239.
102. *Ibid.*
103. *Ibid.*, p. 240.
104. *Ibid.*, pp. 240-41.
105. *Ibid.*, p. 341.
106. *Ibid.*
107. Charles Child Walcutt, Sherwood Anderson: Impressionism and the Buried Life, the Achievement of Sherwood Anderson: Essays in Criticism, ed. Ray Lewis White [Chapel Hill: University of North Carolina Press] pp. 163-64.
108. *Sophistication*, Winesburg, Ohio: Text and Criticism, p. 243.
109. Departure, *Ibid.*, pp. 246-47.
110. *Ibid.*, p. 247.
111. *Ibid.*
112. Malcolm Cowley, *Introduction to Winesburg, Ohio; Winesburg, Ohio: Text and Criticism*, p. 367.

CHAPTER – 4

Young People's Initiation into Adulthood in Some Post-Winesburg Stories

This and the next two chapters, Chapter Five and Six, are concerned with some of Sherwood Anderson's post-Winesburg stories, particularly those written in the middle and later years of his career, in which he ventures beyond the limits of a small country town like Winesburg. However, many of the Winesburg themes continue to engage his creative attention. As in the case of the Winesburg stories, a deep and boundless compassion for his fellow human beings, be they grotesques or not, permeates every one of these stories. Anderson, as seen already, is more interested in the inner life than in anything else. His remarkable ability to get close to ordinary life, look deep into buried lives, probe beneath the dark surface of lie to get at its essence, and transform his perceptions into memorable fictional art continue as ever before in these later stories.

Thematically, the present chapter is a continuation of the previous chapter (Chapter Three) in that it also is concerned with Anderson's handling of the theme of growth and formation in some of the post-Winesburg stories. But there is a difference to warrant a separate study of these stories. Chapter Three is all about the formation of one character, young George Willard, the much sought after newspaperman of Winesburg. Therefore attention is naturally directed on him and the different stages of his growth-mental, moral and physical- from boyhood to adulthood, as it takes place during his contact or encounter with a number of people-men and women, young and old alike-in the small town of Winesburg.

As George appears in different capacities in the several stories of Winesburg, Ohio, his development is not traced linearly. But it is his presence in most of the stories that links them altogether directly and indirectly to form a unified whole. And hence it is possible to map out his growth and formation. On the other hand, the stories of growth and formation with which the present paper deals with growth and formation of separate discursive stories each with its own protagonist and depicting or delineating a particular or special problem faced by the protagonist as a growing boy or adolescent. Further in each story the protagonist recalls one particular experience of his boyhood or early youth, which made such an impregnable impact on his consciousness that the memory of it he cannot erase. Moreover, it created when it happened an elemental crisis in his life, attitudes. As the protagonist looks back at that experience, because he feels that inner compulsion to do so, it appears to him now "to have been crucial to his life", marking a moment "in which he took one of those painful leaps that climax the process of growth", as Irving Howe so well puts it.[1]

The stories considered and linked thematically together are *I Want to know Why* and *I' am a Fool, The Man Who Became a Woman, An Ohio Pagan*, and *The Sad Hornblowers,* all of which are regarded as among Anderson's major post Winesburg stories. They are not taken up here for analysis in the order of their composition or publication, as a measure of convenience. Moreover, this procedure does not seem in anyway to affect one's understanding of Anderson's handling of the theme of growth and initiation in these stories. While thematically they form a unit, they are not repetitive. Each story presents one particular and what seems to its protagonist to be a unique experience. Taken together the stories are found to be complementary to each other. Of the stories selected here for analysis, the first four- *I Want to Know why, I'm a fool, The Man Who Became a Woman,* and *An Ohio Pagan* - are horse racing stories and said to be "based on Anderson's memories of his own youth. One of his many jobs was as a groom or 'swipe' in a livery stable in Clyde, and in the summer and fall of 1895, he travelled on the racing circuit in the area tending to the horses of a local farmer".[2] But it may not be necessary to point out that the interest of these stories lies in their intrinsic quality as short friction rather than in their biographical dimension, although it is very tue that he learnt much about human nature and life in general during his close association with horse racing men and trainers. They are also noteworthy for their narrative art. In each story the mode of narration chosen is most appropriate to the character of the protagonist.

Charles Modlin has described these stories of Anderson's as "stories of adolescent initiation into adulthood".[3] The term 'initiation' as used in the present context has to be explained, since it has been defined variously. It has strong religious, ritual and even occult associations, which as is obvious, is not relevant to the present context. In each of the stories the protagonist experiences something, which he has not experienced or known before. It is such an experience that it compels him to take serious note of it. And it marks the beginning of his getting to know chiefly about himself, his nature, and human nature about which he had no knowledge earlier. In this sense it is an 'initiation'. Others, much older and more experienced than himself, may have red this knowledge. But as far as he is concerned it is entirely new and disturbing. He is puzzled, even baffled. Maxwell Geisman has said of the youthful protagonist of Anderson's that he is a "puzzled and baffled spectacular standing in owe not all the mysteries of life".[4] It is equally important to note that the implication of these stories of Anderson's extend far beyond adolescent's initiation into adulthood, and touch significantly upon several perennial dilemmas and dichotomies of life which remain for most people unresolved and tease them out of thought.

In four of the stories selected here for a close look, a remembered crucial experience is narrated by the protagonist himself. In the other two (*An Ohio Pagan* and *The Sad Horn blowers*) an omniscient third person narrator tells the story. But in all of them the experience is detailed and the story told solely from the protagonist's point of view. In each case the narrator stresses the strangeness of the experience narrated. After undergoing the experience the protagonist is not any longer what he was before. The chief interest in each tale is in his reaction-puzzled, baffled or bewildered to the event itself, which constitutes the action of the story. As Irving Howe puts it, "The true action of these stories is—not perceived object but the perceiving subject".[5] Each story reveals the protagonists experience of the pain of entry into adult life and the frustration of growing up, in "the perplexity he feels at seeing for the first time the ambiguities of life".[6] However disturbing the experience be to the protagonist and whatever be his reaction to it, it certainly results in "an enlargement of his consciousness" which is "refracted' in his story.[7]

Of his Mid-American Chants Anderson is reported to have said, "I sang the ugliness of life, the strange beauty of life pressing in on the mind of a boy". Rex Burbank, who quotes this statement of Anderson's comments:

> *Such was to be the theme of his finest fiction. Sudden glimpses of the strange mixture of beauty and ugliness in life had characterized George Willard's growth to maturity in Winesburg and also the slow movement toward sympathetic consciousness of those defeated by the ugliness of life—Anderson brought his vision of the puzzled boy or boy-man to near perfection controlled point of view with a painstaking attention to the subtleties of the colloquial diction of the narrator, who betrays both a touching naivete and a profound sensitivity to the confusing paradoxes of the adult world.*[8]

This lengthy passage has been worth quoting as it serves as an excellent introduction to the three stories about adolescents. *I Want to Know Why, I'm a Fool,* and *The Man Who Became a Woman* - to be examined hereafter, one after another. These stories form a convenient group for more than one reason. First they tell stories of youthful experiences in horse racing and training. Though each protagonist narrator is crazy about thoroughbred horses, the central concern of each story is the protagonist himself, not the horses. The focus is on him. What the horse symbolizes for each protagonist may be considered in the context of the story itself. Each of them is jolted, as it were, into the adult world and caught up in it by an unusual experience (that is, from his point of view). He discovers that in the adult word which is full of perplexes, the simple values and beliefs on which he has been brought up since childhood, are shaken and unsettled, and that they cannot be preserved and sustained in their simple form. His attempts to make categorical judgments only leave him more perplexed and confused. He is forced to analyse in retrospect what happened to him and relate that experience to himself and his potential listener or reader, whom he takes into confidence, so that the may sort out the sense and meaning of it. Thus each story reads like a confessional monologue. One also gets the impression that each narrator appears to be anxious to disburden what is weighing on his mind and in doing so find an "occasion for symbolic cleansing and relief".[9]

Anderson could not have chosen a more significant title for his story, *I Want to Know Why,* a classic tale about an adolescent's inquisitiveness that leads to his initiation. More importantly, it is also a story which "voices a youthful, desperate plea for insight into the imponderability of human life",[10] about which the protagonist narrator becomes initially aware because of an unexpected troubling experience he has had at a race track. The nearly sixteen year old boy, son of a none too prosperous lawyer recounts what happened on a trip to the racetrack at Saratoga, about a year earlier where he went with three of his friends. The experience he recalls is not only very vivid and fresh in his memory but has been so unsetting and shocking to him that the world no longer seems to him what it was before. What is more, it leave him so irritated, perplexed and indignant that, to cite his own words, "sometimes I'm so mad about it, I want to fight someone. It gives me the fantods".[11]

Anderson gives this story, as he does several of his successful stories, the structural base of an oral narration. The adolescent first person narrator of this story is naïve, simple, but certainly not lacking in sensitiveness and intelligence. In telling his story he is hesitant, humble and anything but all knowing. Therefore he readily wins the listener's confidence. The success of this story considerably depends upon this strategy. In the seemingly rambling opening of the narration, which ultimately is seen to move unobtrusively and steadily towards the inevitable close of the story, the essential traits of the protagonist are "revealed through several neatly economical touches".[12] His life is dominated by his fondness for race horses. He is so crazy about them and feels such a strong sense of kinship with the Negro swipes that as boy that he had wished that he were "a nigger" and even toyed with the idea of becoming "a stable boy".[13] Therefore he is going to the races at Saratoga, which is entirely his idea, is prompted by his love of horses and swipes, rather than a hunger for adventure. For his friends who go with him and who are more or less of his own age, however it is little more than that.

Even at Beckersville his home town, such is the narrator's absorption in the thoroughbred race horses, trainers and training tracks that, more than a thousand times he has got out of his bed before daylight, walked two or three miles to the training tracks to watch them. His intense adolescent feeling and exhilaration for them all is revealed in more than one passage in the story. But to cite one of them:

> *Well, out of the stables they come and the boys are on the tracks and its lovely to be there. You hunch down*

> *on top of the fences and itch inside you. Over in the sheds the niggers giggle and sing, bacon is being fried and coffee made. Everything smells lovely. Nothing smells better than coffee manure and horses and niggers and bacon frying and pipes being smoked out of doors on a morning like this. It just gets you, that's what it does.*[14]

Once at Saratoga, where the nigger Bildad Johnson gives the boys good food and shows a shed for the nights, the people and the horses at the racetrack and the entire atmosphere there enthrall the protagonist:

> *The horses are sweaty and nervous and shine and men come out and smoke cigars and look at them and the trainers are there and the owners, and your heart thumps you can hardly breath.*[15]

The prospect of the two horses, Sunstreak which is a stallion and Middlestride which is a gelding, about which he knows a great deal, and which are to run the race the next day, excites him so much that he cannot sleep the previous night. Interestingly a significant hint of the incipient sexuality of the adolescent narrator is given in his romantic view of Sunstreak:

> *Sunstreak is like a girl you think about sometimes but never see—when you look at his head you want to kiss him—there isn't anything as sweet as that horse—It makes you ache to see him. It hurts you—.*[16]

As Papinchak points out, "The story is about the pre-knowledge of sexuality when the boy is not yet a man".[17] It "throbs with often confused, often undefined sexuality" and it "draws a direct connection between horses, men, women and sexuality",[18] as the protagonist's view of Sunstreak and Middlestride makes it clear.

Nothing special happens on the racetrack to the narrator except the usual suspense and excitement just before the starting of the race, until he sees Jerry Tillford Sunstreak's trainee holding it. He has known Jerry for long, and Jerry who has been friendly has let him walk into the horse's stall and watch it closely. It is the love of horses, of Sunstreak in particular, that binds them. The narrator feels for Jerry an adolescent's admiration for his hero. Now on this particular day as they all wait for the race to begin, the boy narrator and the trainer happen to look into each other's eyes, and it turns out to be an unusual moment for the boy:

> *Something happened to me. I guess I loved the man as much as I did the horse because he knew what I knew. Seemed to me there wasn't anything in the world but that and the horse and me.*[19]

The hint of sexual implication here cannot be missed. The narrator finds that Jerry is as much moved as he at watching Sunstreak run. In the trainer he sees a kindred soul who shares his love and understanding of horses. He experiences in this intense absorbing moment a rate sense of understanding and communion with Jerry, which results in joy. He wants to be as near him as possible after the race. He follows Jerry and his companions to the outskirts of Saratoga and sees them entering a farmhouse, which is actually a brothel. What happens to him there is the central episode in this confessional narrative, too which the narrator has been quietly leading his auditor. What he sees and hears there in the farmhouse gives him the rudest jolt of his young life. The youthful protagonist of *I' am a Fool,* another story of Anderson's about adolescent initiation, to be examined next says of a puzzling and unsetting experience of his, "It was a hard jolt for me, one of the bitterest I ever had to face".[18] These words seem much more compelling appropriate to the protagonist of *I Want to Know Why.*

The narrator creeps up along the fence and looks into the farmhouse through a window. He recognizes it at once as "a place for bad women to stay in". His adolescent moral sensibility is revolted. "The women (are) all ugly mean looking, not nice to look at or be near". The place smells rotten, and so is the talk of men, including Jerry's. It is the kind of talk one hears around a livery stable in a town, but one does not expect to hear where there are women around.[19] He is deeply hurt and pained by Jerry's talk and behaviour. He sees him brag 'like a fool' before one of the women and take all the credit to himself for Sunstreak's success in the race.[20] Even more shocking is the jockey's reaction towards the prostitute. As he looks at her eyes, his eyes begin to shine in the same way they did that morning when he looked the narrator and the magnificent stallion Sunstrek which he himself had lovingly brought up as a mother would since it was a baby colt and trained it for the races. How could he fail to distinguish between Sunstrek and the ugly contaminated woman?. His revulsion is to immediate and uncontrollably strong that he begins to 'hate' Jerry, and wants to kill him, if he can. The narrator feels disillusioned and utterly betrayed by his hero in whom he never suspected depravity. He is confused and perplexed and cannot make out how could a man like Jerry who knows what he does and who could see "a horse like Sunstreak run", "kiss a woman like that the same day'. His bewildered question is: "Darn him, what did he want to do like that for?—What did he do it for? I Want to Know Why"[21] This question continues to haunt him because he cannot find an answer to it.

After this traumatic experience, which ushers the narrator into the world of adults, things are no longer to him what they were before. "At the tracks the air don't taste as good or smell as good".[22] The innocent sense of emotional and moral security he enjoyed as a boy is no longer possible for him. Even before he has the disillusioning experience in the farmhouse, the narrator has an awareness of what is 'bad' and what is 'ugly' and he tacitly rejects both. [The women the farm house were both ugly and bad]. He was no stranger to 'rotten talk' heard in livery stables. He rejects that too. Therefore he is free from any taint. Now he is riddled by the co-existence in one and the same person love of the beautiful and of the morally equally ugly. In his inexperience he assumes that beauty and virtue are inseparable. But what crushes and baffles him now is the sudden realisation "that unhinged purity cannot exist in human nature, and that he must accept and live with the fact that lusts degradation and response to beauty can be in one self. But this knowledge destroys forever the romantic idealism of youth".[23] his uncomplicated love for horses and his associating constantly cleanliness with them suggest his adolescent idealization of sex. As yet he does not think much about girls except as disembodied ideas. In his love of thoroughbred horses "his emerging sexuality is diffused and sublimited",[24] as is clear from his attitude to Sunstreak who is 'like a girl you think about sometime but never see'. What he witnesses at the farmhouse shocks him into the realization that "sentences can men lust and degradation as well as response to beauty". And "his initiation into the puzzling adult world in which ideals of absolute purity and beauty are impossible, causes him to respond with the complete disillusionment and bewilderment of the child".[25]

The story revolves, Irving Howe points out, "around two moments of intense perception, are resulting in joy and the other in pain. The first moment is the boy's sudden awareness that he shares his love for horses with the trainer and the second his shock at discovering the trainer's lust for the prostitute. In this play of symbolic action he learns that the extremes of good and evil can coexist in the same person and can elicit a bewildering similarity of response".[25] His feeling of horror at the degradation in the brothel is so strong that he at once turns against the degraded love between man and woman. With reference to this situation Howe says that the boy's just revulsion at what he witnesses also expresses his 'fears' of 'the prospect of all adult sexuality, which can never be as pure as his relation to horses". Therefore "even as he undergoes his 'initiative' into the adult world, he is developing powerful and enduring resistance to it".[27] In general psychological terms, perhaps fears of adult sexuality in growing adolescents is true. But whether Anderson suggests this idea in this story or gives it the kind of emphasis that some critics give it seems uncertain. As Papinchak has pointed out, "By the end of the story— the boy is like Strident, 'a new colt (that) — will lay them all out"[28] To achieve this, of course he has to sort out the confusions in his mind.

I Want to Know Why, to repeat what has already been said, is about an adolescent's growing awareness of sexuality. But it has something more in it, which is equally relevant to one's growth and formation. It is also a story of an adolescent who is "caught up in a puzzling conflict of values" and his "frustrating inability to maintain a simple, inviolate island of purity in a corrupt world".[29] as David Anderson points out, it is "Anderson's expression of the most important of adult tragedies: the inability to understand the complexity of emotions and the confusion of values evident not only in society, but in each individual human being".[30] In his own simple and naïve way the narrator of the story notices the contradictions and illogicalities inherent in life, and the values professed by individuals and society. And at the end of the story he admits his inability to understand them, and he wants 'to know why'.

The first of the contradictions he notices is between a negro man and a white man. A negro swipe in his simplicity respects the trust placed in him and does not report against a mischievous boy. A white man who professes to have certain values of life and standards would not hesitate to tell on the mischievous boy. In this he may be correct but, the narrator seems to imply, he only betrays his inability understand the mind of a boy. For many white men at the racetrack, the boy observes, a racehorse is only a vehicle for gambling, but not a thing of beauty, which it is to the negro swipe. Another contradiction he notices among white men is that a good and generous man is condemned because he is a professional gambler. The father of his friend Henry Rieback, though a 'Sheet writer', is 'a nice man and generous', and an affectionate father. He always sends his son generous gifts. But the fathers of his other friends do not want their children to associate themselves with the son of a gambler and regard the money he earns as tainted.

The narrator does not comment on these contradictions, but he remains puzzled. The most important contradictions he encounters in Jerry the trainer of a beautiful horse. How one could has seen real beauty turn to a cheap and revolting substitute and thus degrade himself? David Anderson aptly remarks: "Man's basic confusion of values is his inability to distinguish between appearance and reality", "the beautiful and the tawdry, the real and the make-believe".[31] The narrator who is outgrowing his adolescence and is on the threshold of adulthood, feels confused being unable to explain it. In protesting *I Want to Know Why* he is voicing forth his frustration. This story pre-eminently succeeds as it gives authentic expression to adolescent feeling in the idiom and tone of an adolescent. Irving Howe observes: "In language that reverberates with echoes of the authentic Twain, Anderson does justice to what is distinctly boyish in a boy". And but for a few minor lapses, "the story thoroughly maintains the tone and perspective native to its adolescent narrator".[32]

I'm a Fool is also, like *I Want to Know Why*, the story of a race track swipe. He grows into manhood from adolescence as he follows the Ohio racetrack circuit. He too retrospectively recounts in a confessional monologue a bitter and jolting experience he had at the Sandusky races, which initiates him into the complexities of the adult world. In this story also as in *I Want to Know Why* Anderson utilizes "the perspective of the naïve adolescent caught up in a puzzling conflict of values", which he is not able to resolve. Further, like the other protagonist, he "has an uncomplicated, uncritical love for the free, unsophisticated life among the trainers and grooms, and he also becomes initiated into the complexities of life through betrayal of his own simplicity". But there is an important difference between the two. Whereas the other boy who is just sixteen or a little is "betrayed by unsuspected depravity in a man he admires", this one who is nineteen is "defeated by circumstances and by his own ignorance and inferiority complex".[33]

The bitter experience the protagonist narrator recalls retrospectively happened when he was already "a lumbering fellow of nineteen",[34] much older than his counterpart in *I Want to Know Why*, and very close to adulthood and working as a swipe at Sandusky for a master. At the time of narration he is much older and carries into his manhood the bewilderment of his adolescence and the unresolved dichotomies of life. In the experience he recounts which has filled him with a sense of shame unforgivably, he is trapped in a net of seemingly harmless lies he himself has woven. He outsmarts himself through an excess of shrewdness. He discovers that he cannot disentangle himself from the net and has to take the consequence of his own action from which there is no escape. He realizes that it is all because of his own foolishness. By faithfully narrating the story of his folly and thereby making himself look cheap in the eyes of his listeners he derives some satisfaction. In the process he also lessens some to the burden weighing on his conscience.

The meaning of the story, as Rex Burbank has pointed out, is in the conflict between the value f the protagonist's upbringing and the values he acquires in the racetrack. His dilemma is caused by the two conflicting ways of life.[35] Having chosen, much against the wishes of his mother and sister, the life of a swipe in the company of a negro moving from one racetrack to another and enjoying its freedom, he believes he has turned his back on the genteel notions of propriety, respectability, social stratification of his class and the value it attaches to college education. He talks dismissively about those who have lived respectable life and had education and makes the claim that he knows much more about the world and its ways and people than they because of his life in the world of horses, swipes, trainers and racetracks:

——the boys who are raised regular in houses, and never have a fine nigger like Burt for best friend, and go to high schools and college, and never steal anything, or get drunk a little, or to learn to swear from fellows who know how, or come walking up in front of a grandstand in their shirt sleeves and with dirty horsy pants on when the races are going on and the grandstand is full of people all dressed up—Such fellows don't know nothing at all—[36]

The irony is that at the racetrack and the saloons at Sandusky and elsewhere he adopts the very social norms and behaviour he claims to despise. The tension between the demands and expectations of the class of his birth, which he has not really outgrown and the uninhibited gratification of the world of racehorses and the track, comprises the conflict in him. As a result his self confidence seems shaken, especially when he is understandably drawn to a young woman of his own class. It is then that he makes, to his eternal regret, an utter fool of himself. And that is his story.

This is how it comes about. On his day off at Sandusky, the narrator dresses up elegantly like others, wearing his 'good clothes', his 'new brown derby hat' and 'a stand up collar' to go to the races as a mere spectator. On his way he goes to a big hotel, which is crowded with horsemen, strangers and dressed up people standing in the lobby and in the bar. He mingles among them. There he sees a young man "with a cane and a Windsor tie on". For no particular reason he resents him, and to show his contempt for the like of him, he roughly pushed him aside and has more than one drink to show how superior he is.[37] At the racetrack he takes his set in the grandstand feeling grand, important, and superior to all those gathered there. There unexpectedly he meets Lucy Wessen, her brother Wilber and his girl friend from Ohio. Lucy and he take to each other at once: I blushed when she looked right at me and so did she".[38] To impress her further he tells her a pack of lies about himself and his background. Finally it is his lie "built on a series of small truths that catches him out".[39] Knowing as an inside man of the tracks which horse really wins, he advises Lucy's brother to bet on the winning horse about Ben Ahem. To impress her further, he explains that he knows so much about the winning horse because it belongs to his father, Mathers of Ohio, who owns a large estate and a stable of horses which he races in another man's name because their family pride is against racing. Once the narrator starts lying he has to go the whole hog and keep up the diction, particularly because Lucy seems impressed.

It was not the first time that he had indulged in lying. He himself admits that on an earlier occasion he had done it for fun and free drinks, and it seemed harmless then. He and his "nigger" friend Burt, who together led Harry Whitehead's horses from one race meet to another, unhesitant lied in the town saloons to impress the hangers on: "—you went into a saloon, — and there was always someone pretend he was horsy and knew things and began asking questions, and all you did was to lie and lie all you could about what horses you had—".[40]

The narrator is sensible enough to know that Lucy "wasn't stuck on (him) because of (his) father being rich and all that". He realizes that he has made a fool of himself by his lies and whishes that he had "some way of getting(himself) on the aquare".[41] Even then he prolongs the pretence and continues the romance not realizing that because of his lying it is going to be both brief and frustrating. After the race the young people go to Cedar Point where Lucy and he finds himself more involved with Lucy than he had thought possible. Before parting she express confidence that they would keep in touch with each other: "It won't be long because you'll write and I'll write to you".[42] The bitter irony is that the letter she writes to Walter Mathers (the name the narrator has given himself) would come back to her because "there am not any such guy". What is more, in the course of the evening he comes to realize that Lucy would have liked him even if he had not tried to pass himself "for a bigbug".[43] By lying he has made it impossible for himself and got into a rap he cannot get out of. The inescapable conclusion is that he has made an utter fool of himself and that he alone is to blame for it. Had he not met in the saloon the 'dude' with a Windsor tie on who provoked his contempt, and had he not drunk 'the booze' to show himself off, probably he would have conducted himself differently. But this thought brings him no consolation.

Actually the root cause for his innocent deception lies elsewhere. It is not just "adolescent though he is old enough-inn his own words, he at that time "a lumbering fellow of nineteen" and had seen people and places- the inconsistencies and contradictions in his values and behaviour. They are by no means complex or difficult for one to understand. He is able to keep apart the genteel values of the class of his birth and upbringing and those of the horsy people in the racetrack, until he meets Lucy at the racetrack. The urge to impress and the need for love in hi clash, because he fails to reconcile them. They are, in fact, not impossible of reconciliation. He could have impressed the young woman without presenting a false front. He realizes this when it is too late. His regret and remorse over his frustrated romance is genuine. This experience has been an eye opener to him and he is able to see himself as a 'boob'. But ne fails to rouse our sympathy because of his "stolid inability to discriminate among his allegiances". At times "his ignorance comes close to incredibility".[44] He is not able to distinguish, for one of his age, between appearance and reality within the limited area he is familiar with.

Yet another reason for the protagonist's failure to win our sympathy is his mode of narration. There are more digressions than necessary even for a rambling oral narrative. The narrator protests a little too much to be convincing. At the time of his confessional narration he is close to his adulthood, no longer the adolescent of the days of the experience he recounts. In his attempt to give an authentic feel of his state of mind when he went through the unsetting experience, and "to adopt the mask of a love-sick youth", he uses an idiom and style of narration "more forced, more deliberately and consciously adolescent than in *I Want to Know Why*".[48] It is as if he deliberately tries to inject significance into the narrative. Therefore his success is only moderate.

The Man who Became a Woman is "the finest of the horse-and man tales", and it exceeds *I Want to Know why*, which it resembles a little thematically, "in psychological depth and in symbolic richness".[49] It is, by universal consent, one of Anderson's best stories.[50] Irving Howe has justly said of it that it "is richer in atmosphere than the earlier story, it is more certain in technique and consistent in point of view, it benefits greatly from its narrator's distance".[51] Like the other two racetrack stories this is also a confessional story. It is much longer than the other two but far more tightly organized for all its rambling structure. It is much more pronouncedly concerned with the mystery of sex and the ambiguities of sexual development than the other two. The narrator, Herman Dudley, tells his story not as a naïve, confused boy but as an adult recalling a youthful experience with a sense of shame, degradation and under a compulsion to cleanse himself through confession. Narrating the story as faithfully as he can has a therapeutic value for him. In his own words:

> *There was one experience of that time on the track that I am forced, by some feeling inside myself, to tell—It will be kind of like confession is —like cleaning up the room you live in—this story has been on my chest, and I've often dreamed about the happenings in it, even after I married Jessie and was happy. Sometimes I even screamed out at night and so I said to myself, I'll write the dang story'*—[52].

Like the narrator of *I'm a Fool*, he too wants to sort things out and get everything straight by telling his story.

Unlike the protagonist-narrators of the other two stories, Herman at the time of narration is an adult the bewildering experience he recalls happened to him in the days of his late adolescence. Now, by his own admission he is a happily married man, and has had some experience of the world and ways of people, having been a druggist in a city for some time and a tramp before he settled down to married life, which seem to have given him a sense of emotional security, of his present life he says that he "can think this whole thing out fairly now, sitting here in may own house and writing, and with my wife Jessie in the kitchen making a pie or something".[53] Nevertheless the thoroughly unusual and nightmarish experience he recounts remains a puzzle, an enigma t him, some of its terror still remaining with him. Moreover he has not been able to understand its meaning. He tells the reader directly and candidly, "I'm puzzled—I'm not claiming to be able to inform you or to do you any good. I'm just trying to make you understand something about me, as I would like to understand something about you".[54]

The story "gains greatly", as Irving Howe points put, "from having an adult narrator who is deeply involved in his own sory".[55] "the adolescent of the past and the adult of the present are not completely separated, as they can never be",[56] But the narrator is able to maintain with effort enough distance between his present narrating self and his past experience to tell his story as authentically as possible. His mode of narration reveals "how persistently, and poignantly, the adult mind struggle to control the memories of adolescence", which continue t haunt him. And the story itself subtly portrays a "complex state of adult emotion through a recollection of adolescence",[57] when the issue of a safe passage into manhood seemed very much in doubt.

What Herman Dudley strives to understand is his sexual identity, more precisely, its ambiguity. As the title given to the story indicates, Herman believe that he did become a woman on that particular evening in the saloon where he had more than one drink. Whether the women's fade he saw reflected in the cracked mirror there when he looked into it, was a hallucination r the effect of the drink he had, if left deliberately vague by Anderson. But it is connected with the increasing sexual urges and longings in him as he grows towards adulthood. His youthful experience as swipe at the racetrack until he leaves it for good involve, as in the case of the boy of *I Want to Know Why*, but to a far greater degree of intensity and poignancy, horses, men and women and sex. All these get compounded together in his imagination to confuse and even confound him. He does not know how to cope with it. His confessional narration is prompted by the inner urge to clarify to himself of perplexing problem.

As an adult looking back at those days of his adolescence, Herman feels that much of his confusion about his sexual identity and the emerging sexual urges was due to his being a virgin even at nineteen: "Sometimes now I think it was all because I had got to be almost a man and had never been with a woman".[58] He could not ask a woman of a date much as he tried. He had strong aversion for going with "fly girls" as the swipes, drivers and others did in race tracks. He could never bring himself to doing it. But he did dream of women and thought about them a great deal. As he confesses in his narration, I suppose I'd always been dreaming about a pure and innocent one, for myself, made for me by God, may be—.[59] His view of women, romantic and idealistic ,is very much that of an adolescent. Like the boy of *I Want to Know Why* he identified horses with women. In fact he too is confused about their sexuality. Like him he sees a horse as both male and female. He says of the gelding Pick-it-boy, which he loves: "I wished he was a girl sometimes or that I was a girl and he was a man. It's an odd thing to say but it's a fact".[60] More explicitly, he runs his fingers all over this horse's body, "just because I loved the feel of him and as sometimes, to tell the plain truth, I've felt about touching with may hands the body of a woman I've seen and who I thought was lovely too".[61] Herman' descriptions of his intimate experience of walking his horse after the race, and the queer sensation he felt, is explicitly sexual: "you walk and walk, around a little circle, and your horse's head is right by your shoulder—Perhaps no one ever gets as I was then, except boys that aren't quite men yet and who like me have never been with girls or women".[62]

Herman's peculiar attitude to horses, apart from his own love of them, is largely influenced by his friendship with Tom Means, a lover of horses and an educated swipe, ambitious of becoming a writer and writing about horses. Tom, who is just a couple of years older than adolescent Herman, becomes a sort of hero for him. He is as much enthusiastic as the other about racehorses and shares his idealized and romantic view of them. His excited talk about how and what he would write about well bred horses feels and fills Herman's imaginations so much, that he does not need any other comapnay than Tom's He frankly admits to the reader, "To tell the truth I suppose I got to love Tom Means".[63] In thisconfession perhaps thee is a hint of homosexuality. But this suggestion is kept muted. Tom articulates the noble sentiments he feels about thoroughbreds. "With Means present", as Rex Burbank remarks, "he is able to expunge the impurities form horse racing and to constrain his emerging sexual longings".[64] And "his extreme awareness of the affective values available in horses and men prevents him from moving toward full adult secxuality",[65] remarks Howe.

As long as Tom Means stays with him Herman can comfortably hold on to his adolescent romantic attitude towards horses and women, and feel secure. With his going away for good, Herman loses this sense of security and feels very lonely, if not lost. His sense of loneliness is exacerbated with every passing day because of the absence of a congenial companion and his own inability to seek feminine company as others did in the tracks. Hereafter he is "forced to face the more complex facts of the tracks and of his own sexual maturity".[66] He has to confront some of the brutal realities of life, its ugliness, and its nightmarish quality. Unlike that of the other two protagonists, his growth towards full adulthood involves nightmarish experiences and real struggle, and his acceptance of the sordid and ugly realities of the outside world.

Feeling lonely and rather desolate with little work to do at the stables, since for a week or more there might not be any race in the mining town where they are camping. Herman has the hardest time. He finds it impossible to remain alone at the stables, though for a time he had preferred to be alone there, turning his eyes away from the ugliness he saw everywhere around him. One rainy evening he walks away from the stables and through the countryside aimlessly in an agitated state of mind. In the country side he sees everywhere" stones sticking out of the ground and the trees mostly of the stubby, stunted kind—(looking) wild and untidy and ragged",[67] as if they present an outward image of his own inner sterility, confusion and sense of vague unfulfilled desire. More frightening is the mining town itself where the long rows of coke ovens look "like the teeth of some big man-eating giant lying and waiting___".[68] The sight of it all sends shivers down Herman's spine, and seems to anticipate the nightmarish experience he is going to have soon in the saloon he strays into, to have a drink, and back at the stables that night. He is repelled by the shock of his life when he looks at the "cracked looking glass back of the bar", for he sees reflected in it not his face but that of a woman:"It was a girl's face and a lonesome and scared girl too,— just a kid—".[69] The bewildered Herman attributes this strange experience to his having been lonely for far too long a time. It is significant that the mirror in which he sees his reflection is "cracked". An unknown mirror perhaps would have shown a different reflection. Perhaps it is a hallucination and a projection of his own unconscious apprehensions about his sexual identity. However he is convinced of the reality of the experience and of the transformation he believes has taken place. Had he been less agitated and restless, he would not have had this experience. The atmosphere of the saloon adds to his sense of unreality. Nevertheless this episode brings out vividly the ambiguity in his awareness of his sexuality, before he emerges into his full masculine adulthood.

Scared out of his wits Herman Dudley wants to get away from the saloon and to brace himself up he has a couple of drinks. Before he can leave the place he has to witness a brutal brawl, sickening and nauseating, which drives home to him "how mean and low and all balled-up and twisted up human beings can become, and how the best of them are likely to get that way anytime—".[70] this disillusioning experience reveals human nature in the raw. Shaken by seeing himself as a girl in the mirror and sickened by the coarseness and brutality of the drunken card-playing mining men in the saloon, Herman virtually flees the place despite the rain to the security, warmth and comfort of the stalls and the companies of his horse Pick-it-boy who he had wished was a girl. Then he takes off his clothes soaking wet and settles in the hayloft for sleep in between a pile of horse blankets, feeling soothed that Pick-it-boy is nearby. But it becomes for him more of a 'mixed- up night".[71] He gets another hard hit when suddenly two half-drunk big buck nigger swipes invade the stall, attack Herman and attempt to rape him, mistaking him for a white girl, his "body being pretty white and slender then, like a pretty young girl's body".[72]

The attempted sexual assault on him by the niggers reinforces Herman's earlier experience in the saloon. He is so terrified that he is dumbstruck. It is most astonishing that he even fails to tell out or "show them out of there": "I tried and tried so that my throat hurt but I didn't say a word. I just lay there staring at them".[73] Moreover he even believes in his frightened condition that he has become at that moment the young women he had invented to dream about: "—a kind of princess, with black hair and a slender willowy body—shy and afraid to even tell anything she really felt—And now I was that women, or something like her, myself".[74] He reacts to the drunken men the way he thinks a young girl in such a situation might react: he wriggles like a fish just taken off the hooks, and he squirms. However he manages to slip out of the stables and rum wildly away from the tacks into the roaring wind and rain. He is so much scared that "every tree

I came close to looked like a man standing there, ready to grab me".[75] He runs in terror dodging and knocking against trees in the darkness, believing that the two niggers are still chasing after him. Terrified though he is, he fails to scream or make any sound to save his life, however much he might try. He himself is puzzled and the earlier apprehension that he had become a woman again possesses him: "Just why I couldn't I don't know, could it be because at the time I was a woman, while at the same time I wasn't a woman? It may be that I was too ashamed of having turned into a girl and being afraid of a man to make any sound. I don't know about that. It's over my head".[76]

The narrative acquires the qualities of a Gothic horror story as it approaches the final climatic grotesque episode. Running like a crazy man Herman Dudley comes to a field where there is a slaughterhouse. For him it becomes a night of Gothic horror. For he stumbles, falls, pitches forward into the midst of a horse's skeleton washed, bleached white and clean by the falling rain. As Papinchak remarks, "This terrifying encounter is a pivotal and metaphorical one. Herman must finally confront himself and attempt to discover who he is".[77] A new and strange kind of terror shaking him all over new possesses him: "It was a feeling like the finger of God running down your back and burning you clear—It burned all that silly nonsense about being a girl right out of me—".[78] Papinchak aptly comments: "The boy who wishes his horse 'was a girl sometimes' or that he 'was a girl' so that his horse could be a man, who thinks he has been a woman, finds himself in the carcass of a sexless horse and rediscovers his own sex".[79] Herman lets out a terrific scream spontaneously which he could not do earlier: I screamed at last and the spell that was on me was broken".[80] "His scream", as Rex Burbank rightly remarks, "frees him from his verbal and physical paralysis".[81] He now feels that he is a man and his own self as he crawls out of the bones of the horse, and stands on his own feet. He feels ashamed of making a fool of himself. When he runs back and enters the haystack naked with the sheep, "he is in a figurative sense born again into a new innocence of manhood".[82]

At daybreak Herman leaves the track and race horses for good, without regret. By then he has outgrown his adolescence and attained adulthood and sexual maturity. He appears to have realized that he cannot any longer hold on to the impossible and naïve ideas of his adolescence, nor can be ignore the sordid realities around him. "He assumes his role in the adult world", remarks Rex Burbank, "where pure non-physical innocence does not exit, where innocence compels a discriminating selection from among complex alternatives".[83]

A longish story of two chapters *An Ohio Pagan* is an impressive piece though not one among the outstanding stories of Anderson. It tells the story of a boy growing form innocent boyhood to adulthood, which necessarily involves the awakening of his sexual urges, his becoming increasingly aware of this and the accompanying longings and hesitations. As a story of initiation into adulthood it is poignant enough, but not as a complex, complicated and baffling as the other three stories considered earlier. It presents a variation of the theme of growth towards adulthood. Tom Edwards the protagonist of this story is also a great lover of horses, racetracks, and the world of "horsy' men. He is very much reluctant to leave this world but of necessity has to go away from it, although nostalgic memories told originally formed a part of a novel that Anderson was writing and abandoned. As in the case of many of his other stories, critics point out, this story too is based upon Anderson's own personal experiences. It is said that he was drawing upon his own work experience as a swipe as well as a thresher.[84] But however fascinating the biographical aspects of the story be, for us the focus is on the story itself as an imaginative recreation as fictional art of the experiences of an adolescent called Tom Edwards. The merit of the story depends upon how well does Anderson make that experience real to the reader and enable him to participate in it by exercising his responsive imagination.

The story takes place in and around Bidwell, Ohio. Unlike the other three first person confessional narratives this story is presented as a third person narrative told by the omniscient narrator from the protagonist's point of view. Compared with the other stories of initiation, the plot is simple and the narrative is direct and straight forward, almost linear, with easily traceable beginning, middle and end though it has none of the features of the 'poison plot' that Anderson detested.

Tom Edwards the protagonist, born of respectable Welsh ancestry, is orphaned before he is six, both his parents having died, and is brought up by a benevolent and sporting farmer, harry Whitehead, who loves horses and horse races. The boy Tom is made the special guardian and caretaker of Bucephalus, a black stallion", an ugly-tempered beast, as given to whims and notions as an opera star".[85] Only Tom and Harry could make it behave, tom by his gentle and loving ways and the other by suing his long whip. At the great spring race at Columbus, Bucephalus with slender Tom as its rider, wins the race, and "Tom Edwards became a newspaper hero" with is pictures in the Cleveland Leader and the Cincinnati Enqirer.[86] Tom, a tall boy now, and almost of a man's stature, is very happy to be a horseman in this world of horses and races, and is ambitions of becoming a famous and respected driver of race horses. He does not want anything better. In the race at Columbus, his rival driving a famous horse, a big fierce and ugly looking man, had struck at him with the belt of his whip. But Tom, who won the race, did not tell even harry of this incident, and "felt vaguely" that this fact "had something to do with his qualification as a man".[87]

Tom who is happy and content with his present life receives a jolt when the truant officer who is also the superintendent of the Baptist Sunday School, warns him that "if he did not begin going t school both he and his employer would get into serious trouble".[88] Harry, though not against the law which intended "to keep no-account kids off the streets", is indignant that such a promising horseman as tom should be compelled by law to get educated. As for Tom, he is rendered speechless because he takes it hard. He feels that "he had book education enough. He could read, write and do sums and what other book-training did a horseman need?".[89] Books were alright for rainy evenings or when there were no races and no work to do. It is humiliating to go to school now and sit with the kids, as if he were a child. If he should, "he must give up being a horseman and go everyday to a school and do little foolish sums, he who had already proven himself a man. What other schoolboy knew what he did about life".[90] He suddenly decides to "skip out of town", and leaves Bidwell that very night without telling anyone. He goes to Cleveland and lives thee for some months driving a milk wagon in a district factory workers lives. The school at Bidwell no doubt he has escaped, but not the nostalgic and sharp memories of the farm horses and horse tracks there.

The advent of spring crowds his mind with memories of other springs at Bidwell,

Of thundershowers rolling over fields of wheat, just appearing, green and vivid, out of the black ground-dot the sweet smell of animals about barns at the white head farms. He also remembers very vividly and sharply those days when he slept in the stables and went each morning to jog race horses and young colts round and round the half-mile race track at the fairgrounds—That was a life!—life lived in the company of something fine, courageous, filled with a terrible, waiting surge of life.[91]

Everywhere, within himself, in the animals he lived with, and in nature he felt the surging flow of life and growth.

At the fair grounds, away at the town's edge, tall grass grew in the enclosure inside the track and there were trees from which came the voices of squirrels, chattering and scolding, accompanied by the call of nestling birds, down below on the ground, by the song of bees visiting early blossoms and of insects hidden away in the grass.[92]

Tom obviously lived in a kind of dream world in perfect harmony with himself and the world outside at Bidwell, and looked forward to the future free from apprehensions and misgivings. Though physically we-grown and had almost the build of a man, within himself he was still a naïve and innocent boy. As yet he was not aware of the incipient sexual impulse in him, though one might sense it in his love of the Bucephalus.

In total contrast to life in Bidwell life in the city appears to tom, who lives in a narrow and crowded boarding house companions, who regard him with contempt and as a country bumpkin, a "rube". It is but natural that Tom feels "shy, often lonely and sometimes startled and frightened by what he (sees) and (hears) in the city". He often seeks his escape from it all in long walks. But the lonely walks he takes in the grim streets of working men's houses, breathing the smoke laden air and listening to the roar and clatter of machinery in great factories", only depress him. He is left "half sick with fear and with some strange nameless dread of the life about him".[93]

So, early in his seventeenth year Tom Edwards returns to his own Northern Ohio lake country and finds work with John Bottsford who with his threshing outfit and three sons works among the farmers. This marks the next phase in his growth and emotional development towards adulthood. It may be noted here itself that he does not go through any traumatic experience like his counterparts in the other three stories, before he is initiated into adulthood. In fact his growth towards it is steady and gradual. He is now "a tall strong fellow with heavy features, brown eyes, and big nerveless hands",[94] but alt heart he is still the same tender innocent. His work with the thresherman Bottsford is to drive, ironically, not race horses but a team of plodding gray farm horses to keep the threshing engine supplied with water and fuel and to haul the threshed grain into farmers barns. During his association with the Bottsfords two things happen more or less simultaneously which deeply influence Tom. The first is the impact of the religious fervor of John Bottsford on him, and the second is Tom's friendship with Paul, the youngest son of Bottsford, who strengthens Tom's growing interest in women by talking freely about his own interest in them.

John Bottsford, the old thresh man whenever he is worried about his threshing venture in which he has invested his all and dreads the possibility of going into debt, prays at night fervently to Jesus for support and help. Tom, who has had no religious education of any kind till then, is deeply moved by the old man's prayers to this power outside himself "that was in the clouds, in the roaring thunder that accompanied the summer rain-s that was in these things and that at the same time controlled all these things". And Tom for the first time in his life begins "to think about life and its meaning". Whenever he is free or at leisure he thinks of "God and of the possibilities of God's part in the affairs of men".[95] he makes "himself a figure of Jesus as a young God walking about over the land", and summoning "smiling days" "with a wave of his hand".[96]

This view of Jesus s very much that of an adolescent. In Tom, curiously, his growing interest in Jesus gets linked, with the awakening of sexual impulses in him. There is an implicit suggestion in the narrative that the newly roused piety in him nourishes his new urges. This fact becomes clear by the manner Tom understands the meaning and significance of the Mary Magdalene and Jesus episode in the Bible, as it shall be pointed our shortly. Meanwhile there are significant changes in his physical and mental make-up consistent with his growth out of adolescence towards adulthood. The narrator tells us that a "light" comes into tom's eyes and also 'grace' "into his maturing body". New impulses appropriate to his age also come into him. Wherever he goes he attracts the attention of women and smiling young girls. A "new hunger creeps into his heart".[97]

Paul Bottsford, the fat jolly son of John Bottsford and the only companion tom has, talks freely and frankly to him about his fast growing desires and interest in women. He seems to articulate some of Tom's own feelings and vague stirrings which, shy and confused as he is, cannot put into words. In the church the fat boy stares at the country girls as they come in, which shy Tom dare not do, and goes to sleep when the minister begins his sermon. Tom, on the other hand, listens eagerly to the minister's narrating the story of Mary Magdalene, accused of adultery being rescued from the stoning crowd by the all-forgiving Jesus. Next the priest narrates the episode of Jesus being tempted by the devil on the mountain. Tom, who does not listen to this part of the sermon with any attention, mixes up the two separate episodes and takes that Mary followed Jesus to the mountain and tempted him. To his still adolescent idealizing mind it appears rather odd that a woman should tempt man because he had always thought that it was the other way. Now he confides in Paul: "That would be a fine thing if it could happen to us. Don't you think so?".[98] John Bottsford's piety and faith in Jesus affects Tom so much that he likes to believe that this young and beautiful God is close by him and is looking at him. He understands the ways of Jesus in the light of the hunger and stirrings in him.

The next phase in Tom's life (Chapter II of the story) and his growth towards adulthood begins with the Bottsford's along with Tom going to work for a large farmer called Barton near the town of Sandusky. His thoughts and experiences there leave their indelible impress on his mind and determine the course of life he chooses. As noted already, Tom's experiences and thoughts are nothing in comparison with the complex and convulsive experiences of the protagonists of *I Want to Know Why* and *The Man Who Became a Woman*. He does not face anything like a challenging problem but for the threat held out by the superintendent at Bidwell. He does not have compared with the others any initiating experience as such. However, from his point of view, whatever he thinks and experiences at the Barton farms, is significant and deepens his understanding of himself and others. The narrator indicates the different stages of it with apparent ease and effortlessness.

At Barton the season proves prosperous for Bottsford and he decides that his youngest son Paul should attend school in Bellevue during the fall and winter. Not stopping with that he urges even Tom to go to school, and talks to him of the value of learning: "I have watched you. You don't talk very much but you do plenty of thinking, I guess. Go into the schools. Find out what the books have to say. You don't have to believe when they say things that are lies".[99] it is as if for Tom the wheel comes full circle, because he had bidden goodbye to Bidwell only to escape the very thing this present employer wanted him to do. It is interesting that he does not resent Bottsford's suggestion, nor does he say even t himself that there is nothing for him to learn from school going and sitting among kids. as she did at Bidwell. He would have liked to discuss the question with Paul who was to go to Bellevue the next day to go to school. But he does not give him a chance. He only talks excitedly about women and the aggressive plans he has to possess one of them. Not a word about leaning or education escapes his mouth: He merely says: "I am not going to be like a boy anymore. I'll tell you what I'm as big as a man and I'm going to do like men, that's what I am".[100] Obviously he welcomes going to Bellevue solely for this purpose. This boy has his important role in Tom's growing awareness of sex in him.

Tom first feels jealous and envious of his friend and thinks that he has triumphed over him. He even gets angry. But these feelings wear away. But his body begins to burn with eager out into the night and sees the land lying dim and quiet under the moon, it has a soothing effect on him. Instead of Paul, he thinks of "the God Jesus, going up into a mountain with his woman, Mary". And he wonders "what the God, who had brought the beautiful days for the threshing. Would do with a woman".[101] Both his mind and body relax. Before he slips away into sleep and dreams, he whispers a prayer: "Jesus, bring me a woman—I need her Jesus bring me a woman".[102] What a prayer to make to Jesus! Previously he naively hopes that his prayer would be answered.

After Paul's departure there is a change in the nature of Tom's work. Their work on the farm is simplified by mechanization, and Tom, as teamster has little work to do, and has plenty of leisure. He is left alone for long hours, especially on Sundays. He has none to talk to. A restlessness possesses him. The familiar sounds of animals in the barn and the murmuring song of insects in the leaves no longer appear sweet to him. Above all, "no more did the young God Jesus walk beside him"[103] as though he had let him down. How oppressively lonely he feels can be known from the fact that all those who are on the farm helping with the threshing-farmers from nearby farms their wives and daughters-"laughed and talked together, understood one another. Only he was alone. He only had no one to whom he could feel warm and close, to whom he could draw close".[104] Tom's mind begins to play tricks with him. Thoughts of women occupy him so much as to become almost an obsession. He begins to see visions. For instance, a grove of young maple trees near a barn looks like "a troop of girls, young girls who had walked together down a sloping field".[105] Further, women become to him "something different than anything else in nature, more desirable than anything else in nature, and at the same time everything in nature became a woman".[106] Forms of women float before him. He sees them on land, the sea and the sky. In the evening sky he seems to see huge masses of clouds taking the forms of a man and woman embracing each other. Significantly Tom himself becomes aware of his obsession, and he makes up his mind about what he should do without delay: "I'm obsessed with the idea of having a woman. I'd better go to the city and go to school and see if I can make myself fit to have a woman of my own".[107] In his present employer he finds the authority and moral support for his wish and hope: "Even a good man like John Bottsford had a woman for himself. Could he do that"?. He is excited by this thought. "At the moment it (seems) to him that he (has only to go into the city, and go to the schools for a time, to become beautiful and to have beautiful women love him".[108] It seems as simple as that!.

Tom's resolution to go to the city, made in a half-ecstatic state, reveals that he is still naïve, and betrays his inexperience. But it also shows that he does not seek or look forward to the kind of adventure or gratification that Paul anticipated when he went to the city. His intentions are both honest and honorable. He wants and hopes for love, understanding and companionship. But in his excitement he seems to have forgotten the oppressive and dehumanizing life he lived in the city earlier. It is this innocence, which makes his case poignant. The narrator aptly remarks:

> *In his half-ecstatic state he forgot the winter months he had spent in the city of Cleveland, and forgot also the grim streets, the long rows of dark prison-like factories, and the loneliness of his life in the city—For the moment—he thought of American towns and cities as places for beautifully satisfying adventures for all such fellows as himself.*[109]

The story of Tom Edwards, the *Ohio Pagan* ends at this point inconclusively. What happens to him when he goes to the city, and whether he finds fulfillment there at all remain uncertain matters of speculation. But the odds do not seem to be in his favour, if his previous experience in the city is any guide. David Anderson, however, finds "a note of optimism" in the ending of the story. But even he points out that the young protagonist of the story "must learn to identify" "love and understanding" before he can find fulfillment" through them.[110] At the end of the story Tom is only on the threshold of his adulthood, and he is yet to go a long way. It seems apposite to end the present discussion of *An Ohio Pagan* with an observation made by Charles Modlin who describes it as a "startlingly imaginative story of a boy's growing up":

> *The scenes of Tom's religious and sexual awakenings include some of the most lyrical descriptions of nature that Anderson ever wrote. Although some critics as well as Anderson himself have commented on the*

> *inconclusiveness of the ending, it has effectively understated the poignancy as the young pagan looks expectantly towards the city.*[111]

The Sad Horn blowers is yet another poignant story of Anderson's on the theme of young people's initiation into adulthood and growth towards manhood. It is the last of the stories on this theme to be considered in this chapter, although there are surely other impressive stories of Anderson, which can be profitably read form this thematic angle. *The Sad Hornblowers* presents a remarkable portrayal of the inner groping of a seventeen-year old young man faced with the inescapable but complex problem of growing towards and facing his manhood and trying to understand it in a world of endless uncertainties. This story differs from the other four stories discussed in this chapter in certain respects. It has nothing to do with racetracks and race horses. It is built on familialities and bonds, particularly between father and son, brother and sister and their significant role in the process of one's growth towards manhood. Yet another and conspicuous difference between this and the other four stories are that awareness of growing sex impulses is not one of the problems that the protagonist has to contend with in his struggle towards adulthood. This business of man and woman, as he views it, does not touch him closely, as yet.

The Sad Hornblowers is mainly the story of the seventeen-year-old Will Appleton, the elder son of Tom Appleton a house painter and a widower. It is told in the third person by an omniscient narrator from the point of view of Will the protagonist. The adult narrator's voice is, of course, audible throughout. The narrative meanders reflecting the way Will's puzzled mind works. Tom Appleton has another son, Fred who is fifteen years old and fancies that he is already a man, and a daughter Kate, his eldest child. She is twenty years old. The Appletons are a close-knit family. Both the sons assist their father in house painting, and he is vain and proud of them. The family's misfortunes begin with the abrupt death of Tom's wife. It is hard for the children to adjust themselves to the situation, but it draws the children closer together, particularly Will and Kate, though their attachment to each other is rarely spoken about. Tensions, however, build up between the father and the children, particularly between the widower father and the sons. The sons feel that their father's behaviour in public is rather boyish and wanting in dignity. "Young boys growing up" says the narrator, "and merging into manhood do not fancy their father being too boyish".[112] All the children fear that their widower father may marry again. Will and Kate, in fact, resent the very idea, though they do not speak about it: "It was a wave that didn't make much noise, just crept, as it were softly, up a low sandy beach".[113]

Just about the time Tom Appleton thinks that he is in for a prosperous season, which would free the family form financial worries for a while, another disaster overtakes the family. During the surprise party hold for their neighbors the Bradshares, Tom who likes to have a hand in the arrangements, stumbles and spills right over himself two pots of boiling coffee and is left with severe burns. The immediate result is that the expected painting job slips through his fingers and all the family plans for a comfortable winter are spoiled. It would be months before the deep burns on Tom's body would heal to enable him to return to work. Having tried hard and failed to find employment in Bidwell will decides to go to Erie in Pennsylvania to look for work. He might have waited for a couple of weeks to go, had Kate's reaction to his idea of leaving Bidwell been different. He feels a little hurt that his sister, to whom he is particularly attached, does not seem to understand and appears to be "in an almighty hurry about getting him off", and it is "a shame she could not have a little more heart".[114] For, when he talks with her about his plans, she just says, "Yes, I think that's best, you had better go".[115] In actual fact she does worry a good deal about her brother. But the Appleton children are not given to theatrical gestures and overt demonstrations of concern and affection.

It occurs suddenly to Will during an evening walk that Kate perhaps wants to get married. He had not thought of this possibility. If that is so, his going away from Bidwell might have to be for good. It would be a wrench for him. "On that afternoon, and quite suddenly, all the world outside of WBidwell seemed huge and terrible to him".[116] With effort he blinks back a few secret tears, lest he should become sentimental. When he finds his bundle carefully packed and wrapped by Kate, he feels somewhat reassured. He is touched by her gesture of baking an apple pie for supper, a luxury they could ill afford, for his sake. He thinks that "it might be as a way of showing him how she felt".[117] Further she even walks with him to the freight train to see him off. Little is said on the way and they walk in silence. The one question Will wants to ask her, whether she has planned to marry he cannot bring himself to ask. But this thought and thoughts of the possible consequences if she were to marry, fill his mind all through the night in the freight train, and even afterwards. For him his sister is the strongest bond in the family. The Appleton house remains a home, a safe nest, even after their mother's death, because of her. If she were to go away to make her own home with her husband, the family would fall apart, and the house would not be any longer emotionally a safe and secure place for one like him.

Will remembers very vividly his last evening off in Bidwell, even weeks after his departure from there. When the train arrived he had crept into an empty coal car, while Kate continued to stand silently in the shadow of the warehouse nearby. He leaned out for a last look at her. She too took a few steps towards him. Her lips opened and closed as though in an effort to say something to him. "Was there a more final farewell trembling on her lips at the moment? A kind of dread had swept over (him)". Perhaps Kate too felt the same thing. "At that moment she had become altogether the mother in the presence of her child, and the thing within that wanted utterance became submerged. There was a word to be said that she could not say".[118] He whispered "Goodbye" into the darkness. Perhaps she too wanted to say the same thing. "Outwardly there had been only the silence and in the silence she had stood as the train tumbled away".[119] The narrator remarks on this pregnant inarticulate situation: "In the families of working people the dramatic and vital moments of life are passed over in silence. Even in the moments of death and birth, little is said".[120]

The crucial experience for Will in his life is of course his leaving Bidwell for good in search of employment, which would enable him to assert his self. That is of course a decisive step towards his approaching manhood. But that is not all. It is also closely intertwined with his sister Kate's plans to marry and have her own separate home, its effect on the Appleton family, and Wills own reaction to it. He is certainly not against her plans at all. He readily recognizes that she "has a right to get married"[121] while he resents the idea of the possibility of their widower father's marrying again. But his thoughts are not very clear to him, except that he feels like a displaced person rather lonely and lost without a sense of direction. Throughout the night in the freight train he thinks a good deal about marriage, though confusedly. But it is not about his marriage that he thinks: "It was ll a matter-this business of man and woman that did not touch him very closely not yet. The matter of having a home-that was something else. A home was something at a fellow's back—". Whenever one went off to work all week at some farm and had to sleep in a strange room, the thought of one's home with a sister like Kate moving about and attending to everyone's needs. Was most reassuming and comforting.[122]

On the train to Erie, Will encounters an old man, who like his own father Tom Appleton, a longtime cornet player for whom, as it becomes clear to Will gradually, playing on the instrument was an assertion of his self respect and independence. The old man roused Will's sympathy for him and tells him the story of frustrated life. Will listens to him half-heartedly because he is preoccupied with in own thoughts of Bidwell, his sister, and uncertainties about his own future.

He feels like one standing in "the hallway of a house hearing two voices", one of them taunting him that he is now like " a thing swinging in air" with "no place to put down his feet", since his life in the Appleton house at Bidwell had ended. The other voice is about his uncertain future: "Was he afraid? Of what was he afraid? He had wanted so much to be a man, to stand on his own feet and now what was the matter with him? Was he afraid of manhood?".[123] Will's mind understandably clings on to the life of his boyhood, to the life in the Appleton house, perhaps with his sister Kate at the centre of it. But he sees her as in a dream walking with her young man towards the church. "Her being with him meant— perhaps the beginning of a new home- it meant the end of the Appleton home".[124]

As if to echo Will's own thoughts the old fellow traveler narrating his tale of woe all over, happens to say "I might as well not have any home at all".[125] The tears in Will's eyes are taken by the old man as tears of sympathy for him. The old cornet player's life is indeed pathetic. There is nobody in his own home. His present wife, who is much younger, to whom he has given away his all, runs a boardinghouse for factory workers in Erie. The old man has the feeling that he lives there on difference, and has to depend on his tight-fisted wife for everything. He is not free even to play on the horn lest he should disturb other boarders. He prevails upon Will to live with him in his wife's boarding house hoping to have someone to give him moral support in his revolt against his wife (which of course never comes about) and "some little money". He clings on to the young man and virtually imposes his company on him with little thought of Will's own problems and anxieties, and exhaustion at the end of the day's work in the factory.

Two weeks after Will's arrival at Erie the much expected and dreaded letter from Kate arrives, in which she gives him all the news. She ends the letter with the news of her plans to get married in the spring, "Now that Will had made his start in life, there was no point in waiting longer before making her own".[126] if ever there was any doubt or uncertainty about her plans, it is all cleared. But Will is not able to relish his supper and goes out for a long walk towards the shore of the lake. "There was something to be settled with himself, something to be faced. Could he manage the matter?".[127] At the boarding-house and in the factory he is very much a lonely man. But now, after he sees his sister's letter, his sense of being alone strikes him with tremendous force. "The life (he) was to lead alone had become a strange, a vast terrifying thing. Perhaps all life was like that, a vastness and emptiness".[128]

Will tries to think clearly about his situation. The implications of his sister's letter are very clear that he is no longer a boy:

> *A boy is, quite naturally—connected with something- and now that connection had been cut. He had been pushed out of the nest and that fact, the pushing of himself off the nest's rim, was something accomplished. The difficulty was that, while he as no longer a boy, he had not yet become a man. He was a thing swinging in space. There was no place to put down his feet—.One stood face to face with manhood now- one stood alone. If only one could get one's feet down upon something, could get over this feeling of falling through space, thro do with through a vast emptiness.*[129]

This experience of falling through a never ending emptiness is so unusual and complex that he cannot share it with anyone. And there is none either too make an attempt t understand his plight.

At the factory, as much in the boardinghouse, Will is a very lonely. To brave the situation, he tries to think of himself as a man, doing a man's work in a factory, though the word "manhood" sounds queer and its meaning eluding. The work he does in the factory fails to give him the support and sense of security he needs very badly. He cannot "put down his feet" there. It all appears meaningless and absurd and even dehumanizing: "All day he stood at a machine and bored holes in pieces of iron". The holes he drilled have nothing to do with him and he has nothing to do with them.[130] Men working in the factory are like the pieces of iron in which holes had been bored. Life itself seems to have become "just a procession of days". It appears to him that there is nothing for him to grasp and hold on to life. but it is evident that Kate:

> *had got hold of something that her hands had reached out and had grasped something definite. (She) had swung herself off the rim of the home nest and, right away, her feet had landed on another limb of the tree of life- womanhood.*[131]

In contrast to her, Will, who is now a great fellow nearly six feet, with all the appearance and build of a grown up man, feels utterly lost.

When Will returns to the boardinghouse he finds the childlike old man waiting for him. He eagerly urges the young man to blow the trumpet, since he himself cannot do it, to assert their manhood: "The thing to do is to make a noise, make a dance of a racket, blow like the devil".[132] Will feels very sorry for this helpless frustrated man. He himself was on the verse of crying, oppressed by his sense of vastness and loneliness. For the moment, it seems to leave him. He tells himself that he cannot go on forever being a baby and look for someone to depend upon. Fir "Kate has a right to get married". To oblige the old man he puts his lips to the cornet and blows "two or three notes softly",[133] expressing all his sadness, helplessness and frustration. And at the same time it suggests how mature his thinking has become, worthy of an adult.

Thus ends the poignant story of *The Sad Hornblowers*, two old men and one young man. Papinchak aptly says of this story that it "describes the poignancy of the discovery of self waiting at the threshold of maturity. The story plays for us the still sad music of humanity in the soft, quiet notes of a cornet".[134]

NOTES AND REFERENCES

1. Irwing Howe, Sherwood Anderson (New York: Wm. Sloane Associates, 1951), p. 148.
2. Charles E. Modlin, ed. "Introduction", *Certain Things Last* [New York: Four Walls Eight Windows, 1991], p. ix.
3. *Ibid.*
4. Quoted by Rober Allen Papinchak, Sherwood Anderson [New York: Twayne Publishers, 1991], p. 31.
5. Irving Howe, p. 153.
6. Rex Burbank, Sherwood Anderson [New York: Twayne, 1964], p. 97.
7. Irving Howe, p. 153.
8. Rex Burbank, p. 97.
9. Irving Howe, p. 150.
10. David D. Anderson, *Sherwood Anderson: An Introduction and Interpretation* [New York: Holt, Rinehart and Winston, 1967], p. 66.
11. *I Want to Know Why*, Certain Things Last, p. 17.
12. Irving Howe, p. 154.
13. *I Want to Know Why*, Certain Things Last, pp. 9 &11.
14. *Ibid.*, p. 12.
15. *Ibid.*, p. 13.
16. *Ibid.*, pp. 13-14.
17. Papinchak, p. 33
18. *Ibid.*, p. 32.
19. *I Want to Know Why*, Certain Things Last, pp. 14-15.
20. I'm a Fool, *Ibid.*, p. 48.
21. *I Want to Know Why*, Certain Things Last, p. 16.
22. *Ibid.*
23. *Ibid.*, p. 17.
24. *Ibid.*
25. Rex Burbank, p. 99.

26. *Ibid*.
27. *Ibid*., pp. 99-100.
28. Irving Howe, p. 155.
29. *Ibid*., p. 156.
30. Papinchak, p. 33.
31. Rex Burbank, p. 100.
32. David D. Anderson, p. 62.
33. *Ibid*., p. 63.
34. Irving Howe, p. 157.
35. Rex Burbank, p. 100.
36. *I'm a Fool*, Certain Things Last, p. 48.
37. Rex Burbank, p. 101.
38. *I'm a Fool*, Certain things Last, p. 49.
39. *Ibid*., p. 51.
40. *Ibid*., p. 52.
41. Papinchak, p. 34.
42. I'm a Fool, Certain Things Last, p. 50.
43. *Ibid*., p. 57.
44. *Ibid*., p. 59.
45. *Ibid*.
46. Papinchak, p: 35.
47. Rex Burbank, p. 102.
48. David D. Anderson, p. 73.
49. Rex Burbank, p. 103.
50. David D.Anderson, p. 75.
51. Irving Howe, p. 160.
52. *The Man Who Became a Woman*, Certain things Last, pp. 63-64.
53. *Ibid*., p. 85.
54. *Ibid*., pp. 77-78.
55. Irving Howe, p. 162.
56. *Ibid*., p. 161.
57. *Ibid*., p. 164.
58. *The Man Who Became a Woman*, Certain Things Last, p. 67.
59. *Ibid*., p. 86.

60. *Ibid.*, p. 71.
61. *Ibid.*, p. 84.
62. *Ibid.*, p. 70.
63. *Ibid.*, p. 62.
64. Rex Burbank, p. 104.
65. Irving Howe, p. 161.
66. Rex Burbank, p. 104.
67. *The Man Who Became a Woman*, Certain Things Last, p. 73.
68. *Ibid.*, p. 76.
69. *Ibid.*, p. 72.
70. *Ibid.*, p. 82.
71. *Ibid.*, p. 86.
72. *Ibid.*, pp. 85-86.
73. *Ibid.*, p. 86.
74. *Ibid.*, p. 87.
75. *Ibid.*, p. 88.
76. *Ibid.*
77. Papinchak, p. 37.
78. *The Man Who Became a Woman*, Certain Things Last, p. 90.
79. Papinchak, p. 38.
80. *The Man Who Became a Woman*, Certain Things Last, p. 90.
81. Rex Burbank, p. 105.
82. *Ibid.*
83. *Ibid.*, pp. 105-106.
84. Charles E. Modlin, ed. "Introduction", Certain Things Last, p. xi.
85. *An Ohio Pagan*, Certain Things Last, p. 123.
86. *Ibid.*, p. 124.
87. *Ibid.*, p. 126.
88. *Ibid.*, p. 124.
89. *Ibid.*, p. 125.
90. *Ibid.*, pp. 125-126.
91. *Ibid.*, pp. 127-128.
92. *Ibid.*, p. 128.
93. *Ibid.*

94. *Ibid.*, p. 129.
95. *Ibid.*, pp. 129-130.
96. *Ibid.*, p. 131.
97. *Ibid.*
98. *Ibid.*, p. 133.
99. *Ibid.*, p. 137.
100. *Ibid.*, p. 137.
101. *Ibid.*, pp. 139-140.
102. *Ibid.*, p. 140.
103. *Ibid.*, p. 142.
104. *Ibid.*, p. 143.
105. *Ibid.*, p. 141.
106. *Ibid.*, p. 144.
107. *Ibid.*, p. 146.
108. *Ibid.*
109. *Ibid.*
110. David D. Anderson, p. 78.
111. Charles E.Modlin, p. xi.
112. *The Sad Horn Blowers,* Horses and Men (New York: B.W. Hueseb, 1924), p. 247.
113. *Ibid.*, p. 253.
114. *Ibid.*, p. 256.
115. *Ibid.*, p. 257.
116. *Ibid.*
117. *Ibid.*, p. 258.
118. *Ibid.*, p. 269.
119. *Ibid.*, pp. 269-270.
120. *Ibid.*, p. 269.
121. *Ibid*, p. 282.
122. *Ibid.*, p. 259.
123. *Ibid.*, p. 259.
124. *Ibid.*, p. 267.
125. *Ibid.*
126. *Ibid.*, p. 271.

127. *Ibid.*, p. 277.

128. *Ibid.*

129. *Ibid.*, pp. 278-279.

130. *Ibid.*, p. 279.

131. *Ibid.*, p. 280.

132. *Ibid.*, p. 282.

133. *Ibid.*, p. 283.

134. *Ibid.*, p. 39.

CHAPTER – 5

Stories on Man – Woman Relationship

In the previous chapter five of Anderson's discursive narratives of adolescence and initiation into adulthood were studied. In them he depicts the special problems of youth, as he observed in the context of his society and times. All these stories are remarkable for their variety and insight, and there s nothing of a mere repeat. The protagonists of each story struggles to understand and come to terms with his personal experience of one puzzling aspect of growth form adolescence towards manhood. A significant observation of Irving Howe on these stories of adolescence deserves to be adduced here: "—in Anderson's best stories adolescence becomes a commanding vantage point for imaginative statements about all of human life—only the genuinely mature artist can portray immature life".[1] In the present chapter and the next one (Chapter Six) some of Anderson's noteworthy post-Winesburg stories, which are concerned with adults, grown up men and women, are examined. It seems both logical and appropriate to move on from the stories of adolescents to those of adults. Only as a measure of convenience these stories of adults chosen for analysis here may be broadly grouped into two: those in which the focus is on the tangles and convulsions of the relationships between married men and women and those which depict the loneliness, isolation, frustrations, disappointments and thwarted potentials of adult men and women, married and single alike. It has already been pointed out that Anderson's themes, including those mentioned above, are recurrent in his works from first to last, overlap and even get intertwined or interwoven with one another, and that they are separated here only for purposes of analysis. The present chapter concerns itself with the former set of stories and the next chapter with the latter.

Anderson was deeply concerned about human relations, about the relationship between men and women, and more often than not, about the failure of understanding between them, especially between the married. The world of married men and women in Anderson's stories sees in general to be a dimly lit world. Enduringly happy and harmonious marital relations are rather rare there. Whatever the cause be, personal, social, psychological, an almost impenetrable wall seems to keep most husbands and wives apart, making any understanding and communication between them almost impossible. This is a recurrent theme in Anderson's stories, early as well as late. In Winesburg, Ohio, as seen already in an earlier chapter, there are several instances of failed and frustrated marital relations. To recall a few, Wash Williams the telegraphic operator (*Respectability*) a sensitive soul who dotes on his wife, turns a cynic and a misogynist and his sensitive and beautiful inward nature is twisted out of shape, because of his wife's infidelity and her mother's callous disregard of all norms of decency.

If Walsh's married life collapse because of his wife's betrayal, Ray Pearson of *The Untold Lie* presents a more complex instance of married life. an act of indiscretion he committed with a girl who waited on trade in his father's bakery shop led to his marriage with her. Even as a man of fifty with half a dozen children, he regrets that he ever married. He mutters to himself in protest, "Tricked by God, that's what I was, tricked by life and made a fool of".[2] At the time he married, he was dreaming of a life of vigorous activity and adventure rather than be trapped and harnessed into a humdrum life as a mere farm hand. Children seem to be the accidents of life. He feels that when he married he made no promise to his wife, and it seems unfair that he or nay one for that matter should be married to pay for promises, which were never made. Curiously when his young friend Hal Winters, who too has got into trouble a young school teacher, asks him the question, "What about marriage and all that? Has a fellow got to do it? Has be got to be harnessed up and driven through life like a horse?"[3], he cannot give him a ready answer. The conventional answer to w

Winter's question is that he should marry. Ray's own experience of married life suggests a contrary answer. But he cannot bring himself to saying it. Whenever he looks at the beauty of the country about Win forgetting his age he runs shouting a protest "against everything that makes life ugly".[4] As he walks behind his sharp-featured and sharp-voiced wife, he even feels like hitting her with his fist. He wonders what has really gone wrong with him and his life. There is no sign of nay love or affection binding them together. However the memory of some pleasant evenings spent with his children seems to restore some of his composure. Therefore when Hal without witing for his advice tells him that he has decided to marry Nell Gunther and "have kids", he feels like laughing at himself and the world. He mutters to himself, "It's just as well. Whatever I told him would have been a lie".[5] That is, he cannot decide about marriage and married life either way. It is and is not a harness, though his own experience has little to make him take an encouraging view of it.

There is in Winesburg, Ohio the pathetic case of Louise Bently (Surrender), which has already been briefly discussed in Chapter Two. Lonely, neurotic and oversensitive from her childhood, Louise hardly knows what parental love and affection is, though she is not an orphan. Naturally she longs for love more than anything else in the world. She wants to be loved and wants to love someone. To breakdown the wall of loneliness that shuts her off form the joys of the world, she makes bold to take John Hardy, the son of her father's friend, for a lover, and then married him eagerly hoping that her dream of love and happiness would be fulfilled. But she draws a blank there. During the first year of their married life she tries hard to make her husband understand her vague and intangible hunger. But for him love between men and women means little more than sex, gratification of the physical urge, rather than a most important means of communication and understanding and expression of love. He hardly allows her to explain what she really longs for. In the bitterness of her disappointment and frustration she denied their son David any of her love, taking it out of him for no fault of his.

The most poignant instance of failed and disillusioned married life, doomed to failure almost from the start, it that of Elizabeth Willard in Winesburg, Ohio. In Chapter Two, her plights has already been discussed in considerable detail while examining the two stories *Mother* and *Death*. Therefore it is enough to recall here that the relations between Elizabeth and her husband Tom Willard fail largely because of clash of temperaments and conflicting values of life between them, and above all because of an insensitive, understanding and stiff-necked husband who has no thought of his sailing wife, her wishes and aspirations, who neither can give love nor understand the longing for it. Disillusioned and defeated Elizabeth Willard in spite of her ill-health retains something of a defiant spirit in her which gives her the stature of tragic character. It may be said now itself, in anticipation, that none of the stories on the theme of relationships between married men and women including those chosen for analysis here, attains the intensity and poignancy of her story. The stories selected for comment drawn from Anderson's different volumes are *The Other Woman, The Door of the Trap, There She Is-She is Taking Her Bath, The Man's Story,* and *Mrs. Wife*. In passing *The Man in the Brown Coat* will also be considered. Each of these stories presents one particular aspect of the often puzzling and problematic relationship between married men and women. In these stories Anderson is naturally and appropriately concerned with the role of sex in the relationship between men and women, before as well as after marriage.

This theme, as we have seen already, figures in several of the Winesburg stories, but it finds a more conspicuous expression in Anderson' later stories. He seems to view the sexual relationship between men and women as a mirror, which reflects the problematic nature of the self.

Anderson is reported to have said of *The Other Woman* that he wrote it 'partly with my tongue in my cheek-bad little boy stuff'.[6] But in actual fact he is much more in earnest in writing this story than this remark of his suggests. The subtle irony and humour in the story enhances it. This is a strange story in which the author sets down for the better part the protagonist's story in his own words with little or no comment, leaving the reader free to draw his own conclusion. The protagonist on whose mind the focus rests "tells, confessedly but without shame or remorse, of his affair with another woman on the night before his wedding and asserts that this experience helped his marriage".[7] But had he not been sufficiently troubled and puzzled by that experience he would not have felt the inner compulsion to describe it confessionally and at some length, unasked for. At it happens in most confessional narratives, the protagonist chooses to narrate his story as a possible way to work through the problem of his relationship to his spouse and to the 'other woman' with whom he had a single evening's affair on the eve of his wedding. His very mode of narration in which he makes a few assertions and then almost withdraws or modifies them betrays his ambivalence. He remains naïve and puzzled as much at the end of his narrative as at its beginning.

It is during a walk that the protagonist tells his story to the author. The incident he narrates which was entirely a single evening's experience, has effected him so deeply that he cannot forget it. It has revealed to him the complexities of human relationships. Especially between married men and women. The focus of the story is appropriately on the mind of the protagonist who cannot adequately account for his irresistible attraction to the very ordinary looking wife of a petty shopkeeper, who is much older than himself and whom he cannot forget, and his love for his wife, who has both beauty of person and beauty of character. Moreover as the daughter of a judge she has the added advantage of belonging to a respectable class.

The particular experience which created the puzzle for the protagonist happened at a time when he was basking under the sunshine of appointment to a new government post, the winning of a poetry prize, and his engagement to a most desirable young woman. He felt like one floating in air as he had never received so much of attention and flattering and intoxicating words of praise from all and sundry, which filled his mind with the most absurd fancies. The excitement he felt was too great to endure. Under such circumstances he naturally wanted to dream of the young woman who was to be his wife very shortly, think out lines for noble poems he wished to write, or make plans for his future career. But surprisingly his mind refused to do any such thing, because just then "a most unexpected and humiliating thing happened" to him.[8] his mind, strangely, was wholly possessed by the wife of a tobacconist who lived at a corner of his street. She who was at least ten years older than himself, was a very ordinary person with nothing special or notable about her. But being in her presence profoundly stirred him. She had so worked her way into his being that when he wanted so much to think of noble thoughts he could only think of her. And "his imagination had taken hold of the notion of having a love affair with the woman".[9] At night when he should be asleep, he thought about her all the time. A couple of days hence, she got into his daytime thoughts muddling him terribly, which people attributed to his fast approaching wedding. Strangely, when he went to see his fiancé, his love for her was in no way affected by his vagrant thoughts as if they belonged to two different compartments of his mind. "There was", he was convinced, "but one woman in the world (he) wanted to live with and to be (his) comrade in undertaking to improve (his) own character and (his) position in the world, but for the moment—(he) wanted this other woman to be in (his) arms".[10] That was the crux of the matter. The narrator reports it with his tongue in his cheek.

So much obsessed was he with this thought about the other woman, that he made bold to invite her to his apartment one night for an assignation, though he was to be married the next day. The woman did respond to his call, and whatever resolution he had made not to be weak, and to make himself worthy of the noble woman he was going to marry soon vanished the moment she entered his room. When he took her into his arms, his hands no longer trembled with nervousness, and he "felt very happy and strong". This evening's experience had a strange effect on him. Prior to it, when the tobacconist's wife possessed his mind all during the week, he had felt that if anything happened between him and her, her "would not be able to go through with (his) marriage".[11] But when he went next evening to see his beloved he was "filled with a new faith in the outcome of (their) life together", after they were married. Something of the other woman's faith "in her own desires and her courage in seeing things through went with (him)".[12] His bride had asked him in her letter of the previous evening, the eve of their wedding, to delay fulfillment of their marriage until she had overcome her inhibitions. She wrote: "For a long time after we are married, we will forget were are a man and woman. We will be human beings—I am ignorant and often I will be very stupid. You must love me and be very patient and kind. When I know more—I will try to repay you—".[13] Rex Burbank has remarked that paradoxically the protagonist's union with the other woman "has released his inner instinctive life-hitherto inhibited by conventional moral pieties and has helped him conquer his fear of it".[14]

All this is, of course, true. But there seems to be something more to make the situation complex. For, though more than once the protagonist asserts emphatically that he is very much in love with his wife and that his marriage is to him "a very beautiful fact".[15] He has not been able to forget the other woman though he never saw her again after that evening or went to her street again. Contrary to his assertion that he never thought of her again at all, every now and then when he is alone walking in the street or park, "the feeling of her comes sharply into (his) mind and body" and "a quick sharp earthly feeling takes possession of him. It is as though (he) were a seed in the ground and the warm rains of the spring had come. It is as though (he) were not a man but a tree".[16] He is yet to experience a similar feeling in his married life. Speaking about the other woman, he says, brings him a kind of relief. However there seems to be something more in it. Although it is quite some time since he is married, he has not yet experienced its consummation. His wife it still "an awakening woman".[17] She continues to sleep in the room next to his, and "the door is always left open".[18] He has not yet reached the point of frustration and seems to live in expectation and hope of fulfillment. What seems to sustain him is the memory of (his) life he had with her. His confusion and puzzlement and his ambivalent attitude to the two women become apparent in what he tells the author:

> *I shall think of the other woman tonight. My thoughts will not take the form they did during the week before I was married. I will wonder what has become for the woman. For a moment I will feel again myself holding her close. I will think that for an hour I was closer to her than I have ever been to anyone else. Then I will think of the time when I will be as close as that to my wife. She is still — an awakening woman. For a moment I will close my eyes and the quick, shrewd, determined eye of that other woman would look into mine. My head will swim and then I will quickly open my eyes and see again the dear woman with whom I have undertaken to live out my life. Then I will sleep and when I awake in the morning—the other woman will be utterly gone.*[19]

The idealistic, self-deceived protagonist naively believes that his wife would 'wake' up soon and all will be well. But it is not quite certain when it would happen for him to forget once for all the other woman. Rex Burbank has justly remarked that this story "exemplifies the felicitous combination of wonder, sadness, and perplexity surrounding an incident that has revealed the complexity of life to a rather simple protagonist".[20]

The Door of the Trap is also a story of unfulfilled love and frustration in married life, though of a different kind. A sophisticated narrator tells the story from the point of view of the protagonist. Hugh Walker, who is a professor of mathematics in a small college in Union Valley, Illinois. The focus of the narrative is on him and what goes on in his mind. He has been a teacher for six years. He is married and has three children. His wife Winifred, a woman of ordinary intelligence and sensitiveness, is quite satisfied and content with her married life, her husband and children, and all the comforts of life her husband has provided- a large house comfortably furnished, two negresses to take care of the children, to cook and do housework. Therefore she seems to have little to do. She sits either sewing or reading novels: "All the time she read novels. She read the novels of Robert Louis Stevenson. When she had read them all she began again",[21] Obviously, she sought her excitement and entertainment in Stevenson's tales of adventure and romance. The narrator's remark about her, "Marriage was marriage to her",[22] sums up her attitude to herself and her life. She has no further expectations from life and therefore no perplexing questions to trouble her or destroy her peace of mind or complacency. "She has the air of something accomplished",[23] thinks her husband.

Hugh Walker is a complete contrast to his wife Winifred. A restless soul even form his youth, he remains one even now. Had he, like his wife, accepted his "marriage as marriage", he might have mitigated much of his undefined suffering. He sees himself as one put behind iron bars in a prison, and thinks of himself "as a living thing inside a shell, trying to break out"[24] but in vain. He is very much of a lonely man with hardly any communication with his wife or with anyone else for that matter. The conversation between them is either "fragmentary" or it is inane. His inability to communicate with anyone worsens his situation. There is no love in his married life, which appears to him sterile and purposeless. So too seems his profession as a teacher of mathematics. "Young men and women had come into a room and he had taught them. It was nothing. Words and figures had been played with". The old question, "For What?"[25] always comes back wanting an answer and he has none. He feels that his is an unlived and unfulfilled life, and that he stands still, static, while "everything goes on". He wants to know why it is so. "There are certain facts in life", he tells himself, "and I must face facts— I must get my fingers on facts I must live by them and with them. It's the way lives are lived".[26] Poor irresolute man that he has been since his youth, he is distraught and puzzled. He has sought escape from his problems and his restlessness in long never-ending walks, walking insanely for hours. But walking solves nothing. It only tires his body. But when his body is tired he could sleep. In his youth however, when life seemed to have stepped out of his grasp long walks restored his composure and he could work and live among men. Now he has become a lonely grotesque.

This introvert, self-absorbed married man, father of three children, accidentally develops an interest in one of his pupils, Mary Cochran, a young girl from Huntersburg, Illinois. She becomes a new source of his restlessness.[27] He becomes jealous of the young man who sits next to her in the class grows suddenly and furiously angry with him and feels miserable afterwards. He himself is amazed at his strange behaviour, which is in fact a measure of his frustration in his lonely, loveless married life. He decides to invite Mary to his house ostensibly to get acquainted with and know more about her. Winifred accepted her as she accepted everything, the service of the two negresses, the coming of the children, the habitual silence of her husband".[28] The children are happy to have a friendly companion to play with. She seems to understand them better than their mother or father. Soon Mary becomes "almost a fixture in the Walker household".[29] For her, whose parents are dead, it is comforting to be in the presence of children. She, "developing rapidly into womanhood" looks upon Hugh Walker "as something that stood completely outside her own life". They have little to say to each other, despite his sudden and interest in her.[30]

Hugh walker likes to believe that he thinks of Mary "in quite an impersonal way", and that he has "not selected her to think about for any particular reason". She is like a young tree which would soon grow out of childhood, and will go away from his sight. She does not belong to him unlike his wife and children with whom he has to stay on and on: "We are imprisoned by the fact that we belong to each other". Mary on the other hand is free until she makes her won prison, but tha is none of his concern. However she has rendered him the service of bringing him back to life from which he had been drawing away.[31] thus the emotionally starved teacher tries to justify his interest in his pupil. Without being aware of it he seems to seek the fulfillment he had missed in his married life, in patronizing Mary.

Much of Hugh Walker's restlessness, neurotic worry and the oppressive feeling of an unlived life is due to his inability to communicate in which he is locked. One can understand why he cannot communicate with his wife Winfred, and even sympathise with him, if silence between them has lasted all through their married life. But, as noted already, it is not just with his wife hat he cannot communicate. Even his children do not see to interest him. However, with his interest in Mary increasing, suddenly and unexpectedly he breaks up his silence, stops to speak to men in the street, gets into a violent quarrel with a fellow teacher, and even whistles and sings when he putters about in the garden.[32] One afternoon when the family including Mary is assembled in the living room, he startles both Mary and his wife by snatching and throwing into the fireplace with an oath, the book Mary has been reading. Then a flood f words runs from him. In this strange outburst he curses books, people and schools: "Damn it all. What makes you want to read about life? What makes people want to think about life? Why don't they life? Why don't they leave books and thoughts and schools alone?"[33] Almost immediately after this alarming expression for his rudeness to them. he is aware that his explanation is not the truth. Not only to the women but also to himself he has lied. To his question, why should he have been deceiving himself continual lying, he has no answer.

Mary, who had left the Walker's place frightened by Hugh's rudeness, visits them again two weeks hence when he apologetically appeals to her not too "desert" them. Hugh who had felt defeated and crestfallen on the earlier occasion now feels like a victor. He now sees in her a young woman, almost like his wife. One who had earlier thought that he had looked at her in an impersonal way, now deludes himself by the thought that he has a claim on her: "She is almost like a person who belongs here, who belongs to me and my life".[34] It is rather incredible that this very man brings to an abrupt end Mary's visits to his household by an astonishing gesture quite uncharacteristic of him. All of a sudden he becomes bold, leads the frightened girl into his room on evening, kisses her and them almost commandingly asks her "to go out of this house and never come back".[35] There is no way of knowing what prompts him to this rash step. When Mary actually leaves his house, "a strange quivering light" comes in to his eyes and he seems to feel triumphant. With grim pleasure he tells himself: "She is no longer like a young tree. She will be imprisoned but I will have nothing to do with it. She will never belong to me. My hands will never build a prison for her".[36] In these words of his there is a suggestion of having accomplished something worthwhile. If one were to ask him what is it that he has accomplished, he may not have a satisfying answer to the question.

This story of Hugh Walker is not one of Anderson's really successful and impressive stories on marital dilemmas. The author does not render convincingly the complexities and confusions of his protagonist's thoughts and behaviour. One can understand and even feel sympathetic with Hugh Walker's disappointment with his wife Winifred, and with his feeling that marriage for him has been a prison. But his dissatisfaction and frustration seem to stem from deeper causes, which remain vague even to him. Even from his days of youth he has a tendency to seek an escape from the problems of life. He makes only feeble attempts to find answers from them. So he remains a lonely anchorless man and a drifter, wanting in will and resolution. If a loveless married life makes him take an increasing interest in his pupil Mary, it is not clear perhaps even to himself whether he wants from her love or mere gratification of his biological urge. It cannot be said that his wife denied him the latter in his married life, as the three children are there to prove it. If he wants to have an affair with Mary, he does not have the courage for it. Again, it is not clear why he rouses her sexual desires and orders her not to come to his house again. It is nothing but self-deception if he thinks that he has saved here form a life of failure and the jeopardy of being emotionally imprisoned by this gesture. He seems to make use of her without considering what might happen to her. If marriage has been a prison house for him from which there is no escape, then there is little comfort in the thought that he cannot be held responsible for opening the door of the trap if Mary were to enter that prison house sooner or later. Whatever illusory feeling of accomplishment he may have, Hugh Walker sadly "remains trapped in what he sees as the prison of his marriage and the reality of his life".[37]

There She Is- She is Taking Her Bath is a far more convincing and satisfying story on the theme of marriage dilemma and the problematic relationship between married men and women. Years after he wrote this story Anderson seems to have referred to it as the story of a 'timid and absurdly jealous' husband and his 'quite innocent wife', and his hiring a detective to watch her to be assurd.[38] But the situation in the story is far more complex. The story is told by John Smith the protagonist, himself. He is a rambling and ambivalent narrator, as he is "torn between the desire to know the truth (i.e. about his wife) and his inability to face it".[39]

John Smith who tells his story, though not in a confessional vein, is an ordinary man and has nothing special or remarkable about him. Anderson's interest in such people, particularly in what goes on in their minds, is well known. Almost he rouses the reader's sympathy for such people, as the many stories in Winesburg, Ohio make it abundantly clear. But there are a very a few, among whom are Hugh Walker of *The Door of the Trap* and John Smith of the present story, who rouse a mixed reaction. Smith's is the story of a lonely, frustrated man who is a combination of jealousy, suspicion, timidity, cowardice, want of courage, boastfulness, false sense of honour, naivety, self-centeredness, vanity, and self-deception. He makes himself miserable, pathetic as well as ludicrous, all at the same time by his absurd attempts to prove the infidelity of his wife. Smith is also a puzzled and confused man, which is obvious in his rambling, incoherent manner of his story-telling, going forwards and backwards and sometimes going off at a tangent.

The apparently matter of fact opening paragraph of the story implies a great deal. The first two short sentences- "Another day when I have done no work. It is maddening"- suggest that the speaker has not been able to work for several days continuously and is so much agitated over something that it is "maddening". Soon it becomes clear that he is obsessed with jealousy and suspicion regarding his wife's fidelity, which has caused his impotent anger. That all is not well between him and his wife in their married life is obliquely hinted by the piece of information he gives: that he is ten years older than his wife and that they have no children. Had there been a few children and less disparity of age between the husband and wife, probably their relation would have been harmonious, and there might not have been any ground for suspicion or jealousy. Even in the midst of his agitation he is vain about himself as a man of "honor", personal discipline, and regular habits who went to his office every morning and returned home in the evening "at the regular time". However it is touching to see him half-aware of his own foolishness and have doubts about his understanding and judgment: "If I could only decide whose honor has been really been tempted with, I shall be quite all right".[40]

Smith says that all his troubles and agitations concerning his wife began "just seventeen days ago".[41] He implies that till then he was a happy man enjoying domestic felicity. But it is difficult to believe a man of his nervous temper who by nature is inclined to be suspicious and jealous. That particular evening when he reached home he found lying on the floor in the little hallway a scented envelope addressed to his wife, Mabel Smith, in a bold man's hand. It was a brief letter inviting her for a tryst when her husband was away, and signed by Bill, a name as common as Smith or Jones. When he walked into his apartment he found a tall young man sitting opposite his wife. His suspicious already strongly roused, he assumed that this young man was "Bill" and was there pretending to sell her a patent carpet-sweeper. They both, his wife in particular, seemed to have become self-conscious on seeing him. After the young man left, Smith tried to call out to his wife, question and find out form her at once the bitter truth. By then he had convinced himself that she was guilty. When he tried to speak two or three times words just not come out of his mouth. Lacking the courage to force her to confess the truth at the risk of personal violence, although he regarded himself as a fighter who could fight to vinclicate his honour when the occasion called for it, as a boy he had fought another boy in the school yard and loosened one of his teeth, to protect his own honour he decided instead to use "fitnesse" seems to be his word for evasion of action. When he could muster enough courage and strength to speak to her all that he could do was to ask her" in a calm voice", the inane question, what was she doing. Pat came her calm reply that she was taking her bath.[42]

His wife's prompt reply left Smith so unnerved and helpless that he sought his escape in walking for hours in the park. In his indignation he even "swore", despite his being "a deeply religious man".[43] Going out for a walk alone in the park is his practice whenever he has a problem hoping to think about it frankly and clear it up. He tells himself and the reader of his narration: "There is no use my not facing everything frankly. By facing everything frankly one gets everything cleared up".[44] but that is exactly what he failed to achieve. Nor could he remain cool and collected. Instead he found himself growing angry. His anger, obviously, was an expression of his helplessness. To make up for it and to boost his morale he fancied in imagination fighting with the young man and breaking his cane over his head only to warn him against playing with innocent married women. Going a step further he even thought that the men who were walking in the park like him were perhaps in the same position as himself, sailing in the same boat as he.

Though not a male chauvinist, Smith believed that women were like children, had little experience, were easily flattered, and knew nothing about the ways of the world, especially those of young blades who took advantage of their credulousness and tricked them by their tender looks easily he believed as a man of honour, "that we men must protect the integrity of our homes and our firesides".[45] his strategy to meet the present crisis in his domestic life was to remain and se finesse instead of a confrontation with his wife. But at dinner his hand trembled and he spilled the dissert on the table cloth. That he had lost control over his faculties ever since his suspicions about his wife were roused, was proved on more than once occasion. Even on the morning of his narrating his story he bumped his head against the bathtub while shaving. To exasperate him, almost every evening he turned home from his office, he got from his wife more or less the same reply, "I am taking a bath". In the course of his narration Smith in fact refers to seven other times when his wife was taking her bath. Papinchak points out that just as

Hands in Winesburg, Ohio "depends on the image of hands to give larger meaning to the story of Wing Biddlebaum", this story "depends on the narrator's wife being repeatedly in the bath tub when he arrives home from another day at the office where he has done no work".[46]

Unable to bear the suspense any longer the troubled Smith hired a detective to collect evidence of his wife's infidelity. But having done it he felt "ashamed of what (he) had dome and at the same time ashamed of (himself) for being ashamed".[47] He could not decide whether what he had done was an act of folly or manliness. The immediate effect of this state of uncertainty was that he lost sleep. He even regretted that he ever found that note: "No matter what my wife was up to I could sleep if I hadn't found that note".[48] He began to feel afraid of what the detective might find. He would be obliged to act once the proof of her infidelity was delivered to him. Exercising his finesse once again he returned to the same agency under the name "Jones" pretending sum and told him that of his own reasons he wanted him to get a report that his lady love (that is his own wife) was all right, since her husband, a man named Smith, had hired a detective from the same office to watch her. The money he offered to pay him was effectively a bribe to falsify the report of the other man. Of course he got from both separately the kind of report he wanted. But what he could not get was his peace of mind nor could he free himself from his jealousy and suspicion. When he returned home determined to tell her of his suspicion and force a confession form her, he found her taking a bath as she did on other evenings. With his face "blanched" a little he had to seek an escape in the park till dinner time, confused, puzzled and unsettled as before, his dilemmas are unresolved.

Having come close enough to know about the truth about his wife, whether she was really an adultress or a faithful wife, Smith backs out unwilling or unable to face the truth. He lacks the necessary courage for it like Hugh Walker of the other story, and evades truth. Like him he deceives himself. Repeated references in the narration to his wife's taking a bath may make one ask whether she takes her bath immersed in innocence or to cleanse her impurities. While Smith's jealousy has certainly clouded his perception, he has some plausible ground to doubt his wife's faith. Robert Morse Lovell has argued that "the story is not about whether Mrs. Smith is unfaithful but about her husband's insistence that life to conform to codes of behaviour. Smith admires 'men who, like myself—keep the world going'—Rules are very important to Smith, in fact it is not jealousy that stirs him but the thought that his wife believes she can cheat with impurity—with 'young squirt' who flouts the work ethic and thus makes fools of those who shoulder responsibilities—.[49] But his argument of Lovell's is not tenable. For if Smith's stand was as straightforward as Lovell maintains, nothing prevented him from demanding frank explanation from his wife for her conduct. There was no need for his "finesse" at all, hide and seek for the stealthy strategy of detectives he adopts. Obviously Smith is a far more complex character, as the foregoing analysis has tried to show. Given his nature Smith could never establish harmonious relations with his wife, and be happy man in his married life enjoying a stable and durable companionship with his spouse.

The Man's Story, in contrast to the three stories considered, tells the story of an unusual and unconventional relationship between a man who is a poet and a married woman who runs away with him from her uninteresting and suspicious husband to live happily in Chicago despite their ramshackle apartment and rank poverty. But their brief spell of happiness suddenly ends with her murder by a half-crazed man. Both happen to be peculiar and unusual characters and their relationship challenges ones understanding. Many of Anderson's characters, as we have seen already, are in search of something that would give them a sense of purpose in life and the feeling that they have lived their lives. More often than they are disappointed and frustrated, the causes being several. They are left lonely, isolated estranged with few who can understand them. Though called a Man's Story, this piece is equally a woman's story despite the focus being on the man. Her name is not revealed but she is decidedly the more powerful and determined personality, and as long as she is alive, she proves to be the prop and mainstay of the man Edgar Wilson. She sustains him till the end of her life and remains self-effacing, self –sacrificing and in her own way heroic. With her death Wilson virtually collapses.

The narrator of the story is a newspaperman and an amateur poet. He is both observant and naïve. He frankly admits that he is puzzled by Edgar Wilson the man and his poems, which fascinate him and at the same time make him "feel just a little woozy".[50] He is impelled to tell the story of this poet and the strangeness in the relationship between him and his woman companion in the hope that he may himself understand.[51] this modesty of the narrator leaves the reader free to form his own views about them. The narrator gets interested in Wilson during his trial on the charge of having murdered his wife and after he is cleared of it through the confession of the crazy little man who actually committed the murder. It is his indifference to the entire process of trial and the possibility of his being hanged to death, his abstracted air, and his indifference even after he is released, that attract the narrator to know more about him. Wilson does not even care to give a consistent account of his life, true or false. What is known about him in Chicago is that he had come from a town in Kansas running away from that town with another man's wife.

The narrator has comparatively more information about the woman. Her life before she met Wilson was rather "messy". Her home background was somewhat insecure. Her father, a small official, accused of misappropriating some money and jailed, killed himself. Her mother had already died. She happened to marry a man, a druggist, honest, frugal but rather uninteresting. She had something about her, which appealed strongly to men. Several men of the seedy little town smitten by her wrote her unsigned letters inviting her for a tryst. She made the mistake of telling her husband about one of the letters. He grew silent. They did not have any children.[52] When Edgar Wilson came along and stopped in the town for a couple of days, they got acquainted with each other. Her neighbours saw this woman who had grown habitually silent talking to this stranger for two hours. Suddenly she had become articulate in his presence. Gathering her few belongings she walked with him to the railway station. They came to Chicago, took shelter in the anonymity of the city and lived there together "apparently very happy",[53] though they could not be married. As Wilson did nothing bowls with young towards earning, they were miserably poor and had to live in the upper room of an old farm house. To make both ends meet she managed to get a place as ward robe woman in a theatre nearby. She was literally the breadwinner.

As for Wilson, he wrote poetry of a sort, which is "Greek" to the narrator, as he honestly admits. When he reads it at leisure, every line of it seems "crazy stuff", and yet fascinates him in a way. It is all about walls and deep wells and great bowls with young trees erect in them. It is not surprising that he feels "a little bit woozy". But when he reads through several verse of Wilson's he finds running through them a particular theme obsessively:

> *That men had erected walls about themselves and that all men were perhaps destined to stand forever behind the walls on which they constantly bet their fists, or with whatever tools they could get hold of— Men had themselves built the walls and now stood behind them, knowing dimly that beyond the walls thee was warmth, light, air, beauty, life in fact-while at the same time, and because of a kind of madness in themselves, the walls were constantly being built higher.*[54]

Loneliness, isolation, estrangement and failure of communication and the resultant frustration are recurrent themes in Anderson's stories, early as well as late, as noted already on more than one occasion. These acquire a sharpness and intensity in the lives of married men and women of several

Anderson stories. In *The Man in the Brown Coat*, which is more of a sketch than a short story, the protagonist who is an historian and has written three histories of peoples, which stand up like sentries on the shelves of libraries, cannot communicate meaningfully with his wife, nor can she with him. His agonized confession is:

> *We sit together in the evening but I do not know her. I cannot shake myself out of myself. I wear a brown coat and I cannot come out of my coat,. I cannot come out of myself. My wife is very gentle and she speaks softly but she cannot come out of herself.*[55]

Both are trapped in their narrow, limited selves. As man and wife they hardly know each other, though they have been living together. Theirs have been unlived lives. That is precisely what the historian protagonist says:

> *Why do I not say a word out of myself to the others? Why, in all our life together, have I never been able to break through the wall to my wife?- Are there no words that lead into life?—.*[56]

To return to *The Man's Story*, Edgar Wilson the poet holds people themselves responsible of this state of affairs, and for the "going away" of "the light and the warmth of life" because of their "blind refusal—to understand each other".[57] In one of his verses, which the narrator cites Wilson expresses his quiet confidence in man's ability to cut down "all the falseness" in people and "cut and rip through all the ugly husks in which millions of lives are enclosed". In another piece he says speaking for himself: "My fruit shall not be my fruit until it drops from my arms into the arms of the others over the top of the wall".[58] Edgar Wilson seemed to have won this confidence in himself and in man during his association with the woman of Kansas who had risked running away from her husband defying convention and living with him violating accepted codes of married life. in her company, moreover, and let in light and warmth to their lives.

Theirs was a strange kind of relationship, romantic no doubt but in a special way without any of the paraphernalia usually associated with conventional romance. Theirs was not just a domestic household either, which was a little down in its luck. As may be gathered from his poems cited by the narrator, despite their woolliness and vagueness, Wilson was obsessed with the relationship of all people, not necessarily between himself and his companion. He had "a half-mystic conception" about it. He felt the need for a helping hand to explore it further. Before he met the Kansas woman, he "had been going aimlessly about the world looking for a mate", and when he found her things cleared for him,[59] or so he thought. He had other curious notions too, not easy to understand. He believed "that in the field of poetry he had something to express that could not be expressed until he had found a woman who could, in a peculiar and absolute way, give herself in the world of the flesh-and that them there was to be a marriage out of which beauty come for all people", and that woman "had to be untainted by self-interest".[60] In the wife of the Kansas druggist he had found such a person.

Disappointed and frustrated in life, and perhaps deeply hurt by the baseless suspicious of her husband's the Kansas woman must have felt drawn to Wilson. He was a powerful personality to fascinate and attract people, especially women. Not only the Kansas woman but the hunchback girl to whom two little backroom in Wilson's flat had been sublet, also had felt a sort of romantic attachment to him. They are all admiration and devotion to him. The narrator too felt his power so much that he was urged from within to tell this crazy poet's story. The Kansas woman was so completely involved in Wilson that "she was absolutely and wholly happy with him in a strangely inexpressive sort of way". If he "wanted her quite absolutely" for himself, "she was in her own way greedy",[61] and had her hold on him. She helped the poet in Wilson to realize himself by her self-effacing understanding and loving companionship.

The woman's death came about rather unexpectedly. A half-crazed stagehand, who worked in the same theatre where she was employed, had fallen in love with her and written many silly letters to her which she ignored. One evening when Wilson and she were walking across the city, he totally abstracted in thought and she walking beside him, silent and satisfied as always in his company, the stage hand appeared out of the fog, shot her and ran away. But it made no impression on Wilson who walked along as though nothing had happened. The woman, with remarkable presence of mind, gathered herself and managed to walk beside him without saying anything. When a policeman came there, strangely she told him a lie and sent him away in the wrong direction. She managed to lead Wilson to their apartment, walked to the fireplace and lit a fire with the bits of waste paper "making a little flare of beauty" filling the room with light. While this almost ritual like act was on, the poet stood, "blind with his own purpose". Then she walked softly and silently towards him and fell dead at his feet. If she struggled before she died, she struggled in silence.[62] This was the climax to her three-year long, silent self-sacrificing, loving devotion to him and his poetic endeavour. Setting the fireplace ablaze in the context of her life with him, has the force of a symbolic gesture to impress upon him that he must keep the poet in him alive and ablaze, to articulate his deepest feelings and convictions.

Wilson's behaviour at the time of her death is both shocking and "inhuman", to say the least. He stood for sometime, as if looking into nothingness, oblivious of what had happened to the woman he had loved. On an impulse he walked out of the room into the street, stepping awkwardly over her body. He walked for some blocks calmly and nonchantingly, and even stopped on the way to buy a cigarette as if nothing had happened. Then he strolled on until he walked into the midst of a crowd. Then he 'looked anxiously about for a moment, and suddenly began shouting in a loud voice", "shouting, and trying to tell the story of what had happened". This he did once again until he was taken into custody by a policeman.[63] During and after his trial for murder, and acquittal he continued to behave for a time as if he had nothing to do with what had happened. That was strange indeed. But inwardly the man had collapsed. It took some time for him to become aware of the significance of what had happened to him. The narrator assesses peoperly the impact of the death of the woman on Wilson. Before he found the woman he "had been sunk far down into a deep sea of doubt and questioning. Before he found (her) no expression had ever come from him". He had wandered from place to place looking at people's faces wanting to come close to them, but did not know how. "The woman had been able to lift him up to the surface of the sea of life for a time, and with her he had floated on the surface of the sea, under the sky, into sunlight". She was the boat in which he had floated, "and now the boat had been wrecked and he was sinking again, back into the sea".[64] Once he began t be aware of what had happened he started talking to people in the street, in their houses, perhaps in "an effort—not to sink back forever into the sea". "It was the struggle of a drowning man".[65]

The woman from Kansas gave her all to Wilson and became the anchor of his life, expecting nothing in return for herself except the satisfaction of sustaining him and his art. She found the fulfillment of her life in helping him. She made the poet in him possible by taking him under her protective wings. She made the poet in him possible by taking him under her protective wings. Though not married to him in the sense society understands it, her love and devotion to Wilson wee not only exceptional but far more than any married wife could give. Secure under her care he could afford to be absorbed and abstracted in the world of poetic creation. However, all said, Wilson cannot escape the charge of being an egotist who took the woman and her service to him for granted. There is no indication in the story that he ever thought of her. But for her he could not have come anywhere near self fulfillment. His life became a "lived life" as long as she was alive and with him. Had her life not been cut short, may be, Wilson's story would have been different and had taken a different turn. Viewed as a whole, their unusual relationship remains a puzzle. However, during a short spell, each experienced a sense of fulfillment and of living a worthwhile life.

Instances of long happy married life, of enduring happy relation between man and woman are very few in the stories of Anderson, especially among those considered in the present study. If it is a happy one it is invariably short-lived. In *Paper Pills* of Winesburg, Ohio Dr. Reefy marries a deceived young woman who seeks his help as she has none to help her, she discovers in him, the "sweetness of twisted apples". But she dies after an illness, ending their all too brief married life. instances of frustrated and disillusioned married life in Anderson' stories have already been pointed in the earlier chapter. *Mrs. Wife,* (published in Redbook 70, December 1937) and justly called "one of the best of Anderson's later stories" by Modlin[66], stands apart from all the other stories of Anderson's which are concerned with the theme of man-woman relationship among married people. For, it seems to be the only story among those selected for study, in which a harmonious, enduring and happy relationship between husband and wife is a mark of true maturity. It is possible only in the basis of mutual respect, understanding, transparent honesty (free from any guile, hide and seek). This relationship is based on integrity, and has to be striven for and earned. It has to be kept in constant repair, if it should endure, by both man and wife. This view of mature relationship is borne out by the manner in which the story is told at a steady, unhurried pace and a quiet voice. The story concerns a doctor and his wife. A friend of the doctor's to whom the doctor himself tells his story, particularly about a crucial and revealing experience in his married life, narrates it. When a version of this story of Anderson's was first published, it was given the title *A Moonlight Walk*. But the author while publishing the final version of the story gave it its present title, *Mrs. Wife,*[67] a most appropriate one. Etymologically the word 'wife' meant 'help-mate', which fits most aptly the doctor's wife, Martha. She remains his helpmate through thick and thin.

The doctor practiced in a country town and his patients, whom he visited, lived over a wide countryside, valley and hills. He was a sensible and sensitive man of deep and true culture, full of true feeling. Human, humane and honest in his approach to his patients, competent and unpretentious, he was naturally popular. He was "a rather large, very strong and very handsome man",[68] "so very male, virile,—naturally quick and even affectionate in all his relations with people and particularly with women".[69] In his practice he came into intimate contact with a good many women. He could have been easily a women's man had he chosen to be. But he resisted it though it was a great struggle for him and despite some neurotic women patients being very persistent and determined not to be put off. He loved his wife and was very much devoted to her, though he did not speak much about her. "She was rather small and dark, a woman very beautiful in her won way—the way—of a good deal of suffering".[70] the doctor and his wife had known much suffering in life. their daughter, the only living child of their marriage was a cripple, as she was a victim of infantile paralysis, and moved moving about with great difficulty in a wheel chair. The two sons born to them had both died in the outbreak of the same dreaded disease, which had paralysed their daughter. There were no secrets between the doctor and his wife. Such was the transparency of their relationship built on mutual respect and trust. He had a gift for laughter, loud and hearty, while she only smiled. Whenever she smiled her great beauty came to life. In joy and sorrow they stood together.

The doctor had very little money. He was indifferent to either saving or accumulating it. His wife undertook the job of sending bill, as he was very careless about it. Often he "forgot", "purposely", to report to his wife many calls he received, one of his patients, a very rich woman, who came from a city for a short stay in the country town of the doctor, took a fancy for him and urged him to come to the city where he could succeed as doctor and also get rich. When he would not see her in his office, she wrote letters to him and sent flowers in big boxes to his office. He threw them out of the window into the alleyway. Everyone, including his wife, knew it. But she was not perturbed by it. As the doctor told his friend, "—my wife has a head. She knew well enough I was not be caught by one of that sort".[71] The city lady was not the kind to give up easily. Once she wrote to him making a fantastic offer of a hundred thousand dollars, provided he moved to the city, became a doctor to rich women, and agreed to see her daily as his patient though not as her lover. The doctor was not taken it. He knew that at best he could only be fairly good country doctor. The city woman tried yet another bait very difficult to resist. She suggested in a letter that with plenty of money at his disposal possibly he could sent his crippled daughter to some famous physician and get hr cured. The understanding between the doctor and his wife and their mutual trust was such that when he showed the letter to her "she read it and smiled". He vowed solemnly to himself, "By this woman, hard or soft, hurt or unhurt, I will stand until I die".[72]

As if to challenge and test the doctor's resolve, another woman seemed to enter his life and create a real crisis in his married life, It happened unexpectedly. A city manufacturer of sorts, came into the country for the summer with wife, his only child a crippled daughter like the doctor's own, and a nurse who was a Pole. On the instruction of his city doctor, the manufacturer engaged this country doctor to visit the crippled girl on his regular rounds and be at hand in case of an emergency, although there was precious little that any doctor could do to help the sick girl. It was the Polish woman that completely held the doctor's attention. She was perhaps thirty years old, a very strong woman, "in every way physically full and rich". He who was forty-seven years old at that time, physically very strong, became "subject to very direct and powerful sex calls which were similar to the "storms" suddenly descending on "peaceful fields". Later he learnt from the nurse herself that she too had a similar, equally intense and explosive experience on seeing him.[73]

The doctor describes this crucial experience frankly to his friend, the narrator of the story, in a quiet voice without any exaggeration melodramatisation. He felt spellbound in her presence. It was "pure lust" in him and nothing else, as he himself realized. He never had a like experience. "It was almost as though (he) had, in that moment, in the child's (i.e. the sick girl) presence, actually taken the woman. It seemed to (him) that she was something (he) had all of (his) life been wanting with a kind of terrible force-with (his) entire being". During that spell he had become completely oblivious of his wife, her love for him, and the suffering he and she had gone through together over the loss of their sons and the incurable sickness their only surviving child. For the time she was utterly out of his life. it was a terrible struggle within him to resist the temptation. He was in a muddle and failed to attend to his patients. It seemed to be a desperate situation to him. While describing this situation to friend while they were fishing together the doctor, seemingly going off at tangent , recalls significantly a fishing trip he took alone on a moonlight night in a wild mountain stream, "on the night after he had buried his second son". "himself fighting all the night, not to be overcome" by the loss of his son.[74] The fight was "to save himself from despair". Was he doing the same thing now in this struggle between the Polish woman and himself,[75] he wondered.

The doctor's wife was perhaps "deeply aware" of the confusion he was in and the probable cause for it. Having waited for a few days he went out again to meet the nurse. He had thought out a plan to take her out. He lied to his wife that though there had not been any call for his service, some voice had been calling him to go to the crippled girl. Whenever he went out at night to answer a call, it was his custom to go to his wife and kiss her before he left. Such was his obsession with the nurse that he forgot about it that night. When his wife reminded him of this omission, as he was hurrying through her room, he retraced his steps but could not bring himself to kiss her. But he could not help telling her, their relations being always transparent, "I cannot explain. This is a strange night form me. I will perhaps explain it later, I cannot kiss you now".[76]

The doctor got the Polish woman. She told him plainly that she too had felt when she saw him as he had felt about her. A woman of independent judgment and sensitiveness, he knew her mind. She had make enquiries about him and found about his crippled daughter, the loss of his two sons, and about his wife. While she was ready to oblige him on that occasion, she had other thoughts also. She told him candidly: "I do not want you to be unfaithful to her— you are not going to take me. I am a woman of thirty and have never been taken by a man. I had never wanted to be until I saw you. It may be that now I never shall be".[77] Although he had nothing to say in reply, he realised the maturity and wisdom of her remark. "It was the great moment of his life', making him feel that her remark had made him a matured man.[78] After returning home he gave his wife the kiss he had denied her that night, which was a most regard for his wife: "I was in love with her as I had never really been with the Polish woman and in the same way. In a way until after that time I never had been".[79] Not only did it bring him closer to her, but brought him a better awareness of her character and its strength.

The doctor's wife's reaction to the entire episode, summed up in the concluding paragraph of the story, is even more illuminating and sheds light on their relationship. After receiving the reassuring kiss form him that night, she told him: "we have been through it again, haven't we?". Then she, who generally only smiled, for some reason "laughed", a laughter very different from that of the hearty laughter for which the doctor was known. To him, "it was the nicest laugh (he) had ever heard from her lips".[80] It seemed to come from the depths of her being. It was obviously an expression of her sense of tremendous relief from the anxiety and tension she had been experiencing, and of her joy. Ever a woman of few words, her quiet laughter could express her happiness of the moment. The few words she said to him (cited above) hint that there were probably in their married similar experiences of suspense and anxiety for her, the doctor being a very attractive, virile man open to temptations. They had successfully tided over them. the latest episode with the Polish woman was perhaps the most challenging, from her point of view. Luckily she had regained what she feared she had lost forever. Her laughter, far better than demonstrative gestures and words, suggested her renewed understanding, trust and confidence in her husband whom she loved deeply. It was the reaction of a prson of real maturity. But for her restrained and mature response their relation would have been strained beyond recovery It is to the credit of the doctor that he realized and respected her integrity and his own indebtedness to her. She was, as he tacitly acknowledges to his friend the anchor of his life and thought and his moral being.

Mrs. Wife is not only a refreshing departure from the other stories of disappointed and frustrated husbands and wives, but also a true love story. This point has to be emphasized. The doctor and his wife Martha emerge as mature husband and wife, who have grown gracefully with age and experience, discovering the meaning and significance of married love.

NOTES AND REFERENCES

1. Irving Howe, Sherwood Anderson (New York: Wm Sloane Associates, 1951) p. 173.
2. Winesburg, Ohio: Text and Criticism, ed. John H. Ferres (New York: Penguin Books,1966), p. 200.
3. *The Untold Lie*. Ibid, p, 205.
4. *Ibid.*, p. 207.
5. *Ibid.*, p. 209.
6. Cited by Charles E. Modlin (ed), "Introduction", Certain Things Last, (New York, Four Walls and Eight Windows, 1992), p. xii.
7. Rex Burbank, Sherwood Anderson (New York: Twayne, 1964), p. 95.

8. *The Other Woman*, Certain Things Last, p. 20.
9. *Ibid*.
10. *Ibid*.
11. *Ibid*., p. 24.
12. *Ibid*.
13. *Ibid*., p. 33.
14. Rex Burbank, p. 96.
15. *The Other Woman*, Certain Things Last, p. 25.
16. *Ibid*.
17. *Ibid*., p. 26.
18. *Ibid*., p. 25.
19. *Ibid*., p. 26.
20. Rex Burbank, p. 95.
21. *The Door of the Trap*, The Triumph of the Egg, (New York: R.W. Huebsch,1921), p. 127.
22. *Ibid*., p. 120.
23. *Ibid*.
24. *Ibid*., p. 118.
25. *Ibid*., p. 122.
26. *Ibid*.
27. Mary Cocharan Figures in Another Story Titles *Unlighted Lamps* in which she Appears One of the Two Chief Characters. This Story will be Considered in the Next Chapter. In the Present Story she is a Secondary Character, Since it is Mainly the Story of Hugh Walker, the Puzzled, Confused and Frustrated Teacher of Mathematics, Husband of Winifred and Father of Three Children.
28. *The Door of the Trap*, The Triumph of the Egg, p. 129.
29. *Ibid*., p. 128.
30. *Ibid*., p. 125.
31. *Ibid*., pp. 127-128.
32. *Ibid*., p. 129.
33. *Ibid*., pp. 129-130.
34. *Ibid*., p. 131.
35. *Ibid*., p. 132.
36. *Ibid*., p. 133.

37. Robert Allen Papinchak, Sherwood Anderson: A Study of the Short Fiction (New York: Twayne Publishers, 1992), p. 47.
38. Cited by Charles E. Modlin, "Introduction", Certain Things Last, p. xii.
39. *Ibid.*
40. *There She Is- She Is Taking Her Bath,* Certain Things Last, p. 179.
41. *Ibid.*, p. 184.
42. *Ibid.*, p. 187.
43. *Ibid.*
44. *Ibid.*, p. 181.
45. *Ibid.*, p. 188.
46. Papinchak, pp. 28-29.
47. *There She Is-She Is Taking her Bath,* Certain Things Last, p. 189.
48. *Ibid.*
49. Cited by Papinchak, p. 112.
50. *The Man's Story,* Certain Things Last, p. 106.
51. *Ibid.*
52. Though Anderson does not say in so many Words, he does Imply that the Presence of Children could make a Difference to Domestic Life and Save a Married Life. In *The Untold Lie* in Winesburg, Ohio, for Instance, it is the Presence of his Children, Thin – Legged Though they might be,, that helps to Sustain his Married Life.
53. *The Man's Story,* Certain Things Last, p. 105.
54. *Ibid.*, p. 107.
55. *The Man in the Brown Coat,* The Triumph of the Egg, (New York: B.W. Heubsch, Into, 1919), p. 99.
56. *Ibid.*, pp. 100-101.
57. The Man's Story, Certain Things Last, p. 108.
58. *Ibid.*, p. 109.
59. *Ibid.*, p. 112.
60. *Ibid.*, pp. 112-113.
61. *Ibid.*, p. 113.
62. *Ibid.*, p. 118.
63. *Ibid.*, p. 120.
64. *Ibid.*, pp. 118-119
65. *Ibid.*, p. 121.

66. Charles E. Modlin, Introduction, Certain things Last, p. xx.
67. *Ibid*.
68. Mrs. Wife, Certain Things Last, p. 271.
69. *Ibid*., p. 273.
70. *Ibid*.
71. *Ibid*., p. 274.
72. *Ibid*., p. 275.
73. *Ibid*., p. 278.
74. *Ibid*., pp. 278-279.
75. *Ibid*., p. 280.
76. *Ibid*., p. 284.
77. *Ibid*., p. 285.
78. *Ibid*.
79. *Ibid*., p. 286.
80. *Ibid*., pp. 286-87.

CHAPTER – 6

Stories About Frustrated Men and Women and Unlived Lives

The focus of the previous chapter (Chapter Five) was on five of Anderson's post-Winesburg stories which dwell on the puzzles and confusions in the relationships between married men and women and their experience of failure, unfulfilled love and the consequent disappointment. Only in one of the stories, *Mrs. Wife*, the protagonists- the doctor and his wife Martha-are able to triumph over them and rediscover the significance of married love and establish a mature and stable relationship. Te present chapter is also concerned with some of Anderson's stories about adult men and women written after Winesburg, Ohio. In gene.al they also explore the familiar Anderson territory of loneliness, isolation, failure of communication, unfulfilled love etc., among adults. As seen in the previous chapters, Anderson has many stories spread over his entire career which are about people young and old, whose lives are filled with frustrations and disappointments for one reason or other, and who feel emotionally crippled, suffocated in their environments. However in the tales selected for a close study in this chapter are *The New Englander, Seeds, Unlighted Lamps, Out of Nowhere into Nothing,* and *The Egg,* all from Anderson's famous volume *The Triumph of the Egg* the emphasis is on the protagonists' incisive experience of suffocation, frustration, defeat and failure, and their sense of unlived, wasted and buried life.

There is a variety in these stories. They have, however, "in common", as Rex Burbank points out, "sensitive souls who want desperately to break out of the isolation of their inner lives". Further, they "present a picture of waste, of human sensitivity never fully developed, of physical and spiritual potential untapped, or of a sensitive nature crushed".[1] They are stories of people longing for something, about which they may or may not have a clear notion, and groping and painfully striving after it, and invariably ending in futility, as attainment of fulfillment of what they desire and seek always eludes them, whatever the causes be. In these stories as in many others of his, Anderson's attempt is to understand sympathetically his characters rather than judge them or presume to offer social or psychological or other solutions to their problems and puzzlements.

To begin with *The New Englander*, the title Anderson gives this story, calls for some comment. He has a few other stories the titles of which include the name so of the place or region to which their protagonists belong: for example *An Ohio Pagan* (which has been considered in chapter four) and *A Chicago Hamlet*. Obviously Anderson intends to suggest that the place or region to which the characters belong or live in affects them and their attitudes in several ways and therefore has to be taken note of. The indefinite article in the titles of their stories implies that the protagonists- Tom Edwards of *An Ohio Pagan,* and Tom the advertising writer of A Chicago Hamlet- are not viewed as typical or representative of the places associated with them. But in the case of *The New Englander*, the definite article "the' in the title implies that Elsie Leander the protagonist is typical of those who live in the "New England" region, and that of others of her age in that region. Whatever New England might have been or meant to those of the earlier generations, progressively it had come to be looked upon as a region which had lost all its former vigour and vitality, become stagnant, sterile, narrowly conservative, coarse and repressing in its morality, its Puritan ethic having become hardened into inflexible social codes and conventions insensitive to human nature and its essential needs. Its prevailing environment hardly made for life, all cisterns of life having gone dry. At least, this is the impression one gathers from Anderson's about the New Englander.

The New Englander, is the story of Elsie Leander told by the omniscient third person narrator. At the time her story is narrated she is a spinster of thirty-five, obliged to live in a large farm very close to a town in Iowa in the West, after having lived for long in her father's small farm in the Vermont valley in New England. She is the only daughter and youngest of four children born to her parents. Her three brothers had already gone away from the place well before she was born, the oldest brother to New York City, and the other two to the distant West to live with their uncle. Therefore Elsie grew up virtually alone in the Vermont house. Of the brothers the one who went to New York City and one of the two who went to live with their uncle had already died even before she could ever see them. shw saw the surviving brother Tom for the first time only when she went with her old parents to live in Iowa where this brother of hers had settled. Her oldest brother had a son, a young man of twenty-three, who visited the Leanders only once in Vermont. He too had died, though Elsie carried with her tender memories of this cousin of hers for long. These few facts mentioned above are enough to indicate how lonely and lonesome her life must have been. The focus of the story is one what goes on in her mind, and whatever action there is in it is psychological. Outwardly very little happens. There is no scope for any outward experiences of happiness in her life. Anderson very ably traces the different stages or steps of agitation, turmoils and short-lived feelings of relief and joy in her.

Before going into the details of Elsie and her people the narrator begins with a brief but remarkable description of the Vermont House and its surroundings. The house was a small white frame affair. At the back of it was a path which ran up the side of a hill into an orchard, in which all the trees were "old and gnarled". At the back of the orchard there were "bare rocks". "Inside the fence a large gray rock stuck high up out of the ground" and Elsie often used to sit there with her back to it. Seemingly at a short distance away from that point there were "several large mountains". In between "lay many tiny fields surrounded by—stone walls".

> *Everywhere rocks appeared. Large ones, too heavy to be moved, struck out of the ground in the center of the fields. The fields were like cups filled with a green liquid that turned gray in the fall and white in the winter. The mountains...were like giants ready at any moment to reach out their hands and take the cups one by one and drink off the green liquid. The large rocks in the fields were like the thumbs of the giants.*[2]

As it can be seen, the details of the landscape are chosen selectively by the narrator to evoke the cramped barren fields. Though it may not have been exactly a place of 'stony rubbish', it is certainly dry and sterile. The description becomes the outward image, emblematic of the inward sterility experienced by Elsie and her kind. This landscape stands in sharp contrast to the vast, rich fields of Iowa described later in the story vividly.

At home life, of Elsie was passive, inert and she had hardly anyone to talk to and communicate with. In general, the girl child was not cared for and was taken for granted, as if her role was fixed, unchanging and undeveloping. Elsie hardly received any attention from her mother and father, both hardworking. Her mother "rarely spoke to the daughter".

> *(She) did house work in the mornings and in the afternoon sat in the rocking chair in her tiny living room and thought of her sons while she crocheted table covers and tidies for the back of chairs. She was a silent woman, very thin and with very thin bony hands...when she crocheted her back was as straight as the back of a drill sergeant.*[3]

Elsie's father was slightly better, and exchanged once in a while a word or two with her, but little more. A hardworking old man with a half worn-out body, when he laughed, "his laughter was like the creaking of a rusty barn door hinge and the hand he laid on her shoulders was thin like her own hands and like her mother's hands".[4] If he felt any concern for his daughter-perhaps he did-he never gave expression to it. It is as if silence reigned in the house intensifying Elsie's sense of loneliness.

Unexpectedly there was a change in the life of the Leanders and therefore in Elsie's life. Her father and mother decided after long deliberation to go west to lie with Tom, their surviving son. In this decision Elsie had no part, although the narrator does not explicitly say so. She did not think much about it. This brother of hers whom she was yet to see, had married the daughter of a neighboring farmer who brought him some money. They moved to apple Junction in Iowa where they opened a grocery, which was efficiently managed by tom's wife. This venture prospered as his matrimonial venture. When Elsie's parents decided to join their son, he was already the father of a daughter named Elizabeth and four sons.

Stay put as Elsie was for years in the rocky Vermont, from which she had probably not stirred out at all any time and had stoically resigned herself to an isolated life and loneliness, "the t rip west on the railroad train jolted (her) out of herself", and "she became excited"[5] 'in spite of her detached attitude towards life". it was entirely a new experience for her. She could not sleep at night, and during daytime sat all day "looking at a new kind of land" as the train went through towns and cities which appeared and disappeared, crawled up the sides of hills or fell down into forest clad valleys, and passed through flat land where every field was as large as a farm in her own country. The land was so continually changing as the train moved west that it was unlike anything she had ever known at home where nothing changed. The contrast between the two regions hit her hard:

In the valley where she had been born and where she had lived all her days everything had an air of finality. Nothing could be changed. The tiny fields were chained to the earth. They were fixed in their places and surrounded by aged stone walls. The fields like the mountains that looked down at hem were as unchangeable as the passing days.[6]

As the train passed from one state to another through varying landscapes she began to feel relaxed, physically and mentally. She even felt that she had been released from the prison she had been in for years. She was "filled with joy at the thought that the train was still going on into the west" and "wanted to go on forever—into the unknown". In childlike fashion she fancied to have "become a winged thing flying through space".[7] Such was the impact of moving away from Vermont and of the fast changing landscape on her sensibilities. Ironically Elsie did not and could not know or anticipate that her excitement and sense of exaltation would not last long.

Elsie's brother who had settled and prospered in the town of Apple junction in Iowa settled his parents in a huge but unfinished house in the midst of a large farm of cornfields. When the Leanders moved in it was April and the fields were gray and empty and the exaltation Elsie had experienced on the train wore away in their presence. But "something of the effect of it remained with her for months".[8] Always sensitive to her surroundings she could see how different was the place they were in. the house was much too big and looked very old for her to feel comfortable. But outside it was different. There was no gnarled orchard surrounded by a half-ruined stone fence. The freshly ploughed fields stretched away in all directions as if they would go on and on forever. While her father and mother settled down to their routine activities, Elsie sitting on the top step of a small stairway at the back of the house, leaning against the locked door, watched fascinated and undisturbed men who came to plough and plant and giant houses which moved in a procession across the priaries, which looked like a vast sea. She was particularly attracted by a giant like young man who drove six horses in the field and swore at them vigorously startling this pale New Englander whose religion had forbidden swearing. Gradually she got accustomed to his presence in the field. "Sometimes when he drove his horses down to the wire fence he smiled and nodded" to her.[9] This was indeed a new experience for her. In Vermont there were few young men for her to see and nod, all having gone away to seek their fortune.

The time for cultivating corn passed. The men and horses went away. Corn in the fields of Iowa grew so tall that corn stalks resembled young trees, and the cornfields looked like forests. Elsie was affected deeply by what she saw, and by the change of season. New sensations were roused in her. Her mind "partially awakened by the strangeness of the railroad trip, awakened again. She did not feel like a staid thin woman with a back like the back of a drill sergeant, but something new and as strange as the new land into which she had come to live".[10] There were mixed feelings and sensations in her. First, as the corn in the field grew so high as to look like a wall preventing her from seeing into the distance, she felt that her father's house there was like a prison and that she was locked up there more closely than ever. But immediately a new impulse driving the other out, came to her and "she got a sense of release" as she could see through long tunnels under the rows of corn where there was a soft carpet of green formed by the weeds growing there. They looked like "warm passages running out into life", to her who had lived in a prison-like place where no life was possible and precious years of her life had been spent unlived all hr natural impulses and desires suppressed. How difficult it is to free oneself from accumulated inhibitions and fears which condition it is to free oneself from accumulated inhibitions and fears which condition one's life may be seen in her behaviour. She timidly walked to the wire fence and held for a moment a strong young stalk in her hand. But suddenly she grew afraid, her body trembled and she ran back to the steps where she had been sitting as if she had done something wrong, and forbidden. "the thought of trying the experiment fascinated but at the same terrified. She got quickly up and went into the house".[11]

There were vague but strong stirrings in Elsie which she could not understand nor resist. They all had sexual over tones. One night "a murmuring began in the corn and murmuring thoughts and memories awoke in her mind.".[12] She thought that she heard a thousand voices like the back of the voices of children coming from far away. She became excited over the fancy. And then the pale sensitive figure of Young Leander, her dead cousin, son of her older brother of New York, who had visited them Vermont came to her mind. It was as though the young man had come suddenly into the room" and she "sat writing, intense and expectant". This young man went with her every afternoon to the rock at the back of the orchard and sat with her there. She vividly remembered a particular moment in his company, which "marked, high spot in her life". "A strange trembling eagerness for something she had not realized in her experience of life had taken possession of her".[13] Now in her lonely room in Iowa, after so many years she thought or fancied that she heard her cousin's voice once again asking her to kiss him as he had done at Vermont. Her body trembled violently.

The change from Vermont to Iowa and the changed scene of vast spaces and environment from cramped surroundings gave Elsie a feeling of release. Otherwise she was as lonely as ever. There was little communication between her and her parents. Her brother and energetic sister-in-law did not take any note of her presence, nor their children, a noisy lot, during their Sunday visits to them. her sister-in-law brushed her with a move of her hand as she dismissed her own children. The children went tearing through the fields following their dogs in pursuit of rabbits, and silent cornfields rang with their shouts and the baring of dogs. Left alone Elsie sat on the step outside the house to watch the fields and the screaming shouting and wildly running children, such spontaneity of action she had not known in her isolated and lonely life in Vermont. An almost overpowering desire to run with them, "shouting, and playing along the corn rows took possession of her".[14] It may be assumed that in the years past in Vermont never had an occasion or opportunity or stimulus for such an abandon. She timidly climbed awkwardly over the fence and went a little way along one of the rows of corn. But fear and inhibition overtaking her she dropped to the ground and stayed for a long time listening to the voices of children in the distance.

Without Elsie being aware, a new factor entered into the scene of her observation to cause her a lot of emotional disturbance. Among the children was Elizabeth her brother's sixteen years old daughter, very strong and alive and full of energy. When this girl got into the country along with her brothers, she herself became a boy scrambled over the fences and outdid the boys in roughness and noisiness.[15] She was all that Elsie could never have been in her lonely isolated life. The Sunday, as Elsie, silently waited amidst the corn stalks, there was summons for dinner. As she rose to go she saw young Elizabeth Leander and a young ploughman walking slowly along the rows. This was the same young man whom Elsie had seen a few months earlier planting the corn in the field. She could see that "an understanding" between the two young "had been established".[16] The narrator does not say what Elsie felt when she saw them. But the "heavy lumbering silence" during the dinner is suggestive of what the parties concerned felt. After the dinner, Elsie suppressed the desire t go gain into the fields. Instead she adventured into one of the many unused rooms in the upper part of the house. She did not know what she was looking for or what she expected to find there. "She wanted something and did not know what it was. Her own mood frightened her". A bird had flown into this windowless room and become imprisoned. The thought that she too was a prisoner gripped her. She became restless and wanted to go outdoors. Climbing over the wire fence she run along one of the tunnels, into the vastness of the cornfields, "filled with but one desire": "She wanted to get out for her life and into some new and sweeter life she felt must be hidden somewhere in the fields".[17]

As Elsie lay quiet and passive under the corn, tired after the long run she strangely became vaguely hopeful and expectant, probably because of the sense of relief she felt after the free outdoor exercise.

> *Deep within her there was a feeling that something was about to happen, something that would lift her out of herself, that would tear her away from her past and the pat of her people. Her thoughts were not definite. She lay still and waited as she had waited for days and months by the rock at the back of the orchard on the Vermont farm when she was a girl.*[18]

These thoughts and expectations area measure of how oppressively frustrating her life had been in the past, and how intense her longing was for relief and change. But this mood of hope was short-lived. The rapid approach of a thunderstorm made all the children run back into the house form the field. "An odd feeling of disappointment" took possession of Elsie. Distraught and feeling weak she too began to walk back. On her way she chanced to see unseen by them Elizabeth and the young ploughman embracing and kissing each other. The impact of what she witnessed on her was immediate betraying her natural and suppressed sexual desires: "—her tense hands grasped one of the corn stalks. Her lips pressed themselves into the dust".[19] Unable to walk to the house though it was within sight she sat on the ground unable to understand the agonizing agitation in her: "something within herself was being twisted and whirled about as the tops of the corn of thunder announcing the approach of the storm would seem to articulate her unexpressed feelings and silent agony.

When her brother and his family drove away from the place, to Elsie: the farm house in the midst of the cornfield rocked by the winds seemed the most desolate place in the world" When the storm actually broke out, she would not move and allowed the sheets of water to sweep over her. She was so unbearably miserable that "sobs arose out of her throat". "The storm that had for years been gathering in her also broke—She abandoned herself to a storm of grief that was only partially grief. Tears ran out of her eyes and made little furrows through the dust on her face".[20] Even though she heard her mother and father calling to her, in their thin voices, she preferred to stay where she was and get drenched rather than go into the house. She recognized the futility of her efforts to find the understanding she needed. Commenting on the ending of the story Brom Weber remarks that "The story closes with a bitter symbolic rejection of the New England past Elsie weeping in the fields as a rainstorm drenches her—refusing to take shelter in her father's house".[21] The story, it is time, rejects whatever New England in its decadence had come to mean, particularly the repression and inhibition it had fostered and encouraged. However there seem to be implicit in the story something more than a critique of New England, and something of general human relevance. Anderson is concerned with sex as well as human relations. What Elsie Leander had been denied and deprived of was not just sex but affection and love, which no one gave her, neither her parents nor her brother and his family. She was a lonely and isolated person from first to last. She was neglected and taken for granted at Vermont as well as Iowa. The hopes and expectations roused in her by the new free, spacious environment of the farm in Iowa, and the sense of release she experienced there, all turned out to be temporary and short lived. An environment of love and affection and the presence of someone sensitive and understanding who could draw her out and communicate with her would have made all the difference to her life. These she was denied. In this regard spacious Iowa was no different from the narrow Vermont as far as she was concerned. She had no opportunity to happen, not knowing what it should be. Thus Elsie Leander's becomes a sad and deeply moving story of futility, disappointment and unlived life. By going from Vermont to Iowa, she was, like Rosalind Westcott of another story to be examined shortly, going *Out of Nowhere into Nothing* though in a different sense.

The 'seeds' in the title of the story *Seeds* refer to "old thoughts and beliefs – seeds planted by dead men"[22] which spring up in one's soul and choke it. The young woman of the story is one among the many, according to one of the characters in the story, who are "choked" by "climbing", "crawling creeping vines".[23] The young woman of the story who is not given a name, could be easily dubbed as a pervert if one did not know more about her plight with sympathy. Like Leander's hers two is a defeated, frustrated and unlived life but of a different kind. She is more of a prisoner of her fears, ambitions and crippling beliefs nurtured in her environment than Elsie longing for love which sadly is not gratified.

Seeds begin with a conversation between the author-narrator and a psychoanalyst. The psychoanalyst, having practiced for long the method of psychoanalysis to cue people of illness, is now tired and wearied of it and decides to be cleansed. Having tried to go beneath the surface of the lives of men and women he has had to realize that he himself is as much cramped and choked as others by the vines of old thoughts and beliefs which are no longer valid. He has been "an amateur venturing timidly into lives",[24] and has been rather rash in assuming that he could minister to people who are ill. He is spiritually exhausted. The psychoanalyst's friend, the narrator, too shares this view that " it is given to no man to venture far along the road of lives".[25] "The point of the story", as Rex Burbank puts it succinctly, "is that the inner life is a myriad of often conflicting impulses of love and hate, revulsion and attraction, beauty and ugliness. And the inner life has been choked by old thoughts and beliefs seeds planted by dead men', by efforts to control it, or understand it".[26]

To illustrate his view the psychoanalyst tells the author narrator the experience of one of his young friends Le Roy by name, a painter and a man devoted to ideas, who told him this story. In a rooming house in Chicago where Le Roy lived a woman from Iowa also lived for about three months. She was about twenty-seven years old and looked like a thousand other women one saw every day except that she was a little lame and walked with a limp. She taught music to girls in the place she came from, and had come to Chicago ostensibly to study advanced methods of teaching music. In the rooming house she was the only woman except the landlady. The men in the house became curious about this woman who kept herself aloof. They all laughed and whispered and said among themselves that she wanted a lover: "She may not know it but a lover is what she needs".[27] But she was mortally afraid of men. Nothing would induce her to walk with a man or accept invitation to dinner or the theatre. When a young clerk who also lived there induced her to sit with him on the steps before the house, and put a hand on her shoulder, she shook with terror and began to scream.

Naturally the men there began to hate her. But, her behaviour was abnormal and she would not leave them alone. In a hundred ways she continually invited approaches. She would stand naked in the bath room facing the hallway and left the door slightly ajar. Men who passed up and down could not but notice her. Sometimes when men were present in the living room, to their utter embarrassment she would enter silently, throw herself down on the couch there, and keep string at the ceiling. "Her whole physical being seemed to be waiting for something".[28] The land lady had to order her to leave the house. If this were all, this woman form Iowa, would have been no different from other abnormal and perverted young women, and would have been a fit case for a psychiatrist. Le Roy and Anderson of course-who narrated her story to his friend did not view it as a simple matter of psychoanalysis. He saw in it something more serious, because he got involved in her problem rather unexpectedly, though he had hardly noticed her.

Soon after she was ordered to leave, the Iowa woman ran into Le Roy's room like a wounded bird, putting her face on his knees, frightened, said to him tremblingly: "Take me quickly... I can't stand the waiting. You must take me at once".[29] To the indignant landlord who showed up Le Roy, said, acting on impulse to save the situation: "We have been engaged to be married. He have quarreled— She has been unwell and excited. I will take her away—".[30] Once they were out of the house, the Iowa woman stopped weeping, and put her land into his. He found a room for her in another house. Then they went to a park, where he talked with her until midnight. He saw and talked with her again many times later. "Nothing came out of it". Why did she behave in this fashion, having rushed to Le Roy impulsively and surrendering herself to him, remains a puzzle. Certainly it was not a calculated move to involve Le Roy. Having taken a forward step impulsively under pressure, she seems to have stiffened up and shrunk back as if she had done something very wrong. Le Roy however could understand her dilemma and the causes for her inhibitions and fears, and her inability to make up her mind and act accordingly. It was for him a deeply human rather than in clinical issue.

Le Roy gives his friend an account of the familial circumstance and upbringing of this grotesque woman, on the basis of his long conversation with her. She the youngest of four sisters all orphaned when the eldest was fifteen years old. They had a house and a garden. All were quiet capable women. The woman in question became a teacher of music, and all day taught music too young girls. Theirs was entirely a woman's house. For years no man came near it. None of them had a lover. At home they talked only of women's affairs. This utterly feminine quality of their lives visibly affected the young music teacher. She began to think and dream of men. "During the day and day the through the evening she talked with women of women's affairs, and all the time she wanted desperately to be loved by a man".[31] She came to Chicago with the hope of finding a man who would love her. But years of isolated existence, accumulated inhibitions and suppression of desires led to her strange behaviour in the rooming house. She "thought too much and acted too little. What she wanted she could not achieve". Le Roy's explanation of her conduct is that when "the living force within could not find expression", it expressed itself in another way. "Sex spread itself out over her body" and "permeated the very fibre of her being". The touch of man's hand, even the mere sight of a man in the street "did something to her".[32]

If this were all, the young woman would have been no more than, no different from a sex-starved person. Le Roy could understand that. Therefore he grows indignant at the psychoanalyst's suggestion that he, of whom she was not afraid, could have played the role of her lover and cured her of her sickness. But professionally induced synthetic love which psychoanalysts practice to cure psychic maladies according to Le Roy, goes against the very nature and significance of genuine love. Therefore he tells his elderly friend: "It isn't so simple — you miss the whole point. Nothing in life can be settled so definitely".[33] Mere gratification of sex would not do, although it had its place in mutual understanding of men and women. This woman first of all had to be freed from the hard crust of out model ideas and beliefs which had made her and others, including himself, grotesques. She, it is true, "needed a lover" but the "need of a lover was—a quite secondary thing". For "she needed to be loved, to be long and quietly and patiently loved".[34] Only such love would cure her of her malady. But it is rare to find it. It is Le Roy's contention that the disease she suffered from is "Universal". "We all want to be loved and the world has no plan for creating our lovers".[35]

The story closes with Le Roy's expression of his spiritual exhaustion. It has to be assumed that the Iowa woman continues to live the same unlived life of loneliness, frustration and futility, becoming more and more of a grotesque, as there seem to be no redeeming features inn her environment, and no support of any kind. Like Elsie Lender in the *The New*

Englander, she too is trapped within herself and is unable to satisfy the demands of her inner imaginative life to communicate with others.

Unlighted Lamps is the story of Dr. Lester Cochran of Huntersburg, a small town in Illinois, and his eighteen-year old daughter Mary Cochran. Mary appears as a secondary character in another story, *The Door of the Trap*, which was already been considered in a previous chapter. The present story is poignant, and us much more effective and moving, as it probes deeply into the sensitive nature and dilemmas of Mary as well as the doctor, her father. In the other story Mary has a more or less passive role. She is made use by Hugh Walker in an attempt to sort out his own needs and problems. In *Unlighted Lamps* both father and daughter are utterly lonely for different reasons and their experience of isolation, both physical and psychological, is excruciating. The store of love each has goes waste because it remains untapped and without an outlet. The inner life in each case fails to find outward expression. The doctor's in particular is a buried life. Between the ageing and sick doctor and his young daughter there is silence rather than nay communication. It is too late by the time they both resolve to break through the wall of silence that has kept them apart, and that is the irony of their lives. The title given to the story points to it. The lamps could have been lit and at least some of the darkness enveloping their lives been cleared, but they were not.

The narrative situation is the impending death of the doctor due to a heart ailment which sets both the father and daughter examining their lives in the light of this eventuality. It brings them the painful awareness that they have failed to free themselves from their inner isolation and fulfill their emotional potential. Anderson develops the theme by means of shifting narrative perspectives, by alternating the thoughts of father and daughter as they assess their lives, and by a series of contrasts in character and scene.

The omniscient third-person narration begins with Mary Cochran going out for a long walk on a Sunday evening after dark. She wanted to think seriously about her future as her affairs were approaching a crisis. The previous evening as it was growing dark her father Dr. Cochran had told her "quite suddenly and abruptly" that "he was a victim of heart disease and might die any moment".[36] He did not know that his words would prove prophetic. Conversations between the father and daughter were rare and always brief. He made the announcement of his approaching death "in a cold quiet voice", devoid of any expression of feeling or emotion. It had seemed to her that "everything concerning her father must be cold and quiet".[37] Finding his daughter turning pale at the announcement, he tried to assure her that there was no need to worry since the experts were not always right in their prognosis. While reassuring her, "he had wanted to put his arm about his daughter's shoulder— but never having shown any feeling in his relation with her", he "could not sufficiently release some tight thing in himself".[38] He also remembered in his rumination that it was not only in the case of the daughter but of his wife Ellen too, when she was living with him, that he had shied away from all forms of expression of concern and feeling and tenderness. Afraid of expressing emotion, he had often as a young man "sat in the evening in silence beside his wife" although "his hands ached to reach across the narrow space that separated them and touch her hands, her face, her hair". He had let her think, as he had done his daughter, that he was" cold and unfeeling", while "something in him was straining and straining to tear itself loose".[39] His marriage and his life, both had filed, because of this strange fear, and this inhibition against communication, against speaking out what one felt.

Dr. Cochran, was anything but an insensitive and unfeeling man. In fact, he was sensitive and deeply human. His marriage itself with Ellen, Mary's mother, who was stranded in Hunterburg, and became ill at the same time, the young doctor attended to her and when she recovered married her. Having lived a hard life, she welcomed the idea of a quiet life in a small town. But the marriage did not succeed. For, after their child Mary was born, she "suddenly found herself unable to go on living with the old man", and desired to resume her acting career. Lester Cochran, who understood her state of mind, himself took her to Chicago where she got work in a company. But, one who had shown so much of understanding, took her to the door of her hotel and put money into her hands, walked away from the place" in silence and without even a farewell kiss". The doctor had several such other "intense moments" in his life when he was "deeply stirred". He remembered them all but concealed them under a cool and quiet surface. Later in his life he recalled and lived them over again".[40] He never forgot his wife though he did not see her again. But few knew about it.

Another experience of the doctor's during the first year after his marriage had etched itself on his mind unforgettably. As he and his wife were driving home one summer evening after visiting a farmer in the country, she told him of her pregnancy, about "the great adventure of their marriage". Though he had been stirred as never before, he "remained silent because he had thought no words he could utter would express what he felt", and assumed that she would understand what he felt without words".[41] He has allowed his lips and tongue lie idle. After his wife went away, he had taken the same attitude of remaining silent and inarticulate even in the case of his daughter Mary who had now grown to be almost a woman and resembled her mother. It was this inarticulateness which was actually his camouflage for is fear of expressing his deep emotions, his un demonstrativeness, and the mask of a cold exterior that had led to his building unwittingly an almost impenetrable wall between himself and his wife and daughter. With time he himself became aware of the sheer folly of his attitude and the self-centeredness and cowardice involved in it: "I've been a fool and coward. I've always been silent because I've been afraid of expressing myself- like a blundering fool. I've been a proud man and a coward".[42] But by the time he could resolve to make amends at least in the case of his daughter, it was too late in the day.

Mary who had set out after dark for a long walk hoped to sort out her thoughts regarding her future. Her mind was crowded with thoughts about herself, her father and her standing among the people of the town. She was aware that she was a victim of town gossip, and that there was a kind of prejudice against her in the community because of the scandal associated with her father and mother. It was mistakenly thought that her mother has run away with a young sport of the town. The attitude of the town towards herself and her father ought to have brought them closer, but it had not. The doctor himself would not tell her the actual facts about her mother's disappearance. His habitual silence and the prejudice of the local people against her had made her life lonely at home as well as outside. She was starved for love and affection. But she resented strongly the attention Duke Yetter was showing her, and the efforts he was making to impress her. She suspected that he thought her to be an easy catch. These circumstances of her life had encouraged in her a "dogged determination to in some way think her own way through the things of life she could not understand".[43] Her determination had given her courage to walk alone boldly and proudly in the evening in the fast growing factory district of the town, a thing girls of her age and class would not have dared.

In those parts of the town where she and her father lived Mary felt a secret antagonism to herself. But in the Wilmott street where she walked alone frequently, as she did now, where workers who spoke in foreign tongues lived, she felt at home and free though they were all strangers. "The hubbub of life always stirring and asserting itself" in that part of the town "had a strong fascination for her".[44] As she passed through the street, she was greeted politely once in a while by housewives and others. Where she lived the atmosphere was becoming constantly more and more oppressive and stuffy. She wanted to get away from the place and into the world to be her own self when the time came. She went to her favourite haunt on the top of a small hill, a decayed orchard, and sat on the rock against the trunk of an old apple tree to think out in that quiet place some plan for her future. The time for taking a decision, she felt, had come. Her quiet was rudely disturbed by Duke Yetter's call. He had followed her to the place, very sure of his conquest. Mary did not want him to reach her. She sprang forward and gave him a sharp blow on his check threatening to get him killed by her father if he dared following her again. Rather than go home, she went straight to a bridge across a creek at the edge of the town and stood watching a couple of boys fishing there. Their father, who recognized her as Dr. Cochran's daughter, joined her. It was a very touching and significant meeting. "It was the first time she had ever heard a citizen of her home town speak with feeling of her father".[45]

This farmer helped her to see a dimension of her father's personality hidden from view by his cold and silent exterior, his goodness, and his kindly, gentle and generous nature. Once this man had been ill for a long time and was down and out". One of his sons just then got his head badly hurt from a fall. The doctor not only took particular care of them but gave the family money to buy groceries and medicines. When they got well, the doctor would not take any money from him. Instead he said: "You know how to live with your children and with your wife. You know how to make them happy. Keep your money and spend it on them".[46] The slow moving stream in the black shadows under the bridge seemed to Mary an exact image of her father's life which always was in shadows never coming into sunlight. "A great new love for her father swept over her and in fancy she felt his arms about her". As child she had continually dreamt of receiving caresses from her father. Now she resolved to make that dream come true that very night.[47]

Meanwhile the doctor too, who had been revolving inn his mind his past, had arrived at a similar resolution to set things right at once. He declared to himself aloud, sitting in the dark quiet of his room, "Tonight I'll do it. If it kills me I'll make myself talk to the girl".[48] This thought occupied his mind throughout the evening, while returning from the country, after having helped successfully a farmer's young wife in her first but difficult labour and his resolve to tell his daughter everything was redoubled. "—he would tell the whole story of his marriage and its failure sparing him no humiliation". He would help her understand her mother in whom there was "something very dear and beautiful". This knowledge would help Mary "to be a beautiful woman". This thought gave him "full confidence in the strength of his resolution".[49]

Mary who waited for her father t home also thought on similar lines. She thought only of him as he had thought of her. An incident which had taken place when she was fifteen now haunted her. On his suggestion, she had gone with him to visit a sick woman in a farmhouse. On the way, unusually he had talked with her "a little". His behaviour that evening was very unusual. He appeared to be "boyish and almost gay". After supper in the farmhouse he walked with her around the house. He stood before he for a moment and "laughed almost heartily". He then speculated aloud what would happen to her when she became a woman, what kind of life was she going to lead. All this expressed the concern of a father for his child. Then he sat beside her. For a moment it seemed to her that "he was about to put his arm around her". But he "jumped up and went into the house leaving her to sit alone in the darkness". As Mary recalled this incident, she also remembered that on her part "she had met her father's advances in silence". Had she made some gesture of warmth, it would have made a lot of difference to their silent lives. It seemed to her now that "she, not her father, was to blame for the life they had led together".[50] She had not given him love to receive love in return from him. Love and affection were always reciprocal. The sons of the farmer-laborer, she recalled, knew how to give themselves to their father and received in return his warmth. In her retrospection she also remembered that, evening long ago when she rode with her father, while returning her father "had made another unsuccessful effort to break through the wall that separated them". He had even told her, "I'm going to tell you about your mother and myself".[51] But as ill-luck would have it, just at that moment their horse plunged forward frightened by the breaking timber of the bridge. By the time the doctor regained control of the horse, they were already in the town, and "his diffident silent nature had reasserted itself".[52]

When Dr. Cochran returned from his visit Mary, who was eagerly and expectantly waiting for him sitting in the darkness, noticed a change in his behaviour. Instead of walking directly into his room as on other occasions, he lingered for a while near the door listening to the heated conversation of the loiterers there. Then he cheerfully shouted "Good Night" to them all before reaching the stairway. Mary, was so much surprised by his behaviour that she "became half-convinced that not her father but some other man was now coming up the stairway".[53] Obviously his resolve to tell everything too his daughter had made him cheerful, as if a load weighing on his conscience had been taken off. His "strange cheerful hearty mood" continued as he dragged his heavy steps on the stairs. But his mind was in a confused riot and began to wander. A stream of words of protest came from of that his lips. "It's strange that my hands should have helped a baby be born while all the time death stood at my elbow". He was struck by the irony that he a dying man should have helped in the birth of a baby. His last words before he collapsed and died were: "The woman struggled and now I must struggle".[54]

Unlighted Lamps ends with "unresolved relationships and incompletely lived lives",[55] as Papinchak remarks. The hunger of both father and daughter for love remains unsatisfied. What makes their story poignant is that, when both are about to reach a point of understanding, resolve to make amends and make up for what they had missed in life till then, and reach out to emotional attachment they should be denied the only opportunity for fulfillment. The "forgotten cigarette" the doctor held between his fingers at the time of his death, from which faint light "danced up and down in the darkness",[56] perfectly symbolizes the life he had lived ever between light and darkness but always in the dimness of a shadow. Both father and daughter fail to penetrate their isolation. Mary seeks love and understanding from her father. Had Duke Yetter the crude young man who was moving heaven and earth to win her had been a different man, she probably would not have repulsed him. At the end like her father she too is alone, lost and unfulfilled.

The story works by several contrasts, the most apparent being the contrast between the buried and unlived lives of Dr. Cochran and Mary, the father and daughter, and the vibrant and spontaneous lives of the town people, particularly the immigrant labourers through whose section of the town Mary passes in her lonely walk into the country. Supporting this contrast, and of day fading into evening, all of which blend together...to form a single impression of unfulfilled potential".[57]

Out of Nowhere into Nothing, the very last of the stories in the volume *The Triumph of the Egg,* is a very long tale like *An Ohio Pagan.* It is in fact a short novel rather than a short story, it seems needlessly and tiresomely long. The omniscient third person narrative is prolix and meanders. There are inadequately prepared shifts of points of view and attention is divided. The flashbacks are rather abrupt and not always well connected. As a result the focus gets blurred and an otherwise intense and poignant story of three different people who struggle hard but in vain to make sense of their lives, gets diluted. It fails to convey the sense of compelling urgency felt by the protagonist Rosalind Wescott who is faced with a challenging crisis in her life and has to choose between two difficult alternatives. This story illustrates how Anderson is more at home in the limited compass of a short story than a long tale. Rex Burbank rightly regards it as inferior to *Unlighted Lamps.*[58]

The title, *Out of Nowhere into Nothing,* gives the essence of the story which presents another variation of the theme of unlived, unfulfilled, emotionally deprived and buried life. Loneliness and isolation are a recurrent refrain in it. As in all the stories of Anderson, the interest here is psychological and lies in the probing of the interior of the consciousness of the characters, their hopes, expectations, and confusions, rather than in outward events, which are few. *Out of Nowhere into Nothing* is mainly the story of Rosalind Westcott, a young woman of twenty-seven who is beautiful, strong, vital somewhat romantic in her temperament and in search of freedom and fulfillment.it is her lot to draw a blank despite her endeavours. The focus of the narrative is chiefly on her. There is another character, Melville Stoner, a long-nosed bachelor who is past forty, who looks like a huge seabird, alternatively like a vulture. He is Rosalind's next-door neighbor in her home town Willow Springs, Iowa. He is very much a lonely man but assumes the role of a reflective observer of life and people. In spite of the mischievous twinkle in his eye, there is sadness deep down in him and a sense of failure. Stoner is a forceful personality. In some respects he and Rosalind are kindred spirits in the sense that they are sensitive, imaginative but lonely and feel isolated from others though for different reasons. Both crave for freedom and grope for meaning in their respective lives but with little success. There is yet another character in the story, Walter Sayers, who in comparison with the other two seems rather a pathetic soul totally wanting individuality. He too is lonely and frustrated. A timid man that he is, he is convinced that he is a defeated man in life, born only to be defeated. He is Rosalind's employer in Chicago. He is thirty-eight, married, and has a couple of children. It is Rosalind's involvement with him that plunges her into an un resolvable dilemma and creates a crisis in her life. Marriage with him is out of the question. It is Sayer's suggestion that she could be his mistress.

The narrative begins with Rosalind Wescott's coming home to Willow Springs from Chicago unannounced after a gap of several years, and ends with her equally abrupt and unannounced departure to Chicago after a three-day stay.

Her ruminations during that short interval, her fears and misgivings, her hopes and expectations about her relations with Sayers, her unexpected encounter with her neighbor Stoner, her disappointment with homecoming, her unsuccessful attempts to resolve the crisis in her life-these fill the interval between her arrival and departure. Apparently she came home because she was "homesick", but actually she had come hoping to be able to talk with her mother about the crisis in her life and seek her advice. She wanted to think over Sayer's proposal as a way to find meaning in her life. At Chicago she "hadn't been able to talk with anyone"[59] about this problem. To clarify the issues involved in the lives of the chief characters, attempt is made in the following paragraphs to reconstruct in a linear fashion their story and also analyze their characters. As in the analysis of the other stories of Anderson, some form of retelling the story in a linear and connected form is unavoidable here, to draw attention to what goes on in the mind of each character.

Rosalind had been a city woman for the past six years and had changed. Having come home with expectations she felt rather disappointed. Willow Springs, a rather meaningless, dreary town at any time, now appeared to her "more dreary" largely because of the disturbed state of her mind.[60] The monotonous sameness of life at home, and her father and mother going about their daily chores mechanically, got on her nerves. "Everything in the house was just as it had always been".[61] Conversation with her taciturn mother-her father hardly spoke and when he did, felt awkward-was dull and consisted of the routine questions about her life in Chicago. Rosalind began to wonder whether she really wanted to tell her mother about her problem. She found it difficult to stay at home all the time with them. She did not go to meet her friends either, as she was conscious of the gap between herself and them. Instead she hurried away out of the town to walk along the railroad tracks and beyond t recall and reflect on the course her life had taken particularly since she graduated from the high school at Willow Springs.

The three years after her schooling until she was twenty-one were "trying" years of "wanting" at home "waiting for something", like other young women of her age. "There was nothing to do but wait", but what for, neither she nor they knew. Some of them had young men friends who visited them "Others joined the church, went to prayer meetings, became active members of some church organisation".[62] They fussed about but Rosalind had none of these. She was very much alone, at home as well as outside, "strangely nervous, eager for something to happen that never would happen".[63] She filled her waking hours with day-dreams of people of all ages; but they were all moving away from her, underlining her listless loneliness, she received little help from her father and mother who lived in their own world. If they gave any thought to their daughter, it remained unexpressed.

A chance had taken Rosalind to Chicago. Her only brother who lived there asked her to visit him and his wife. Having gone there she stayed on, learnt stenography took lessons in acting, acquired other skills and worked in more than one office. She was glad to be away from Willow Springs. Chicago might be no more than "a big noisy dirty village" but there was "something alive there'. And occasionally she saw men or at least heard of men who "had kept some precious thing alive in themselves". She felt that "she had learned a little something of life".[64] During the weekends she like many other young people went to places seeking excitement, saw new faces and colorful crowds, and saw men and women together. She was awakened out of the torpor of her hometown. But she also became "hungry" like others, "hungry for companionship", and "wanted to possess—a man—, be sure of him,— own him".[65] She also read books which she could not have read at Willow Springs. Some of them claimed that "sex" held the "key—to the secret chamber of life" and if one understood sex all the mystery surrounding life would be untangled.[66] But Rosalind soon got tired of such books and "the subject". Her question was, 'would it solve her problems of loneliness? She had felt alone in Willow Springs, and continued to feel it in Chicago too: "If the sex impulse within had been gratified, in what way would my problem be solved? I am lonely now. It is evident that after that had happened I would still lonely".[67] Rosalind train of thought indicates that she had grown. What she wanted was love, someone who loved her and whom she could love.

Rosalind's life took a new turn when she became the secretary of Walter Sayers, who was treasurer of a piano factory. She made his acquaintance "at just the time when her awakening became a half realized thing". "For the first time she became really interested in the work that ate up her days".[68] She felt that she was no longer a drifter form office to office in Chicago, moving from rooming house to rooming house, "striving feebly to find something about life by reading books, going to the theatre and walking alone in the streets. In the new place her life at once began to have point and purpose".[69] In Sayer's presence she became articulate and the talks with him "had awakened her"."She felt they had made her a woman, had matured her".[70] Obviously Sayers seemed to have met one of her most deeply felt needs. In turn, Sayers also found in hr one who brought cheer to his dreamy life, self-confidence and much needed moral support in addition to love. But their reciprocal need threw them, Rosalind in particular, into a "perplexity" which sent her running to her mother for advice and support.

Walter Sayers was a slender, rather small man of thirty-eight, his eyes always clouded and troubled. Temperamentally he was unfitted for the task of treasurer of the company and made costly mistakes. He did not inherit any fortune. He owed his position in the company to his wife whose money had been invested in the business. His ambition was to be a singer but his voice was not large enough to enable him to make singing his profession. He gave up music, and even apparently surrendered his interest in it, going against his grain. His attempts to build up interest in his work had not been successful. Very much unlike him, his wife Cora seemed self-sufficient. She was quite happy, satisfied with her life and herself and was completely absorbed in raising flowers and vegetables in her garden with the help of a young negro gardener. She derived a sensuous delight from this work and talked glowingly about it. Her enthusiasm only irritated Sayers. Slow fires of hatred of his wife began to burn beneath the surface of his life eating away his vigour and energy. Very much of an introvert that he was, impotent rage possessed him. To escape from his house, is wife, her talk, her garden, and her eternal planning, he tried to cultivate an interest in photography and vanish with his camera into the woodlands during the weekends. Even this strategy would not work, because his heart was not in it and he was cheating himself. "He did not want to be a photographer. He had once wanted to be a singer".[71] In the frustration, he smashed his camera to pieces.

There was little conversation between Sayers and his wife. He was given to a lot of brooding about his failures in life, and to self-pitying. When he thought of his wife, he did not want to be unfair to her enthusiasms. But he envied her little triumphs in the backyard garden. He felt that she was very possessive, and possessed him as she possessed the garden. He could not but surrender to her. Indulging in self-pity, he felt that in his wife's eyes he was no more than a weed she plucked and threw out or a vegetable she was determined to grow there in its place. He had no right to exist otherwise and be himself. "Something was plucked out of him and another thing grew in its place-something she wanted to have grow".[72] When he smashed his camera to pieces and felt as though a song had suddenly come between his lips, it was his helpless protest against his wife's hold on him in a life with little fragrance of love in it, and his timid effort to assert his self.

Rosalind entered the life of Walter just about the time he was in this confused and perplexed state, and she extended a hand to grasp. Before long they ceased to be the conventional employer and employee in their relations. In her presence the silent brooding introvert became articulate. He found in her one "to whom he could talk, to whom he wanted to talk", and felt that he in turn had "opened" the "doors of life" for her.[73] In her presence the habitual tenseness of his body relaxed and he felt relieved. He fell into a confessional mood and told her of his failed ambition to be a singer and his having to give up music altogether. He would not, he told her; blame his wife and children for it. They could perhaps have lived without him, but he a "defeated man" "could not have lived without them". For he was "a dependent" and "needed something to cling to".[74] Surprisingly in Rosalind's presence Sayer's music seemed to return to him, though he had believed that he could never be a singer. In her company he felt: like a new man in a new world" and could burst into song.[75] She was happy and proud too and thought that she had given him the courage to sing.[76] The two wanted to be lovers and had discussed the issue but could not resolve it. It was a struggle for both. Sayers was "honest enough in fighting off the intensification of their relationship".[77] He had told her that it would not work out but would bring unnecessary unhappiness to them. But in Rosalind the struggle continued and he knew about it. He also knew that she had abruptly gone to her mother for counsel and support. As for himself, he need her very much and at the same time in a half-hearted way wished that she never came back,[78] because the situation was hopeless.

About the same time as Walter Sayers was worrying himself over his plight, Rosalind too, who had been walking away from her mother's house, and walking along the rail track, was thinking of him and the problems that had brought her to her mother. She was also revolving in her mind the people whom she knew in Willow Springs. In particular she was thinking of her immediate neighbor Melville Stoner, a bachelor, who lived alone and had none to keep the house for him. He was thirty-five when she went away to the city: "He had a long, hawk-like nose and his hair was long and uncombed".[79] This man who was grotesque in appearance was also a "grotesque" in his mental makeup (the Andersonian sense), as Rosalind was to discover soon. Occasionally he used to greet her when she sat alone on the front porch, when their eyes met. She had thought about him at times. Otherwise there was no contact or conversation or communication with him. Generally he kept himself to himself. He did not work anywhere as he had a small income. He ate his meals in a hotel. On some days he was seen sitting all day in a chair reading a book. As Rosalind walked along she stumbled upon Melville Stoner, the very man she was just then thinking about.

Stoner struck her as an unusual person, the like of him she had not met anywhere. Frank, uninhibited but never crude in his speech Stoner was in some ways childlike and spoke what he felt. She was surprised that as a young man he had thought of her for quite sometime as she herself had about him and wanted to know more about her: "—it's nothing specially personal, my wanting to get at you and understand you a little, I'm that way about everyone. Perhaps that's the reason I live alone, why I've never married or had personal friends. I'm too eager—"[80] Rosaling ws caught by this new view point. Her surprise was greater when he said that they both really had been friends because they "have had the same thoughts", although they had hardly spoken to each other. Sensitive observant and imaginative, Stoner could imaginatively enter into the minds and thoughts of others. He could tell Rosalind what her father and mother thought and did everyday. She felt that perhaps he could invade or had already invaded the secrets of her mind. She felt fascinated and frightened by his talk. It was strange that one who had such gifts of mind and understanding had been alone, lonely and had not chosen to come close to any other person or marry. He was tired of the dullness and stupidity of life whether in the city or in a small town, and the eternal sameness of talk there.

Like Walter Sayers, Stoner too became articulate in Rosalind's presence and spoke to her confessingly, but without any trace of self-pity like Walter Sayers, of his futile struggle to overcome his loneliness: "Sometimes I forget to eat. I read books all day, striving to forget myself and then night comes and I cannot sleep".[81] That was not all. Sometimes unable to endure it, he grew to "hat" himself and felt like running out of town. This experience was so bewildering that during one winter he feared he was "going insane". He walked into an orchard and buried his head in the frozen grass where bees crawled drunk with a kind of "ecstasy". They reminded him of what he had missed in his life: "The bees were in an ecstasy of life and I had missed life. I have always missed life. It always goes away from me. I always imagined people walking away".[82] Rosalind was so much moved by his despair that she felt an irresistible desire to touch his hand and shout that she was there very much. But instead she stood string silently at him. Stoner who had recovered in the meanwhile laughed it off, making her wonder whether he was not laughing at her. However meeting him unexpectedly and talking to him while walking back home with him, made her feel relaxed and free as if she had found something, which she could not find at home. Stoner had made an impact on her, although their meeting lasted for a couple of hours only. She had discovered that he was, far from being a dull citizen of a dreary town, one who knew a great deal about life. He had opened up for her a new world of thought and gave her hope that she could understand people, including her father and mother. She felt that she could understand the reason for Stoner's being what he had become: he had not opened the locked gateway of love. If one could do that, Rosalind thought, "Life might after all be a rich, triumphant thing",[83] not ugly and dirty as it once had seemed to her: She had tasted the love of a man. She felt now confident that she could approach her mother to discuss her problem, for which she had come to Willow Springs.

As a young girl it was Rosalind's habit to go to the orchard nearby to sit leaning against an apple tree and daydream about the "white wonder of life". Now as a grown mature woman she looked at the world differently. Her life of loneliness in Chicago, and her relationship with Walter

Sayers had brought about a change in her outlook. And her present unexpected meeting with Melville Stoner and the couple of hours spent with him had added another dimension to her perception. But when she looked at her mother's heavy, sagging face at the supper table, her confidence to approach her mother sank a little. Her tenseness was back again. She retired to the orchard to sit in the shadow to sort out her thoughts. The spirit of Walters Sayers and Melville Stoner dominated her mind. They seemed to approach. She asked herself whether she suddenly had begun to love two men, both older than herself.[84] Both, she felt, had a knowledge of life and death that she did not have.

Calling a halt to her thoughts Rosalind returned to her mother who was waiting for her daughter in the porch. Now was the opportunity to tell her about her love for Walter Sayers and her wish to offer herself to him. Having told her story, she felt relieved, and waited in silence for her mother's reaction. She lay tense and still at her feet, her lively mind active once again with disturbing thoughts. She already wondered if what she told her mother could be quite true. For "her own desires and impulses were not clearly realized within herself". "Men had always confused" her. Could she not get what she wanted in life in some sort of communion with another woman, her mother for instance?[85] What did men and women want from each other? Was it their fate to be consumed: women by men and men by women? She thought of the two men whose spirits seemed to be hovering around her. Of them, Stoner seemed "bold and cunning". He was too close to her, knew too much of her. He was unafraid".[86] There was no escape from him. He would invade her secret thoughts and mockingly laugh at her. She felt afraid of him, and wished that he could be destroyed with a thought. She forcibly pushed the figure of Stoner from her mind. But no sooner was he out than Walter Sayers came in. He seemed gentle, a man of understanding, less aggressive and less assertive. When he sang sweet solace had come to her, she had suddenly become alive and life coursed through her body.

"Song was the true note of life, it was the triumph of life over death".[87] It was after listening to his song which was about life and death, defeating each other forever, that she had decided to come closer to him. "It was in expressing physically her love for the man she would find the white of life—which as a clumsy and crude girl, she had dreamed".[88]

At long last Rosalind's taciturn mother broke the tense silence and spoke in a weeping, choked voice. She muttered over and over again, "God, Rosalind, don't do it, don't do it".[89] It was, as much a test to her as it was to her daughter. Hr brief reply seemed to condense all the sadness, anguish disillusions, defeat, failure and frustration she had gone through in he married life. She was convinced that what she had experienced would be the fate of all women. She could not tell her daughter all that she wanted to say. In brief, there was no such thing as love; the word was a "lie"; life "perpetuated itself by the lie called love"; sex was "sin" and both men and women were condemned to commit the sin which destroyed them"; "men only hurt women" because they were made that way; letting a man touch her dirtied a woman; and finally, "There is no love. Life is a lie, It leads to sin, to death and decay".[90] Mrs. Wescott gave vent though incoherently to all the despair and frustration she had bottled up over the years. Hers too was an unlived, defeated and unfulfilled life. in a different way Henry Wescott too lived a lonely, defeated and unfulfilled life.

Rosalind did not get the understanding and support she expected from her mother. Instead she warned her daughter not only against her lover employer but against all men. Rosalind could not accept her mother's view of men. The song Walter had sung about life and death, sung by a man, did not sound like a lie to her. And there was Melville Stoner, another male, in whom too "was singing the song of life and death". The same song was singing within herself too.[91] All these confused her. She felt a little embarrassed that Stoner must have overheard the conversation between her and her mother and known all that passed between them. but a new resolution rose in her. Her mind became alert and quick, driving out the dead cold weariness that had gripped her. Rosalind decided to return to Chicago at once without telling anyone. Instead of waiting for the train at Willow Springs, she chose to walk to the next town eight miles away, so that she would get out of town first. To be on the move would give her something do. As if Melville Stoner had read her thoughts, he met hr at the gate. She was glad to meet him. For it was he "who lifted—Willow Springs up out of the shadow of death. Words were unnecessary. With him she had established the thing beyond words, beyond passion-the fellowship in living, the fellowship in life".[92] He held out the promise of life to hr. they walked together to the town's edge. He declined her invitation to go with her, and with a laugh before turning back he said: "I'll stay here. My time for going passed long ago. I'll stay here until I die—with my thoughts".[93] His plea was that he was too old to give up his passive role.

In declining to grasp the extended hand of Rosalind, Stoner, though tired to the marrow with the loneliness of his life, was resigning himself to it and would not use the opportunity to establish a permanent contract with another fellow being.[94] Probably he thought that it would be a futile exercise. Apparently he wanted to be a freeman, and craved for freedom as much as Rosalind. But in preferring to stay back, probably he thought that such freedom was not possible. When he walked with her along the rail track, it seemed to her that he resembled "a sea-bird stranded a inland".[95] This image of a stranded sea bird, as Rex Burbank points out, symbolically suggests that "Stoner is a caged spirit".[96] With Stoner's going back, Rosalind went forward swiftly, now running and now walking. In coming away from her hometown she had thrown off the town and her rather ad her mother", as one would throw off "a heavy and unnecessary garment". "Her body tingled with life. She did not ask herself what she was going to do" and how she would meet the problems which had brought her to hr mother.[97] She simply ran forward into a faint streak of light which seemed to became more distinct as she ran further. She half wished that she might run on forever through the land, cities and towns driving darkness away.[98]

With Rosalind running with a sense of joy towards light the long story ends. Where would she go since she cannot be running eternally, remains a question for which the story does not give any clue. There is no answer to her question, 'should she agree to be Walter Sayer's mistress or not. Before she went to meet her mother she very much wanted to give herself up to him. As Rex Burbank has pertinently remarked, "before she leaves for Chicago, Rosalind establishes an almost mystical 'fellowship in life' with Stoner, but Anderson gives us no indication that all the impressions that have come to her since leaving Chicago have added up to anything more than a kind of aimless groping or to nay understanding of life".[99] She is left confused as the insight into life she sought eludes her. In her search for a solution to her problem Rosalind ends where she began: *Out of Nowhere into Nothing*. Like Elsie Leander (*The New Englander*) and the unnamed woman in Seeds, she too is trapped within herself. They are "unable to satisfy the demands of their inner imaginative lives for communication with others".[100] Effectively it becomes a buried life, despite the fact that like Elizabeth Willard, Kate Swift and other women created by Anderson, Rosalind too is intensely alive, more aware and sensitive than those about her.

One of Anderson's own favourite stories and generally acknowledged as one of his most significant and accomplished short stories and supreme achievements, and a classic among American short stories, *The Egg* could have been studied along with Anderson's stories of growth and development towards adulthood, considered in Chapter Four. For, the narrator of this story as an adult recalls in disturbed tranquility and reflects upon a profoundly disconcerting incident of his boyhood in which he, his father and mother were involved, and which initiated his education in human defeat and the futility of human attempts to explain the inexplicable.

However, *The Egg* is chiefly the tragic story of the unlived and defeated life of his father and of course that of his mother in which their ambitions are thwarted by shattered dreams based on false hopes. Therefore in the present analysis of the story the focus is on the narrator's father, who is essentially a simple man, naïve and pathetic whose ambition prods him into a situation he cannot control and thus brings about his spiritual destruction.[101]

The Egg is a seemingly humorous story. Superficially, it is t the story of a grotesque, who is incapable of the kind of success his society expects and respects, making comic and ridiculous attempts to give the public what he thinks it wants. But it is a complex story, in which Anderson probes beneath the surface of the seemingly humorous and ridiculous to know what makes man a grotesque. Even a bare outline of the story of *The Egg* can be "appalling", as Irving Howe[102] has remarked. It begins as a first person retrospective narrative, in which the narrator recalls his father and mother and their contrasting personalities, which led the ultimate conflict. His father, "intended by nature to be a cheerful, kindly man", was contented with the farmhand's life and its harmless and simple pleasures of social intercourse with other farmhands, glasses of beer, and song. He was "quite happy in his position in life" and had "no notion of trying to rise in the world".[103] In his thirty-fifth year he married a country school teacher who had high hopes "They became ambitious. The American passion for getting up in the world took possession of them".[104] Perhaps the narrator's mother who had read a number of books about Americans rising from poverty to fame and greatness, was responsible for their ambitions. This tall silent woman did not want anything for herself but was incurably ambitious for her husband and son. All the miseries and defeats of their lives stemmed from it. The two business endeavours of the family- a chicken farm and a restaurant led to the family's downfall.

As a first step towards becoming wealthy the father gave up his position as farm-hand, and both husband and wife bought a chicken farm and launched into chicken rising. Here, as Irving Howe remarks, "the image of the egg, which is to dominate the story with a crazy and malevolent exuberance appears'.[105] It was during the years of poultry farming that the father collected malformed baby chicks-four-legged two-headed and double-winged grotesques-and preserved these monstrous things in alcohol as valuable treasure. Having struggled for ten years in vain to make the chicken farm pay, the family moved away to a railroad junction at Pickleville near the town of Bidwell to embark on the restaurant business. Thus the discouraged chicken farmer graduated to restaurant keeping. It was again the mother's idea and she was confident that it would be profitable since travelling trains would come to the restaurant. She was ambitious for her son and wanted him "to rise in the world, to get into a town school and become a man of the towns".[106] The father carried with him to Pickleville his grotesque treasure of deformed and dead chicks. It was his firm belief that people liked to look at strange and wonderful things. Therefore in the restaurant "the grotesques in their little glass bottles sat on a shelf back of the counter".[107]

Both father and mother worked very hard, as they had always done, in their new venture. The mother decided that the restaurant should remain open at night to cater to those who came by the evening and early morning trains. A little trade began to grow up. Even the father, possessed by the American spirit of success, became ambitious. He believed that in the past he has unsuccessful because he was not cheerful enough. He conceived the idea of making the restaurant a social centre for the neighboring young people. He and his wife should adopt a cheerful outlook on life, engage the visiting customers with "bright and entertaining conversation", and create "the jolly innkeeper effect",[108] This strategy, he liked to believe, would surely bring him success, fame and fortune. If his wife had any reservations about it, she did not express them. The father thus strove to be entertainer as well as host to attract customers. As he believed that people "liked to look at strange and wonderful things". The grotesques, the bottled aberrations he had so carefully treasured, were placed on a shelf back of the counter as show pieces.[109] Thus a weird element is introduced into the narrative which foreshadows the futility of his attempts to succeed.

Everyone in the family tried earnestly to impress the customers. Smiles took the place of glum looks. The father became feverish in his anxiety to please, and waited for a young man or woman from Bidwell to show what he could do. The wire basket on the counter filled with eggs must have given him the idea of entertaining his guests with a trick or two he could play with eggs. The narrator cryptically remarks: "At any rate an egg ruined his new impulse in life".[110]

It all happened late one night, and the father's dream burst, shattered to pieces, when he hectically tried to entertain a young customer by showing him a trick with an egg. Joe Kane, a young man, son of a merchant of Bidwell, whom the father had not seen before, came to Pickleville to meet his father who was expected by the ten o' clock train. As the train was late by several hours the young man came into the restaurant to loaf about and wait for its arrival. With the other customers going away, Joe was left alone with the father, who was somewhat nervous because confronted by the situation he had wished for so often, he did not know how to proceed. His eyes lighting on the basket of eggs, he began his conversation with the young man, insisting that Christopher Columbus was a cheat because he falsely claimed to be able to make an egg stand on its head. What he actually did was merely a trick. The father, who misunderstood the point of the anecdote about Columbus and the egg-mattered and swore and still grumbling at Columbus, claimed that he could actually make the egg stand without breaking its shell and without any trickery. To the visitor, he seemed mildly insane. After half an hour's trial and effort he did succeed in making the egg stand for a moment. But he found that the visitor was no longer watching him or his feat. Meanwhile the egg had rolled over and lay on its side.

A good deal disconcerted by the failure of his effort, the father with a showman's passion, tried to show his visitor the poultry monstrosities in the bottles he had treasured. The sight of the deformed bodies only made Joe a little ill, and he got up to go. But the father led him back to his set, and suppressing his anger offered to show him another trick. He heated in vinegar an egg and began hastily squeezing it through the neck of an empty bottle even before the egg had been sufficiently softened. He struggled for a long time in vain. He heated the egg again in vinegar and was back at the bottle to push the egg into it. "He worked and worked and a spirit of desperate determination took possession of him".[111] He was angry with the visitor because he did not show sufficient interest in the trick he was struggling to perform. When he thought that at last he was about to accomplish the trick, ill starred as he was, something untoward happened. The delayed train for which Joe was waiting, came in at the station, "and Joe kane started to go nonchalantly out at the door". Making a last desperate effort to make the egg "do the thing that would establish his reputation as one who knew how to entertain his guests", the father who was in panic worried the egg roughly. "The egg broke under his hand" and "the contents spurted over his clothes". The different guest who saw this "laughed".

The father roared in anger and exasperation. "He danced and shouted a string of inarticulate words".[112] In his wrathful acknowledgement of the utter frustration of his ambitions and humiliation of his defeat, he hurled another egg at Joe, just missing the head of the young man as he dodged through the door and escaped".[113] Then the defeated father went upstairs to his wife. There was a half insane light in his eyes, as though he intended to hurl an egg at his wife and son the narrator. But he gently laid the egg on the nearby table and began to cry like a boy, seeking refuge and compassion in his wife. The egg had finally triumphed over him and the family. The narrator, who recalls this incident of his boyhood, sympathizes with his father. Comic as the father's efforts are to triumph over the egg, the son cannot laugh at his ridiculous attempts because he senses that they only compound his father's frustration. He can do nothing but speculate on the causes of his father's despair.

It is possible to read *The Egg* profitably as a "burlesque of American salesmanship", as Horace Gregory has remarked.[114] But there is far more in it than a parody of a favorite American ideal. Anderson does not write from the condescending stance of 'social consciousnesses'. In Anderson's sympathetic portrayal of the father in the story, it is possible to see "a poignant gesture of filial reconciliation", in sharp contrast to his portrayals of fathers in other stories (for example, George Willard's fathers in Winesburg, Ohio). But as Irving Howe has pointed out, the larger significance of the story: "the story must finally be read, not primarily as a social portrait or a filial gesture, but as a parable of human defeat".[115] The narrator's father, who is triumphed over by the egg, becomes typical of all frail human beings who are defeated in life, and who live frustrated, unfulfilled and unlived lives. It is as if defeat is at the very heart of human life. But in the present story, in which the egg is the most pervasive controlling metaphor and symbol, it appears "less as a symbol of creativity and renewal than as a token of all the energy in the universe-arbitrary, unmotivated, ridiculous and malevolent-against which man must pit himself".[116] The father in the story is not merely defeated but tricked in his defeat. His very legitimate hunger shared by his wife to live and prosper in life becomes the source of their humiliation and loneliness.

The irony at the heart of the central episode of the story is that the egg "a maddeningly fragile, refractory and intractable thing in itself",[117] brings about the humiliation and defeat of the father and exposes the same qualities in his life. Nature has its ways of solving deformities easily. If an egg produces a deformed, grotesque chicken the misshapen creature dies. But man the grotesque, whose most serious deformity is spiritual", lives on and is prevented from attaining fulfillment,[118] though he makes futile and frustrating efforts.

The Egg is a grim story about the riddle of life itself, which ultimately appears to be despairing and tragic. It's easy pace of narration and mildly wry tone conceals the view of human life underlying it. The "peculiar virtue" of the story is that "while each paragraph seems comic its total effect is one of great pathos", as Irving Howe[119] has observed. It is remarkable for its artistry. Rex Burbank has the most perceptive comment on the art of this story in which "Anderson achieves perhaps the most nearly perfect blending of contrasting moods and tones, of absurdity and pathos, symbol and object, and action and theme he was ever to accomplish. Nothing in (it) is extraneous to its meaning: nothing in its meaning may be extracted from the facts of narrative—symbol, object, tone, mood, and diction merge in the theme of the defeat of a diffident little man by a world too complicated for him".[120]

All the five stories of adult men and women studied in this chapter, the chief characters in different ways experience defeat and failure. Their lives are wasted as their potentialities; their gifts of imagination and human sensitivity are either crushed or go untapped. The business of life becomes much too complex and complicated for them to grasp. They struggle in vain for fulfillment. The view of human life that emerges from these stories are discouraging if not pessimistic. The rays of light and hope that one could see at the close of Winesburg, Ohio become dim and one is left with a sense of puzzlement.

NOTES AND REFERENCES

1. Rex Burbank, Sherwood Anderson (New York: Twayne, 1964), p. 88.
2. The New Englander, The Triumph of the Egg [New York: B.W.Huebsch,1921], pp.134-135.

3. *Ibid.*, pp. 135-136.
4. *Ibid.*, p. 136.
5. Ibid., p. 137.
6. *Ibid.*, p. 138.
7. *Ibid.*, p. 139.
8. *Ibid.*, p. 141.
9. *Ibid.*, p. 143.
10. *Ibid.*, p. 144.
11. *Ibid.*, pp. 145-146.
12. *Ibid.*, p. 146.
13. *Ibid.*, p. 147.
14. *Ibid.*, p. 151.
15. *Ibid.*
16. *Ibid.*, p. 152.
17. *Ibid.*, pp. 154-155.
18. *Ibid.*, p. 156.
19. Ibid., p. 158.
20. *Ibid.* p. 159.
21. Brom Weber, Anderson and "The Essence of Things", *Critical Essays on Sherwood Anderson,* ed. David D. Anderson [Boston: G.K. Hall and Company, 1981] p. 133.
22. *Seeds,* Triumph of the Egg, p. 32.
23. *Ibid.*, p. 23.
24. *Ibid.*, p. 24.
25. *Ibid.*, p. 23.
26. Rex Burbank, pp. 107-108.
27. *Seeds,* Triumph of the Egg, p. 25.
28. *Ibid.*, p. 26.
29. *Ibid.*, p. 28.
30. *Ibid.*
31. *Ibid.*, p. 29.
32. *Ibid.*, pp. 29-30.
33. *Ibid.*, pp. 30-31.
34. *Ibid.*, p. 31.

35. *Ibid*.
36. *Unlighted Lamps,* The Triumph of the Egg, pp. 65-66.
37. *Ibid.*, p. 66.
38. *Ibid.*, p. 67.
39. *Ibid.*, p. 81.
40. *Ibid.*, p. 82.
41. *Ibid.*, pp. 84-85.
42. *Ibid.*, p. 85.
43. *Ibid.*, p. 70.
44. *Ibid.*, p. 69.
45. *Ibid.*, p. 78.
46. *Ibid.*, p. 79.
47. *Ibid.*, pp. 79-80.
48. Ibid., p. 85.
49. *Ibid.*, p. 86.
50. *Ibid.*, p. 88.
51. *Ibid.*, p. 89.
52. *Ibid.*, p. 90.
53. *Ibid.*, p. 91.
54. *Ibid.*, p. 92.
55. Robert Allen Papinchak, Sherwood Anderson [New York: Twayne publishers, 1992], p. 47.
56. *Unlighted Lamps*. The Triumph of the Egg. p. 92.
57. Rex Burbank, p. 90.
58. Robert Mores Lovett, on the Other Hand, Regards this Story as "a Triumphant Witness to Anderson's Mastery of the Short Story form". See Papinchak, p. 102.
59. *Out of Nowhere into Nothing,* The Triumph of the Egg, p. 171.
60. *Ibid.*, p. 175.
61. *Ibid.*, p. 173.
62. *Ibid.*, p. 176.
63. *Ibid.*, p. 177.
64. *Ibid.*, p. 183.
65. *Ibid.*, p. 202.
66. *Ibid.*, p. 203.

67. *Ibid.*, p. 205.
68. *Ibid.*, p. 206.
69. *Ibid.*, p. 215.
70. *Ibid.*, p. 183.
71. *Ibid.*, p. 213.
72. *Ibid.*
73. *Ibid.*, p. 249.
74. *Ibid.*, p. 249.
75. *Ibid.*, p. 250.
76. *Ibid.*, pp. 250-251.
77. *Ibid.*, p. 225.
78. *Ibid.*, p. 221.
79. *Ibid.*, p. 180.
80. *Ibid.*, p. 189.
81. *Ibid.*, p. 190.
82. *Ibid.*, p. 193.
83. *Ibid.*, p. 200.
84. *Ibid.*, p. 246.
85. *Ibid.*, p. 251.
86. *Ibid.*, p. 252.
87. *Ibid.*, p. 254.
88. *Ibid.*, pp. 254-255.
89. *Ibid.*, p. 258.
90. *Ibid.*, pp. 258-261.
91. *Ibid.*, p. 263.
92. *Ibid.*, p. 265.
93. *Ibid.*
94. Paul Rosenfield, Sherwood Anderson, Critical Essays on Sherwood Anderson, p. 78.
95. *Out of Nowhere into Nothing,* The Triumph of the Egg, p. 266.
96. Rex Burbank, p. 92.
97. *Out of Nowhere into Nothing,* The Triumph of the Egg, p. 266.
98. *Ibid.*, p. 267.
99. Rex Burbank, p. 93.

100. *Ibid.*, p. 89.
101. Irving Howe, Sherwood Anderson [New York, Wm .Sloane Associates, 1951], p. 170.
102. *Ibid.*, p. 168.
103. *The Egg,* The Triumph of the Egg, p. 46.
104. *Ibid.*
105. Irving Howe, p. 168.
106. *The Egg,* The Triumph of the Egg, p. 53.
107. *Ibid.*, p. 52.
108. Ibid., p. 55.
109. *Ibid.*, p. 52.
110. *Ibid.*, p. 56.
111. *Ibid.*, p. 61.
112. *Ibid.*, p. 62.
113. *Ibid.*
114. Mentioned by Irving Howe, p. 170.
115. *Ibid.*
116. *Ibid.*, pp. 170-171.
117. Rex Burbank, p. 96.
118. David D. Anderson, Sherwood Anderson: An Introduction and Interpretation [New York:, Rinehart and Winston,1967], p. 64.
119. Irving Howe, p 171.
120. Rex Burbank, p 96.

CHAPTER – 7

By Way of Summing-up

With this chapter the present analytical study of Sherwood Anderson's short-stories from a thematic point of view draws to a close. Having traversed through more than twenty five of his short stories including the whole of Winesburg, Ohio, which are generally regarded as representative of his genius and achievement, it remains to recapitulate briefly by way of summing-up the main line of argument developed in the preceding chapters. However, it has to be stated at the outset that the present study has no claims to make either by way of new insights or startling discoveries. All that it has tried to do is to respond to Anderson's stories as sensitively as possible and understand his genius and achievement, taking help from accessible relevant published critical commentary on his work. As the number of the short stories chosen for analysis is considerable, the study has confined itself only to them exclusively, and some of Anderson's novels are barely mentioned in passing only, to keep the study from being unwieldy and unmanageable. For the same reason no attempt is made to compare Anderson with other writers of short fiction.

Anderson's distinction and achievement as a writer of short fiction, and his invaluable contribution to the American short story have been now generally recognized and acknowledged. He was a sort of pathfinder and brought in many changes into the American short story in themes, content, form, narrative technique and style, he also opened up fresh possibilities for other writers of his generation to follow. That such distinguished writers as Earnest Hemingway, William Faulkner and others are regarded by critics as among his "prize pupils" is enough testimony for his distinction and for the impress he has left on the short story. Though he tried his hand at other forms of writing, chiefly novels and confessional autobiographical narratives, he found his forte in the short story which most suited his creative genius. In his own practice he rejected as utterly inadequate and constricting the form of the short story with its 'poison plot' as he found it, and broke new ground to extend its scope and make it a flexible artistic medium to encompass fresh themes and new depths of feelings from everyday life in contemporary American society.

Anderson embarked on his career as a short story writer, as a mature man in his late thirties, eminently equipped in range and variety of experience of life to explore the possibilities and limitations of Mid-Western American life, which he knew firsthand. His creative endeavour was to probe, within the limits of the short story, beneath the surface of life and into the interior landscape of people's consciousness and articulate their unexpressed or half-expressed feelings and emotion, and states of mind. He thus brought to the short story an unprecedented psychological depth. He had triple concerns that every responsible writer should have: concern for life, for form and for the creative medium. He was more than usually sensitive to life in the society of his times, the rapid and far-reaching changes taking place in its everyday life and values. He was open to many and varied experiences of life and made this openness the central concern of all his writings. To explore and express everyday experiences, and recreate them imaginatively as fictional art in terms of appropriate form became his objective. He devised for his stories a seemingly formless form without an iron-clad plot structure, which however suggested the halting and hesitancies, surprise and gropings of life in its meandering flow. The ordering and organizing principle was psychological. This new form of the short story required a new way of telling it, a new idiom and narrative style. Drawing upon the native oral tradition of story telling, he forged a style generally simple, colloquial, unhurried in its pace, free from rhetorical flourishes but capable of giving authentic expression to his insights into the lives of the people he concerned himself with. Anderson's devotion and dedication to his art, over and above every other consideration, was total. His lasting allegiance was to it, and he rejected the purely materialistic and commercial values of his society.

Anderson found abundant material for his art in his rich and varied experiences of life in his hometown Clyde, Chicago and elsewhere, and in his sensitive observation of men and women. It is possible to relate certain characters and situations in his works to specific people known to him and incidents in his life. But Anderson rightly did not make the mistake of confusing biography with fiction. He recreated imaginatively in terms of fiction whatever he saw and experienced in his life. His focus was on ordinary humanity rather than the extraordinary or the heroic. He found eminently and meaningfully worthy source of material for his creative imagination in the ordinary and undistinguished lives of average people, whether in a small town or a metropolis, who generally were obscure, ignored, uncared for, disregarded as of no consequence by their own society. He was particularly drawn to those men and women who were naïve, simple, inhibited, frustrated, perplexed and confused, inarticulate and twisted out of shape in mind and spirit by forces beyond their control. He called such people "grotesques: in whom he found a measure f real humanity despite their oddities like the twisted and discarded apples in an orchard which still retained delicious sweetness in them.

Anderson was deeply moved by their yearnings, hopes and expectations, deprivations, unfulfilled aspirations, their incisive sense of loneliness, of being alone and isolated in a claustrophobic and tense environment, their inability to communicate, and their futile struggles to free themselves. He felt deeply concerned for them. He thought of them as distinct individuals struggling to live rather than as an amorphous group. He approached them with sympathy and compassion as one among them. He tried to understand their buried, inarticulate, and unfulfilled lives intuitively rather than from the outside according t any previously definite theory, philosophical. He was convinced that human lives were much too varied and complex to be compressed into a compact theory or idea in the abstract. This approach of Anderson's yielded him remarkable insights into the lives of those whom he called 'grotesque'. To portray their lives authentically in terms in terms of the art of fiction- in terms of the short-story in particular-was his constant effort. He was aware how challenging this task was. He found the themes for his fiction in the lives of these ordinary and average people.

As it happens in the works of most writers, certain themes preoccupy Anderson. He finds them to be of universal relevance in meaning and significance. They not only recur regularly in his short stories but they are all inter-connected, inter- dependent and intertwined. They form a complex as they overlap one another. The more pronounced of them are : loneliness and isolation, inarticulateness and failure of communication, potentialities thwarted, sense of frustration, and defeat, longing in vain for love, unfulfilled and unlived lives, breakdown of human relationships, false notions, outmoded conventions and taboos, groping for values in a confusing world, growth from adolescence towards maturity, and the complexities of sex. These and other themes are of universal interest, as people in other and different societies too have been experiencing them. Anderson considers these themes never in the abstract, but always in the context of the lives and experiences of individual men and women.

Of these several themes the most recurrent and pervasive in Anderson's stories is the theme of loneliness and isolation, the obverse and reverse of the same coin. It occurs virtually in most of his short stories in varying degrees of sharpness and emphasis. Anderson clearly perceives the complexity of the issue and realizes that it at once the cause and consequence of several human problems. Several of the characters he has created illustrative the point. Wing Biddlebaum of *Hands* in Winesburg, Ohio, a sensitive, imaginative and inspiring young teacher is condemned to a life of isolation and loneliness and mortal fear of persecution and premature old age, because the expressive gestures of his hands are grossly misunderstood and misinterpreted by the community. Largely because of the shortcomings of their own temperament and partly abetted by their environment and circumstances, Melville Stoner and Walter Sayers of *Out of Nowhere into Nothing* (The Triumph of the Egg) are lonely and isolated. Stoner, a sensitive thoughtful man, prefers to be a sort of recluse and refuses to have any active relationship with the community around him, even though his sense of loneliness is so oppressive to him that he fears that he may go mad. In sharp contrast to him is Walter Sayers who is an introvert, given to self-pitying, and believes that he is born to be defeated. Timid, cowardly, inarticulate, emotionally dependent, and longing for love which he does not always get, he tends to nourish his loneliness.

In between, there are many others in Anderson's world of fiction, both men and women, old and young, who experience loneliness and isolation in various degrees of incisiveness and intensity. Therefore it becomes the ground bass of his fiction. He explores it in terms of specific, concrete and subtle instances of particular individuals to show how it is not only pervasive in modern life but also twists and perverts sensitive men and women to make grotesques of them. Their lives are grossly impoverished, their gifts and potentialities for a normal and legitimately happy life are thwarted, and their hopes and aspirations are frustrated. Women in particular seem to have the worst share of it, Elizabeth Willard (*Mother* and *Hands*), Elsie Leander (*The New*

Englander), and the young women who is not given a name in Seeds, providing poignant instances of it. As there is great variety among Anderson's lonely and isolated characters, there is no repeat or monotony, The factors causing their loneliness are not only complex but vary from character to character. In his stories up to and including Winesburg, Ohio, Anderson implies that human isolation and loneliness stems largely form shortcomings of human nature and circumstantial pressures such as false values and beliefs, taboos and constricting conventions which betray insensitiveness to elementary human needs, want of understanding, sympathy and compassion, greed and indifference, and denial of love. These build apparently impenetrable and formidable walls between people frustrating all attempts at communication and understanding. However in some of his later post-Winesburg stories Anderson seems to view loneliness built into the human situation itself, although he does not care to advance any metaphysical explanation for it. He believes that however discouraging the situation, it is worth trying to understand, sympathise the empathise with others. The adventure of life lies here.

Anderson's stories on the theme of growth and development of adolescents towards maturity reveal his remarkable insight into the growing adolescent mind under circumstances and pressures, familial, social and cultural, which are not always conducive to a steady and healthy growth. He understands with sympathy the confusions, uncertainties, vague longings, desires and ambitions, and fears and apprehensions regarding incipient sexual urges experienced by the adolescents, and renders them convincingly in terms of fiction without any trace of the condescension, knowingness and complacency of an adult. Often he enables the adolescent protagonists to express themselves in their own idiom and language to reveal how they register their responds to the pressures they are exposed and come to terms with life. *I Want to Know Why* and *The Man Who Became a Women*, among others admirably, illustrative the point. They are acknowledged as among the best short stories of Anderson.

Anderson is deeply and continuously exercised over the turmoils, perplexities and confusions in the lives adult men and women, their vague longings and gropings, their frustration and disappointments and failures, while loneliness and isolation continues as a constant refrain of their lives. Several stories of Anderson's early and late, explore this universal theme. Imaginatively sensitively and insightfully Anderson has recreated their lives and experiences in such stories as *Unlighted Lamps, The New Englander, Out of Nowhere into Nothing* and *The Egg* and brings out their experience of suffocation, frustration, defeat and sense of emotionally crippled, wasted, unlived and buried life.

The relationship between married men and women, which continuously engages Anderson's creative attention, seems to have appeared to him to be almost always uncertain and problematic. Among his stories on this theme, there are far more instances of failed and disillusioned married life than really successful ones. Winesburg, Ohio has quite a few stories of failed marital relations for instance, (*Respectability, The Untold Lie,* and *Surrender*), the most poignant of them being the story of Elizabeth Willard, mother of George and wife of Tom Willard (*Mother* and *Death*). Among the post-Winesburg stories, *The Other Woman, The Door of the Trap, The Man's Story,* and *There She Is-She is taking Her Bath,* present the puzzling relationship between men and women before as well as after marriage, from different angles. *Mrs. Wife* among the stories of Anderson on this theme seems to be a solitary exception in the sense it successfully presents an enduring, stable and mature relationship between husband and wife built on real love. It deserves to be called a true love story.

In these stories in particular, and in other stories too, the role of sex in the relationship between men and women is [resented. It also figures conspicuously in the stories concerning the growth of adolescents towards maturity, in which the protagonists become uneasily aware of the growing sexual urges in them. Some of Anderson's first critics have found fault with him for dealing with these forbidden subjects.

In *Seeds,* one of the later stories, there is a direct reference to psycho-analysis in which Freud's concept of sex predominates. It has been questioned where from did Anderson derive his knowledge of the theories of sex and psychoanalysis, and how much of it did he owe to Freud. It would seem that Anderson's knowledge of Freudian theories came from secondhand sources. But, more importantly, intuitively he seems to have grasped the profound importance of sex in one's life, and in the relationship between men and women. He seems to have argued against the popular taboos against sex, and viewed it as a legitimate urge by properly gratifying which men and women might understand and communicate with each other meaningfully.

In conclusion, it has to be said that reading the short stories of Sherwood Anderson is an enlarging and enriching imaginative experience. They sharpen one's perceptions of the possibilities of life and deepens one's understanding of the eternally recurring human problems. They uphold in strict fictional and artistic terms the supreme value of love, compassion, sympathy and understanding over and above established conventions, ideas and beliefs. Anderson's reverential approach to human life, his determined refusal to project himself as reformer or world-betterer, his integrity as a writer of fiction, and his remarkable gift for providing insights into the lives of those neglected, average and ordinary many whom he significantly describes as "grotesques", all make his works of enduring value and universal appeal. In spite of the passage of time and changing circumstances, they have not lost their freshness not their relevance.

Bibliography

TEXTS OF SHERWOOD ANDERSON USED:

1. Winesburg, Ohio
2. Certain Things Last
3. Trimph of the Egg
4. Horses and Men
5. Death in the Woods

BOOKS ON SHERWOOD ANDERSON

1. Alridge, John: Critiques and essays on Modern Fiction (The Ronald Press Company, New York, 1952).
2. B.W. Huebsch: The Triumph of the Egg (B.W Huebsch, New York, 1921).
3. Brom Weber: Anderson and the essence of things. (G.K. Hall and Company, Boston, 1981).
4. Charles Child Walcutt: Sherwood Anderson: Impressionism and the Buried Life (University of North Carolina Press, Chapel Hill, 1966).
5. Charles E. Modlin: Certain Things Last, (Fourwalls and Eight Windows, New York, 1992).
6. Charles Child Walcutt: The Achievement of Sherwood Anderson: Essays in Criticism (University of North Carolina Press, Chapel Hill, 1966).

7. David D. Anderson: Sherwood Anderson An Introduction and Interpretation (Rinehart and Winston, New York, 1967).
8. David D. Anderson: Sherwood Anderson Moments of Insight (G.K Hall and Company, Boston, 1981).
9. David D. Anderson: Critical Essays on Sherwood Anderson (G.K. Hall and Co., Boston,1981).
10. David D. Anderson: The Grotesque and George Willard, Winesburg, Ohio: Text and Criticism (Penguin Books, England, 1977).
11. David D. Anderson: Critical Studies in American Literature (University of Karachi, Pakistan, 1964).
12. Duffey, Bernard: the Chicago Renaissance in American Letters (Mildniga State College Press, East Landing, 1954).
13. Edwin Fussel: Wineburg, Ohio: Art and Isolation (Virginia Quarterly Review of 1971).
14. Edwin and Robert Grabharm: Sherwood Anderson: the Modern Writer (The Michigan State College Press, East Lansing, 1954).
15. Erich Fromn: Escape from Freedom (Aaron Books, New York, 1967).
16. Erich Fromn: The Sane Voice: A Study of the Short Stories (Cleveland, 1963).
17. Frank O' Connor: The Lonely Voice: A Study of the Short Stories (Cleveland, 1963).
18. Geismer Maxwell: Sherwood Anderson: the Last of the Townsmen (Houghton Miffin, Boston, 1949).
19. George D. Murphy: The Theme of Sublimation in Anderson's Winesburg, Ohio (Modern Fiction Studies, Lonson, 1967).
20. Harcourt: Sherwood Anderson's Memoirs (Brace and Company, New York, 1942).
21. Henry Nash Smith: the American West as Symbol and Myth (Cambridge, 1950).

22. Howard M. Jones and Walter B. Rideout: The Letters of Sherwood Anderson (Boston, 1953).

23. Irving Howe: Sherwood Anderson (Wm, Sloane Associates, York, 1951).

24. Jarris A. Thurston: Technique in Winesburg, Ohio: Text and Criticism (Penguin Books, Hammonds Worth, 1996)

25. John H. Ferres: Winesburg, Ohio (Penguin Books, New York, 1966).

26. K.W.B. Adams: The American Adam (Chicago, 1955).

27. Lord Ragian: Myth and Ritual (Indiana University Press, Bloomington, 1974).

28. Malcolm Cowley: Introduction, Winesburg, Ohio (Viking Press, New York, 1960).

29. Malcolm Cowley: Anderson's Last Days of Innocence, The Achievement of Anderson. (The University of North Carolina Press, Chapel Hill, 1976).

30. Mark Twain: The Adventures of Huckleberry Finn (Penguin Books, New York, 1966).

31. Milton R. Stern and Seymour L Gross: American Literature Survey (Light and Life Publications, New Delhi, 1975).

32. Nancy L. Bunge: The Ambiguous Endings of Sherwood Anderson's Novels (Whiston Publishing Company, New York, 1976).

33. Phillips, William: Sherwood Anderson's Winesburg, Ohio (University of Chicago, Chicago, 1949).

34. Ray Lewis White: Sherwood Anderson: Early Writings (Ohio: Kent State University Press, Kent, 1989).

35. Ray Lewis White: The Achievement of Sherwood Anderson: essays and Criticism (University of North Carolina Press, Chapel Hill, 1966).

36. Rex Burbank: Sherwood Anderson (Twayne, New York, 1964).

37. Robert Allen Papinchak: Sherwood Anderson A Study of the Short Fiction, 1992).
38. Robert Allen Papinchak: Sherwood Anderson; A Study of the Short Fiction (Twayne, New York, 1993).
39. Robert Allen Papinchak: Sherwood Anderson (Twayne Publishers, New York, 1991).
40. Schevill, James: Sherwood Anderson: The Formative Years (The Ohio State University, 1943).
41. Trilling, Lionel: Sherwood Anderson: The Liberal Imagination (Viking Press, New York,1950).
42. Walter Litz: Major American Short Stories (Allied Publishers, New Delhi, 1975).
43. West, Ray B : The Short Story in America (Henry Regency, Chicago,1952).
44. Williams, Kenny.J: A Story Teller and A City: Sherwood Anderson's Chicago (Northern Illinois University Press, 1988).

ARTICLES

1. Baden, AL : The Structure of ht e Modern Short Story (College English, 1945).
2. Beck, Warren: Art and Formula in the Short Story (College English.1943).
3. Edwin Fussel: Winesburg, Ohio: Art and Isolation, Modern Fiction Studies (Vol. VI, No. 2, 1960).
4. Gullasom, Thomas: The Short Story an Underrated Art: Studies in Short Fiction, (1946).
5. Louis J. Budd: The Grotesues of Sherwood Anderson and Wolfe-Modern Fiction Studies (Vol. V, No. 4, 1959).
6. Milovan Djilas: "Alienation", Encounter (Vol. XXXVI, May, 1971).
7. Nirmal Verma: It is Half Way Between a Novel and a Poem (The Times of India, 1982).
8. Peden William: The American Short Story during the Twenties: Studies in Short Fiction, 1973).

9. Pinker Sanford Speaking about Short Fiction, 1981.
10. Sudipta Kaviraj: Alienation and Literature: A Provisional Paradigm (Jawaharlal Nehru University, New Delhi, 1973).
11. Voss, Arthur: The American Short Story (University of Oklohoma Press, Normen, 1973).
12. West, Ray, B: The American Short Story at Mid Century, Critical Approach to Fiction (TATA Mc. Graw Hill Company, New Delhi, 1968).

Index